A Basic Dictionary of Saints

Kathleen Jones is Emeritus Professor of Social Policy in the University of York. She is the author of books and academic papers on social policy and mental health, and of five previous books on saints of the Church, including *The Saints of the Anglican Calendar*. She was a member of the Archbishops' Commission on Church and State, the Archbishops' Commission on Marriage and, for some years, of the General Synod of the Church of England. She lives in York.

T0034640

Also by the same author
and available from Canterbury Press:

The Saints of the Anglican Calendar
The Celtic Saints *(forthcoming)*

Also available in this series:

A Basic Church Dictionary *Tony Meakin*
A Basic Bible Dictionary (forthcoming) *Stephen Motyer*

A Basic Dictionary of Saints

Kathleen Jones

CANTERBURY
PRESS
Norwich

First published in 2001 by The Canterbury Press Norwich
(a publishing imprint of Hymns Ancient & Modern Limited
a registered charity)
St Mary's Works, St Mary's Plain
Norwich, Norfolk, NR3 3BH

A catalogue record of this book is available
from the British Library

ISBN 1–85311–397–2

Typeset by Regent Typesetting, London
and printed in Great Britain by
Bookmarque, Croydon, Surrey

Contents

Abbreviations

A   Anglican
R   Roman Catholic
O   Orthodox

Introduction

References to the saints are all around us. The Union Flag, which consists of the crosses of three martyrs – St George, St Andrew and St Patrick – is regularly waved at promenade concerts in London, and painted on football fans' faces at international matches. Lovers send messages on St Valentine's Day, and Santa Claus (St Nicholas) still arrives much too early in the department stores. We sing of Santa Lucia, and of Good King Wenceslas, who looked out on the feast of Stephen (two saints there). In almost every country in the world, there are places named after saints – British cities like St Albans and St Andrews and St Davids, villages the length of France and Spain, North American cities like San Francisco and St Louis, remote islands like St Helena. Who are these people? What do we mean by calling them 'saints'? Have they any relevance to the modern world?

Who they are is the subject of this *Dictionary*. By calling them saints, we mean that Christians have accorded them special respect for the quality of their lives, and they are commemorated annually. They are not perfect people: some of them, like St Peter and St Paul, were spectacular sinners; but they had the courage to admit that they were wrong, and they learned from their mistakes.

Yes, saints are relevant to the modern world, for at least three reasons: because they offer better models for living than those of our popular culture – the TV stars and the new rich whose doings fill the glossy magazines; because they bring theology down to our human level by focusing it on real people with real problems; and because they are part of our heritage as Christians, helping us to define our values.

The values of the saints are surprisingly modern. Here are people who care about poverty and suffering, stand out against cruelty and bigotry, and find time for contemplation and wisdom instead of the remorseless acquisition of money and power. They love animals, know about herbal medicine, and are at home in the natural world which we call 'Planet Earth'. They understand the essential rhythms of human life, knowing how to live, how to grow old, and how to die. We need to learn about them as a protection against the distortions of the media, the pressures of mass living, the clamour of 'Buy, buy, buy' and 'Spend, spend, spend'. Through the saints, we can see the Holy Spirit at work in the world. They are the authentic voice of Christ himself, calling us back to reality.

There must be many thousands of saints who have lived quiet lives out of the public eye, uncelebrated and unremembered, known only to the mind of God. It must be said that those we do know about have often been very badly presented – as impossibly pious figures, trailing incredible legends and performing unlikely miracles; but that is changing faster than many people realize. Theologians and ecclesiastical historians are working to produce new accounts of the saints, separating fact from fiction, revealing the real-life experience and the human dilemmas behind the legends and centuries of muddled reporting (much of it by oral tradition). There is a new concern to use all the equipment of scholarship in theology, history, psychology, archaeology and other branches of knowledge to set the record straight. Lists of saints (commonly called calendars in the West, but menologies or synaxaries in the Eastern Orthodox Church), are being revised in all the main Churches. New saints are being named, and new prayers and collects (called 'propers') written for their commemoration.

People who have been cautious about some of the excesses associated with the saints in the past – the dubious relics, the superstitions, the exaggerated claims to sources of spiritual power – can come back to the study of the saints, finding in their lives sources of inspiration and opportunities for development in prayer.

Theologically, those who are regarded as saints may be respected (which is all that the word *venerated* means), or seen as models of

Christian living. They may not be *worshipped*. All that we respect or find good in them comes from God; and while some people find it helpful to *invoke* the saints in their prayers, they pray *through* them, not *to* them. We may find parallels between a saint's experience and our own; but this should bring us closer to God himself. We must not substitute the creature for the Creator.

This short text is a starting point for getting to know some of the saints better. It includes great Christians from all the main Christian Churches on an inter-faith basis – Western and Eastern, Catholic and Protestant. Some lived a long time ago, and some are quite recent. Some of them are well known, and some ought to be better known – either because they are of particular interest to English-speaking readers, or because they had a major influence on the development of the Christian faith. They are worth getting to know; and their lives throw some very interesting sidelights on Church history. I hope that readers will be able to use the Dictionary for quick reference, and then go on to discover more about the saints, and the great company they represent.

I am grateful to Sr Anna Huston of the Society of St Margaret, Haggerston, for providing the illustrations in this volume.

A Basic Dictionary of Saints

Individuals who lived before the Reformation are generally listed by their baptismal name or name in religion, and those since the Reformation by surname. A single date after a name is the date of death. Dates of commemoration are given at the end of each entry. Names in the Anglican Calendar are marked 'A'. Names in Roman Catholic Calendars are marked 'R'. Those in the Calendars of the Eastern Orthodox Churches are marked 'O'. Those celebrated in all three traditions are marked 'A. R. O.' * against a name denotes a separate entry for that person.

Adamnán or Adomnán (c. 627–704): abbot of Iona, and chief biographer of *Columba. *Bede quotes at some length from his description of the Holy Places in Jerusalem. He worked for reconciliation between the Celtic and Roman Churches, and was responsible for the Law of Adamnán, which specified that clerics, women and young boys should be treated as non-combatants in tribal warfare. [23 September, R.]

Adrian of Canterbury: see **Hadrian**

Aelred of Rievaulx Ailred (1110–67) was abbot of what was in his day the largest Cistercian monastery in England, with some 150 choir monks and 500 lay brothers. He was noted for his charitable rule, his personal asceticism, and his patience. His biography by

Walter Daniel shows him as a gentle and holy man of good judgement and diplomatic skill. *Bernard of Clairvaux held him in high esteem, and sent him to Rome to protest against the appointment of William FitzHerbert as archbishop of York. He travelled indefatigably, despite poor health, visiting other Cistercian monasteries and exerting an influence on their development. His writings include two celebrated treatises, *Spiritual Friendship* and *The Mirror of Charity*. He also wrote biographies of *Edward the Confessor, *Ninian of Scotland, and the saints of Hexham. [12 January, A. R.]

Agnes (?292–305) was a virgin martyr. Though many medieval legends about her have to be discounted, her basic story is supported by historical evidence. She is said to have been only twelve or thirteen years old when, during the persecutions of Diocletian in Rome, she evaded her parents' protection to declare herself a Christian. She

refused to sacrifice to the gods, and was executed in the Piazza Navona, where the church of Sant' Agnese in Agone now stands. *Ambrose of Milan and *Jerome both wrote about her in the fourth century; Pope Damasus I composed an epitaph in her honour; and the Spanish-Roman poet Prudentius, who visited Rome in 400, wrote a lyrical poem in her memory. In art, she is usually shown carrying a lamb (though her name derives from the Greek *agneia*, 'white' or 'pure', and not from *agnus*), and she was painted by many Renaissance artists, including Duccio, Tintoretto and Fra Angelico. [21 January, A. R. O.]

Aidan of Lindisfarne (651) was a

monk of Iona. He was sent to Northumbria at the request of *King Oswald, who had himself been an exile in Iona, where he had been taught by the Celtic monks. The Roman mission had collapsed after *Paulinus withdrew to Kent, and Northumbria became the centre of Celtic Christianity in England. Aidan and Oswald were personal friends, and worked together to evangelize the people, but Oswald understood that Aidan must have a quiet place for prayer. He gave him the island of Lindisfarne, across the causeway from Bamburgh Castle, and royal protection. Aidan went about on foot in the manner of the Celtic monks, founding churches and monasteries and schools, liberating slaves, and teaching the people. *Bede writes of his inspiring example to his clergy, his generosity, his frugal life-style and his fearless reproof of wrongdoers. Lindisfarne was sacked by the Vikings in 793, and no visible signs remain of Aidan's work, but many visitors to Lindisfarne still find it a holy place. [31 August, A. R.]

Alban (third century) is the proto-

martyr of England. He died in the persecutions of one of the Roman emperors – either Severus (c. 209), Decius

(c. 254) or Diocletian (c. 304–5). Recent studies suggest the earliest of these dates. He lived in the Roman city of Verulamium, where he hid a Christian priest, who taught him. When soldiers came to arrest the priest, Alban confused them by wearing his cloak. On arrest, he declared himself a Christian, and he was beheaded on the site of the amphitheatre outside the city. He was buried nearby, and later the monastery, and the town of St Albans developed on the site. Alban has often been depicted as a Roman soldier (most notably in Sir Ninian Comper's memorial in St Albans abbey to the men who died in

World War I), but the fact that he was accorded a public trial and a public execution suggest that he was a Roman citizen of some standing in the city. The chapel of St Amphibalus in St Albans abbey commemorates Alban's Christian teacher, though that was probably not his name. [22 June, A. 20 June, R.]

Alcuin (?735–804) was probably born in York. He was educated in the Minster school, and stayed on to teach there, helping in the foundation of the Minster Library. He eventually became head of the school for fourteen years. He was not a monk, and never became a priest, though later he was made a deacon. He was pre-eminently a teacher. He wrote textbooks in Latin, and stressed the importance of accuracy, because good Latin was necessary for charters, the taking of oaths and other legal documents. In 781, he moved to Aachen to head a new school for Charlemagne, and this led him into a much wider sphere of work. He became Charlemagne's religious adviser, meeting the most intelligent and cultured men in Europe. When Charlemagne decreed that schools should be set up in every diocese in Gaul to teach on the lines Alcuin had established in the palace school, he supervised the entire enterprise, sending his own former pupils to found the new schools, and having many books copied to provide them with texts. When he retired in 796, he was unable to return to York, because the Yorkshire coast was being ravaged by the Danes. He became abbot of Tours, where he created a distinguished school of learning and wrote a major book on the Trinity. [20 May, A. 19 May, R.]

Aldhelm (639–709) studied at St Augustine's, Canterbury under *Adrian, and became abbot of Malmesbury and first bishop of Sherborne. He was re-lated to the royal house of Wessex, and his verses, which were sung to the accompaniment of a harp to attract people to church, are said to have inspired *Alfred the Great. *Bede commends him for his learning and great energy in administering his diocese. His Latin style was somewhat over-elaborate, and his work *On Virginity* was written for the edification of the unlettered faithful rather than with respect for historical accuracy. His name was removed from the Calendar after the Norman Conquest, but restored as a result of the representations of *Osmund of Salisbury. [25 May, A. R.]

Alfred the Great (849–99), king of Wessex, was the son of Christian parents, and was taken to Rome to be confirmed by Pope Leo IV at the age of four. He spent his formative years fighting the Danes from the marshes of Athelney. He defeated them and drove them out of southern England, building a ring of fortified *burhs* to keep them beyond the boundaries of the Danelaw, and warships to keep them from invading the coast. He was a good legislator, enacting laws to limit blood-feuds and to protect the weak. He started a school of learning at Winchester which translated a number of leading European scholarly texts into Anglo-Saxon under his guidance. He was a scholar himself, adding notes and glosses to their manuscripts. As a result of the Danish wars and the sacking of the monasteries, many clergy were illiterate. Alfred instructed the bishops to train them, setting up schools for young men and founding nunneries. He was buried in his royal capital at Winchester. [26 October, A.]

Alphege (c. 953–1012), bishop of Winchester, supported King Ethelred of Wessex against the Danish invaders, and negotiated with their leaders,

Sweyn and Anlaf, in 994. Sweyn became a Christian, and kept his promise not to invade the borders of Wessex. In 1005 Alphege became archbishop of Canterbury, but new Danish raiders besieged the city and attempted to hold him to ransom, demanding the enormous sum of £3,000 for his freedom. Alphege forbade his people to raise the money, and the pagan Danes, at a drunken feast, attacked him and killed him with an axe. He became a hero to the Anglo-Saxons. Shortly before his own death, *Thomas Becket invoked Alphege in his prayers as Canterbury's first martyr. [19 April, A. R.]

Ambrose (c. 340–97) was the Roman consul for the provinces of Aemilia and Liguria when riots occurred over the succession to the Arian bishop of

Milan. Someone in the crowd (it is said to have been a child) cried 'Ambrose for bishop!' The crowd took up the cry and the emperor agreed to his appointment. He was consecrated within a week, resigning his governorship and giving away all his personal property. His letters to his sister Marcellina, who became a consecrated virgin (there were no religious houses for women at this time), are still extant. On several occasions he opposed the power of the emperors, rebuking them and even forcing one to carry out a public

penance. When another issued a decree enabling the Arians, a dissident sect, to take over churches, Ambrose refused to cede a single church, and he was besieged in his cathedral from Palm Sunday to Easter Day by imperial troops. He kept the congregation singing hymns, and the emperor finally gave way. Ambrose wrote several major treatises, hymns and poems, and is recognized as one of the four Latin Doctors of the Church. [7 December, A. R.]

Anastasia (?304) was probably martyred at Sirmium in Dalmatia during the persecutions of Diocletian. She was honoured in the Eastern Church, and Byzantine officials brought her story to Rome. Their church in the Greek quarter of Rome was called the Anastasis basilica, being, like a church in Constantinople, a copy of the Anastasis basilica in Jerusalem, where the second Mass of Christmas was sung at dawn. The name of Anastasia became confused with that of the basilica, and this Mass is still said in her church in Rome on Christmas Day, which is her feast day. Her name occurs in Eucharistic Prayer 1 in the revised Roman Missal. Later legend made her a Roman martyr, but modern scholars think that her origins were certainly Eastern. [25 December, R. O.]

Andrew of Spello (c. 1254) was one of the seventy-two disciples of *Francis of Assisi, and became chaplain to the Poor Clares of Spello. An early account of his life preserved at Spello tells (in Latin) the story of how, while he was praying in his cell, he had a vision of Christ; but the convent bell rang, and he was faced with a dilemma: it was time for him to feed the poor waiting at the convent gate. Should he go, or should he stay? Longfellow tells the story (with some poetic licence) in his well-known narrative poem, 'The Vision'. Andrew went to minister to the poor, and returned to his cell to find the vision waiting, and saying 'Hadst thou stayed, I must have fled.' [9 June, R.]

Andrew the Apostle (first century): according to John 1:40, Andrew was a disciple of *John the Baptist, and went to tell his brother Simon that 'We have found the Messiah'. He brought Simon to Jesus, who named him *Peter. For this reason, Andrew is sometimes called the *Protoclete* or 'first called'. The brothers lived in Bethsaida, a mile or two from the Lake of Galilee, and shared a boat. They were mending their nets when Jesus called them to follow him on his mission (Mark 1:16–18; Matt. 4: 18–20). He is repeatedly mentioned in the Gospels, particularly in relation to the Feeding of the Five Thousand, where he points to the boy with five loaves and two fishes (John 6:8–10). Many apocryphal stories developed about Andrew, perhaps because nothing definite is known about his life after the Resurrection. *Jerome says that he was martyred in Greece, and other accounts say that he went to Syria or Ethiopia. He became a patron saint of Russia, and the chief patron saint of Scotland – the latter on the basis of a story that the French bishop Regulus was told in a vision to take Andrew's relics to 'the ends of the earth', and deposited them in the city now known as St Andrews. The saltire, or diagonal cross of St Andrew, which now forms part of the Union Flag, was not known until the tenth century. [30 November, A. R. O.]

Andrewes, Lancelot (1555–1626): a prebendary of St Paul's in 1589, dean of Westminster in 1601, and bishop of Winchester in 1619, Lancelot Andrewes was celebrated as a preach-er, and was responsible for much of the work of the commission which produced the King James Bible, or Authorized Version, in 1611. He is remembered as a great Anglican who debated the Anglican position with the Pope's representative, Cardinal Bellarmine. He combined high intelligence with a great lucidity and beauty of expression. He was a man of piety, and his *Private Prayers* (*Preces Privatae*) are still in print. His tomb is in Southwark cathedral. [25 September, A.]

Anne is the traditional name of the mother of the *Blessed Virgin Mary. There is nothing about her in the Gospels, but her name is given in the apocryphal *Gospel of James*, written about 170–80. *Gregory of Nyssa and *John of Damascus wrote about her, and she was greatly venerated in the East. The Crusaders brought a devotion to her to Western Europe, where the most famous representation of her is Leonardo da Vinci's *The Virgin with St Anne and John the Baptist*. A number of English churches are dedicated in her name, and in art she is often shown teaching the Virgin Mary to read. *Martin Luther bitterly attacked her cult. The doctrine of the Immaculate Conception in the Roman Catholic Church is that her daughter Mary was without sin from the moment of her conception. [26 July, A. R.]

Anselm (1033–1109) came from Lombardy and became abbot of Bec in Normandy. After some thirty-four years at Bec, during which time he developed a great reputation as a scholar, he was pressured into becoming archbishop of Canterbury. He came into conflict with King William Rufus, a man of violent temper, almost immediately. Anselm had no inclination to compromise and, against the king's demands, upheld the rights of the papacy over ecclesiastical appointments. William made great efforts to have Anselm deposed, and he was forced into exile in 1097. The death of William Rufus two years later did not ease the situation for long, as the same conflicts developed under his successor, Henry I. In all, Anselm spent seventeen of his nineteen years as archbishop in exile. On the Continent, he was greatly respected for his scholarship, and his reputation rests chiefly on his writings. [21 April, A. R.]

Anskar (c. 801–65) was the first missionary bishop to Scandinavia. He was born in Amiens, and became a monk at the monastic school of Corbie (see *Bathildis) in that city. Though his first missions to Denmark and Sweden met with only very limited success, he became bishop of Hamburg in 832. When Hamburg was overrun by Vikings from Norway, he was appointed archbishop of Bremen, with a general responsibility for missions in all three Scandinavian countries. He set up mission stations in Denmark and Sweden, but was not able to make any headway in Norway. Much of Anskar's work was obliterated after his death, and *Sigfrid, who carried out a mission some two centuries later, virtually had to start again; but Anskar is remembered for his lonely and dangerous pioneer work, and is the patron of Denmark. [3 February, A. R. O.]

Antony of Egypt (?251–356) is the most famous of the Desert Fathers of North Africa, though the distinction of being the first probably belongs to *Paul the Hermit. We have a biography written within a year of Antony's death which tells of his long life (can it possibly have been 105 years?), his great asceticism, and his temptations in his long periods of solitude. He sold his family estates and gave the money to

the poor, lived for thirteen years in a disused cemetery in Upper Egypt, and then moved out into the Arabian desert.

There other solitaries came to live near him, and he founded two monasteries on the Eastern pattern: the monks lived alone, but came together for worship and meditation. Helen Waddell's *The Desert Fathers* reproduces his biography and some of his sayings. In the late fourth century, news of the way of life of the Desert Fathers reached Rome and had a profound effect on Western monasticism, though *Benedict of Nursia was later to introduce a more communal pattern of monastic living. [17 January, A. R. O.]

Antony of Padua (1195–1231): the popularity of St Antony as the saint who can be invoked to find lost articles seems to derive from an incident in which one of his novices stole a book from him. The story is that the novice journeyed as far as a river, and (whether or not inspired by his guilty conscience) saw a hideous apparition on the opposite bank. He made haste to return the book. More reliable records of Antony's life say that he was a Portuguese from Lisbon who became an Augustianian canon and acquired a great reputation for his preaching. He went to Italy, met *Francis of Assisi, and became a Franciscan. His gift of making theology simple and his melodious, compelling voice drew crowds wherever he went. The *piazzas* of the Lombardy towns were crowded with people who came to hear him in the open air, because the churches were not large enough. In Padua he reconciled quarrelsome nobles, secured the release of prisoners, and protected those who were cheated or oppressed. He shared Francis of Assisi's love of the natural world and of animals. He spent his energies unsparingly, and died before he reached the age of forty. [13 June, R.]

Apollonia (249), an aged deaconess of Alexandria, was captured during one of the imperial persecutions in that city. She was badly beaten and her teeth were knocked out. She broke away from her pursuers, who were proposing to burn her alive, and threw herself on the fire. This led to medieval debates over whether she had committed the sin of suicide, or whether, in the extreme circumstances, her deliberate choice of death was justifiable. Her memory was revived by a journal for dentists published in Boston, Massachusetts, called *The Apollonian*. Perhaps a more significant fact about her than the loss of her teeth is that women are comparatively few in the Calendars of early saints, and most of those who were remembered were said to be young and beautiful virgins. Apollonia is an exception, reminding us that the persecutions affected all sections of the Christian community equally.
[9 February, R. O.]

Athanasius (c. 296–373) accompanied the patriarch Alexander of Alexandria to the Council of Nicaea in 324–5, and became a strong supporter of the view of the Person of Christ enshrined in what has since become known as the Athanasian Creed. This view was challenged by Arius, who held that Christ was not co-existent with God the Father, but was only the first created being. Though the Council of Nicaea endorsed the 'Athanasian' doctrine, there followed many years of bitter controversy with the Arians. Athanasius became patriarch in 328, and spent much of his forty-five years of office in exile. Though he was supported by the papacy, he incurred the anger of Arian emperors, and of Julian the Apostate, who was hostile to Christianity. His writing, based largely on the teaching of *Justin Martyr and *Irenaeus, was powerful in advocating the full divinity of Christ, a doctrine restated at the Council of Constantinople in 381, after his death. His best-known works are his treatises on the nature of the Incarnation and against the Arians (both of which may be read in English translation), and his life of *Antony. He supported the desert hermits, and was a friend of *Pachomius. [2 May, A. R. O.]

Athanasius the Athonite (c. 925–1003) was a Greek scholar, born in Trebizond, who became a monk at Kymina. Fearing that he might be called upon by his fellow monks to become abbot, he retreated in 961 to the remote and almost inaccessible Mount Athos near the tip of the most eastern peninsula of mainland Greece, where he built a church and a monastery with money contributed by the Eastern emperor. This became an influential centre for Greek Orthodox monasticism, at one time comprising a loose-knit community of thousands of monks. Though the numbers are now greatly reduced, the monks of Mount Athos still maintain their traditional isolation. [5 July, R. O.]

Augustine of Canterbury (605) was prior of the monastery of St Andrew on the Coelian Hill in Rome

7

when *Pope Gregory the Great sent him on a mission to evangelize the Anglo-Saxons. *King Ethelbert of Kent, who had some claim to being the *bretwalda* or overlord of southern England, had married a Christian princess from Gaul. On the way to the coast of Gaul, Augustine and his party turned back, overwhelmed by the difficulties of the enterprise; but Pope Gregory ordered his consecration as bishop, and sent him on. After a dramatic meeting on the Isle of Thanet, Ethelbert gave the monks an old Roman church in Canterbury, and eventually accepted baptism, along with his household. Augustine's mission did not proceed far out of Kent. London at this time was a city north of the Thames, in the hands of the East Saxons, and seven years elapsed before Mellitus was consecrated its bishop. *Birinus was sent on a separate papal mission to the West Saxons in about 635, and the north of England, with Scotland and Wales, was left to the Celtic Church until the time of the Synod of Whitby (664). Augustine was hampered by the fact that Pope Gregory's maps, from which he planned the conversion of England and the formation of twelve dioceses, dated from the Roman occupation of Britain, which had ended over two centuries earlier, and it was left to *Theodore of Tarsus, who became archbishop of Canterbury in 666, to fulfil the original plan. [26 May, A. 27 May, R. O.]

Augustine of Hippo (354–430) has left a painfully honest account of his early years in his *Confessions*: his profligate life as a student at Carthage (which he may have exaggerated); his years as a Manichaean, which involved belief in the duality of good and evil; his abandonment of his long-term mistress; and his eventual conversion to Christianity under the influence of *Ambrose of Milan. He returned to a ministry in North Africa as one of a group of celibates, was ordained a priest in 391, and became a bishop in 395. Augustine maintained the Christian community in Hippo in the face of mounting attacks from the Vandals, who overwhelmed the city after his death. His preaching, his charity for the

poor of the city, and his judgement in civil and ecclesiastical cases were stabilizing factors at a time when law and order were breaking down. His intellectual brilliance has made him no less influential since his own day. His writings, particularly the treatise on the Trinity and *The City of God*, in which he contrasts Christian political order with that of the secular world, have become Christian classics. Augustine's belief in predestination, which greatly influenced *Jean Calvin and other writers much later, has been seriously questioned by subsequent theologians, but he remains a major figure in the history of the Church, and has long been recognized as one of the four Latin Doctors. [28 August, A. R. O.]

Azariah, Samuel Vedanayagam (1874–1945) was the son of an Anglican priest. He became secretary for the Y.M.C.A. in the whole of South India before being ordained as an Anglican priest. He was appointed to take charge of the mission station of Dornakal in the diocese of Madras, where he worked among the rural population, with a particular concern for the Untouchables. In 1913 he became assistant bishop, and developed clergy training for the rural areas. He made distinguished contributions to the work of the World Council of Churches, where he was a strong advocate of Christian unity, and he was one of the leaders of the movement for a united Church of South India, achieved two years after his death. [2 January, A.]

Barnabas the Apostle (first century) came from Cyprus, and was a Jew of Greek stock. When the apostles decided to 'have all things in common', he sold his land and gave the money to the community fund. His original name was Joseph, but the apostles named him Barnabas, which means 'son of encouragement' (Acts 4: 36–37). He was sent to the small group of Christians in Antioch with *Paul, and they subsequently carried out a mission in Cyprus with John Mark (see *Mark), landing at the great Graeco-Roman city of Salamis. When John Mark left them, they went on to a lengthy mission in Asia Minor, where they faced considerable danger, but established a number of churches. After returning to Jerusalem, they decided to go their separate ways: they differed over the question of circumcision, and while Barnabas was prepared to trust John Mark on another mission, Paul was not. Barnabas continued his journeys with John Mark, and Paul with Silas. Little is known about the subsequent work of Barnabas, but the apocryphal *Acts of Barnabas* (fifth century) say that he went back to Salamis where, like *Stephen, he was martyred by stoning. [11 June, A. R. O.]

Barnett, Samuel (1844–1913) and **Henrietta Barnett** (1851–1936): Samuel Barnett was vicar of the Victorian slum parish of St Jude's, Whitechapel, where he and his wife Henrietta worked together for over forty years, labouring to improve the condition of the people. They were both leading members of the London-based Charity Organisation Society. Samuel Barnett was involved in the movement to develop university settlements and was one of the founders of Toynbee Hall. He worked for a variety of educational causes, and for better housing for artisans. Henrietta, who outlived him by nearly a quarter of a century, was the main founder of the Children's Country Holiday Fund and a member of the Hampstead Garden Suburb Trust. The Henrietta Barnett School at Golders Green commemorates her work for the education of girls, and Barnett House at the University of Oxford is named for them both. [17 June, A.]

Bartholomew the Apostle (first century): 'Bartholomew' means 'son of Tolmar' and is not a personal name. Biblical scholars have identified references to Bartholomew in the synoptic Gospels as relating to the 'Nathanael' mentioned as one of the Twelve in the Gospel according to John. He was a Galilean fisherman, and his original scepticism ('Can any good come out of Nazareth?') swiftly changed to recognition of the Son of God when *Philip brought him to Jesus. He is reputed to have preached in Arabia or Ethiopia after the coming of the Holy Spirit, and to have been martyred. [24 August, A. R. O.]

Bartholomew of Farne (1193) came from Whitby. He was of Norwegian extraction, his original name being Tostig. He changed it because the boys at school laughed at him for being a foreigner. When he grew up, he went to Norway, where he was ordained by the bishop of Trondheim. Attempts were made to arrange a marriage for him (the Norwegians at that time had a married clergy), but he took fright and returned to England, resolving to become a hermit and to follow the example of *Cuthbert. He occupied a cell on the island of Inner Farne, where he grew his own food and led a cheerful life of hard physical labour, prayer and study, singing the Psalms loudly to the accompaniment of the birds. He was visited by the monks of Durham, who commented charitably on his contention that 'the dirtier the body, the cleaner the soul' by saying that he 'made the island fragrant by his virtues'. [24 June, R.]

Bartolomé de las Casas (1474–1566) came from Seville, and his father sailed with Christopher Columbus. In 1502 Bartolomé went to the Indies to make his fortune, but he was appalled by the brutality of the Spanish settlers towards the peaceful Indians, who were dying in their thousands as a result of deliberate massacres and forced labour. He became a Dominican friar and made seven journeys back to Spain to protest against what amounted to genocide. Prominent ecclesiastics were shareholders in the great riches of 'New Spain', and his outspoken denunciations met with considerable resistance. He became bishop of Chiapa in New Mexico, and his work is commemorated by an institute in Lima, Peru. [20 July, A.]

Basil the Great (329–79) was the eldest son of a noble Christian family in Asia Minor, the brother of *Gregory of Nyssa and *Macrina. He undertook a tour of monasteries in Syria, Egypt, Palestine and Mesopotamia, spent a period as a hermit, and founded a monastery on the banks of the River Pontus. This became a model for Eastern monasticism, substituting a communal pattern for the life of solitary asceticism established by the Desert Fathers, and later it influenced the Benedictine Rule in the West. Basil assisted Bishop Eusebius of Caesarea for some years before succeeding him, and became a metropolitan with jurisdiction over a number of dioceses. He defended orthodoxy against Arianism, and was responsible for setting up the *Basiliad*, an institution for the sick and poor which became a model for Christian charity. Basil's administrative ability, pastoral concern and doctrinal writings have been of enduring influence in both the Eastern and Western Churches. [2 January, A. R. O.]

Bathildis (Balthild) (680) was an Anglo-Saxon girl captured in a coastal raid by the West Franks. Some accounts say that she rose to become the queen of Clovis II by her own beauty and intelligence; others say that she may have been of English royal blood, and married as a result of a treaty. She and Clovis had three sons, all of whom became kings in Gaul. The eldest was five when Clovis died in 657, and Bathildis acted as regent for eight years. During this time she supported the Church, relying on the advice of the bishops. She founded the celebrated monastery of Corbie and the royal nunnery of Chelles. *Bede's story (which he got from *Wilfrid) that she was responsible for the death of the bishop of Lyons is incorrect. After a palace revolution, Bathildis retired to Chelles, where she is said to have served in other nuns with simplicity and dignity. [30 January, R.]

Baxter, Richard (1615–91): this Presbyterian divine was ordained in the Church of England. Though he was prepared to accept episcopacy, he was shocked by the low standards of morality and learning among the country clergy. He became a Dissenter in 1640, and ministered to a congregation in Kidderminster. During the Civil War, he acted for a time as a chaplain to units in Cromwell's New Army, though he refused to justify the cause of either King or Parliament, and consistently opposed the execution of *Charles I. Poor health caused him to retire from an active ministry, and he wrote over a hundred works notable for their piety and moderate views. After the Restoration, Charles II appointed him a King's Chaplain and offered him the bishopric of Hereford, which he declined. [14 June, A.]

Beche, John (1539) was abbot of Colchester at the time of the dissolution of the monasteries. He was one of the three abbots (the other two being *Hugh Faringdon of Reading and *Richard Whiting of Glastonbury) who took Henry VIII's Oath of Supremacy in an attempt to save their abbeys, but who were executed for their resistance to the royal divorce. The Roman Catholic Church regards them as 'equipollently beatified' and as martyrs, but has never canonized them. Abbot John Beche was a learned man and a friend of *Thomas More and *John Fisher. He opposed their execution, and spoke out against the king's marriage to Anne Boleyn. In November 1538, commissioners were sent to dissolve his abbey. He made a personal plea to the king, but was put to death at Colchester. [1 December, R.]

Becket, Thomas: see **Thomas Becket**

Bede (673–735) entered the monastery of St Peter's at Wearmouth in Northumbria at the age of seven, and moved to its foundation at Jarrow when he was nine or ten. There he became learned in Latin (his own language was Old English) and the greatest chronicler of his period. He went once to Lindisfarne and once to York, but had no desire to travel further. His *History of the People of England* is the single most important source on Anglo-Saxon history. He also wrote the lives of his abbots, *Eata, *Benedict Biscop and *Ceolfrith, lives of the saints, poetry, sermons and biblical commentaries. His reports on events are detailed and unprejudiced (except for his severity on those who refused to accept the Latin date of Easter – he grew up in the aftermath of the Synod of Whitby). *Boniface called him 'the candle of the Church, lit by the Holy Spirit' and later chroniclers modelled their work on his. His title, 'the Venerable Bede', is a mark of respect (veneration) and not a comment on his age. [25 May, A. R.]

Benedict of Nursia (c. 480–550), the founder of the Benedictine Order, was born in Naples. He became a hermit near Rome at a time when

the Roman Church was studying the Byzantine practice of monasticism, the work of the Desert Fathers, and the modifications introduced by *Basil of Caesarea. Benedict moved to Monte Cassino and developed a form of community life – based on worship, study and manual labour – which was adopted all over Europe. His life is best known through the *Dialogues* of *Gregory the Great. Benedictine monasteries became great centres of learning and healing and were often wealthy and influential. The Cistercian Rule introduced by *Bernard of Clairvaux in the eleventh century was a reformed variant of the Benedictine Rule. Benedict's monastery at Monte Cassino was destroyed by the Lombards in the late sixth century and was later rebuilt. It became so celebrated that both sides spared it in the Italian campaign of World War II. [11 July, A. R. 14 March, O.]

Benedict Biscop (c. 628–90), a Northumbrian who travelled with *Wilfrid on their first journey to Rome. They parted company at Lyons on the way out, and Biscop spent several years in Frankish monasteries, including two at the great monastery of Lérins, where he became a monk and took the name of the founder of the Benedictine Rule. His knowledge of Benedictine life was valuable in the aftermath of the Synod of Whitby, when monasteries in northern England, Wales and Scotland were changing from the Celtic to the Latin Rite. He made six journeys to Rome in all, and maintained his contacts with the Frankish monasteries, bringing to England many cart-loads of books, sacred pictures, vestments and other religious objects. He also brought the first chanter, who was able to teach Gregorian plainsong. Biscop founded the monastery at Monkwearmouth, where *Bede was a boy in the abbey school. [12 January, A. R.]

Bernadette (1843–79), whose family name was Soubirous, was fourteen years old when she had a series of visions of the *Virgin Mary at the rock of Massabielle, near Lourdes. She was the eldest of six children, poor, unedu-cated and sickly. Her simplicity and honesty were not shaken by a series of searching investigations, though her insistence that the Virgin had identified herself as 'the Immaculate Conception' (see *Anne, mother of the Blessed Virgin Mary) concerned those who examined her. Bernadette did not profit from the development of Lourdes as one of the Roman Catholic Church's greatest pilgrimage centres. She escaped from the publicity and the crowds by entering the Order of the Sisters of Notre Dame at Nevers, where she endured much illness and died at the age of thirty-five. She was canonized in 1933 for her simple and holy life, not on account of the visions. [16 April, R.]

Bernard of Clairvaux (c. 1090–1153) was the son of a Crusader. At the age of twenty-two, he entered the monastery of Cîteaux with thirty-nine companions, including his brothers and friends. He became abbot of a new foundation – Clairvaux in Champagne

– and introduced a new and austere Rule involving great asceticism. At this time, Benedictine houses in France had often become wealthy and somewhat lax in their observance. Bernard's reformed Cistercian Rule was adopted in many other monasteries. He rose to great power and influence, particularly

during the pontificate of Eugenius III, who was one of his monks. He attacked the monks of Cluny for their worldliness, opposed the teaching of Peter Abelard, preached two Crusades, and undertook a mission against the Albigenses or Cathars. He was capable of remarkable invective against his opponents, but also of such gentleness in preaching the faith that he was known as 'the Honey Doctor'. At the time of his death, there were over four hundred Cistercian monasteries in Europe, the bare stone walls and plain glass of their churches contrasting sharply with the elaborate Benedictine foundations. [20 August, A. R.]

Bessarion (fourth century): there are several saints of this name (or its Russian variant, Vissarion) in Eastern Orthodox Calendars, and the name was for many centuries a popular one in Eastern Europe. Stalin's full name was Josef Vissarionovitch Djugashvili. The fourth-century Bessarion seems to be the source of its popularity. He was an anchorite in Egypt, a follower of *Antony, who acquired such a great reputation for holiness that he was compared to Moses. He wandered from place to place 'like a bird' (says his biographer and namesake, Cardinal Bessarion), fasting and living in silence. Many legends arose about his physical endurance, his magical powers (he was said to have walked on the Nile) and his battles with demons. His only possessions were his tunic, his cloak and a book of the Gospels. He gave his tunic to bury a dead man, and his cloak to cover a naked one. Then he sold his Gospels to ransom a slave. He is said to have lived to a great age. [17 June, R. 6 June, O.]

Birinus (c. 650): some years after *Augustine's mission to England, Pope Honorius I consecrated Birinus and sent him with a mission 'to go to the remotest areas of England, where no teacher had been before.' He got no further than Wessex, where he converted the king, Cynegils, and his household. It appears that he had no contact with Canterbury, and he was called 'the Romish bishop', which may imply that the Canterbury mission resented his presence. Dorchester, then a flourishing Romano-British town, was his seat. He ministered from there for fifteen years, building many churches. But the population began to decline, and there is no record of any bishops of Dorchester after 660. Presumably the diocese was taken over by Canterbury. [4 September, A. 3 December, R.]

Boethius (c. 480–524): Severinus Boethius was a Roman statesman who translated the works of Plato, Aristotle, Pythagoras, Euclid and other scholars from Greek into Latin, thus making them accessible to Western scholars in the early Middle Ages. He was a philosopher in his own right, his most celebrated work being the *Consolation of Philosophy*, which *Alfred the Great translated into Old English, adding marginal notes of his own. In the time of Theodoric the Ostrogoth, who wanted to free himself from the control of the Eastern Emperor in Constantinople, Boethius was accused of treason and sacrilege, imprisoned and executed. There has been some debate over whether he should rank as a Christian and a martyr, chiefly on the grounds that the *Consolation of Philosophy* is not explicitly Christian; but the consensus of Catholic scholars is that his own faith was Christian and orthodox. He was canonized by Pope Leo XIII in 1833. [23 October, R.]

Boisil or Boswell (c. 664) was a monk trained in Ireland who became prior of Melrose and *Cuthbert's teacher. He was greatly renowned for his learning and holiness. Bede calls him 'God's beloved priest', and he later became abbot of Melrose. Cuthbert was with him when he died of the plague, and succeeded him as prior. Churches were dedicated in Boisil's name on the Scottish border, and part of his eighth-century shrine is kept at Jedburgh. [23 February, R.]

Bonaventure (c. 1218–74) was a Franciscan friar who taught at the Sorbonne in Paris at the same time as the Dominican *Thomas Aquinas. Less

reliant on pure logic than Aquinas, he developed a more devotional theology influenced by the Fathers of the Eastern Church, such as Pseudo-Dionysius and *John of Damascus. He became minister-general of the Franciscan Order when he was only thirty-six, and succeeded in healing the divisions which had developed since the death of *Francis of Assisi. He is known as 'the second founder of the Franciscan movement', because he reinstituted the original Rule in a spirit of moderation and reconciliation. He is known as 'The Seraphic Doctor'. [15 July, A. R.]

Bonhoeffer, Dietrich (1906–45): this Lutheran theologian, trained at Tübingen and Berlin, strongly opposed the persecution of the Jews after Hitler came to power, and was forced to leave Germany. He acquired a great reputation in Britain, the United States and elsewhere, preaching the Christian faith and condemning the activities of the Third Reich. He became one of the leaders of the 'Confessing Church', returning frequently to Germany to lead the opposition to Nazism. He was in the United States when World War II broke out, but caught one of the last ships back to Germany, knowing that his life would be in danger. He was arrested in 1943, and sent to Flossenberg concentration camp, where he was hanged in April 1945, only a month before the Allied armies reached the camp. His *Letters and Papers from Prison* is a moving account of his spiritual sufferings and his abiding faith. [9 April, A.]

Boniface (c. 675–754) was a Devon man, probably from Crediton. His baptismal name was Wynfrith. He studied at the monastery of Nursling in the Winchester diocese and became a teacher there, writing the first Latin grammar in Old English for his students. He was ordained priest when he was thirty, and led missions to Friesia, then largely overrun by pagan tribes. In 722 he was made a regionary bishop with jurisdiction over Germany. He opposed the old Norse gods, often by confrontation with their followers, and succeeded in founding a number of monasteries. He asked the English monasteries for their prayers and support. *Winnibald, *Willibald and *Walburga were among those who responded. English monasteries sent money, books, vestments and holy objects for the new foundations. Boniface became archbishop of Germany and papal legate. He spent some years reforming the Frankish Church, which had grown lax, and then returned to his first love, the conversion of Friesia, when he was nearly eighty. He was killed by hostile tribesmen, and buried in the monastery of Fulda. Boniface

became England's patron, equal in esteem to *Augustine of Canterbury and *Gregory the Great; but, like many Anglo-Saxon saints, he was little respected by the Normans after the Conquest, and he became better known in Germany than in his native country. In recent years there has been a revival of interest in his life, and he is known as 'the Apostle of Germany'. [5 June, A. R. O.]

Booth, William (1829–1912) and **Catherine Booth** (1829–90) were the founders of the Salvation Army. William grew up among the London poor after the early death of his father, and broke his connection with Methodism to convert 'the dark ocean of human wrecks' in the city slums. Catherine, whom he married in 1855, was his loyal partner. She insisted that women could preach as well as men, and the 'Hallelujah Lasses' played a full part in the work. William's methods were robust: his mission halls were 'citadels', their motto 'Blood and Fire' – the Blood of the Lamb and the Fire of the Holy Ghost. His 'shock troops' wore uniform, and their publication was *The War Cry*. Their brass bands and their songs, often sung to popular

tunes, drew the crowds. William Booth's book, *In Darkest England, or The Way Out* shocked the late Victorians by demonstrating the squalor and misery of the 'submerged tenth' of the population. He was 'the General'. Catherine, 'the Mother of the Salvation Army', was fully involved in its work, and also raised seven children, six of whom lived to become celebrated in the movement. The Salvation Army developed into a world-wide organization, offering social care and shelter to society's derelicts as a Christian witness. [20 August, A.]

Bosco, John (1815–88): the founder of the Salesian Order was born the son of a peasant farmer in Piedmont. He grew up in great poverty at a time when northern Italy was suffering from political upheaval and the first effects of industrialization. He became a priest, and devoted himself to working with the homeless boys who were living on the streets of Turin, where they were drawn into vice and crime. He started workshops where they could learn a trade, and, as other priests came to join in his work, he founded an Order named after *Francis de Sales. There was much opposition to the movement – from traditionalist clergy, who found it too innovative; from revolutionary clergy, who wanted it turned to political purposes; and from the anti-clericalist regional government; but Don Bosco's work met an immediate and pressing need. His motto was 'We go straight to the poor.' The Order spread to other parts of Italy, and then to other countries in Europe, the United States and elsewhere. The Salesian Order has concentrated on primary education, technical education and hospital work, and now numbers some 2,000 communities in many countries. [31 January, A. R.]

Botulph (680) was one of two sons of noble Saxon parents. He and his brother Adulf were educated in Germany or northern Gaul, and became monks. Adulf stayed on the Continent, and is said to have become bishop of Utrecht or Maastricht, but Botulph returned to England and founded a monastery in a bleak part of the Fen District in Lincolnshire, said to be inhabited by evil spirits. *Ceolfrith of Wearmouth visited him there, and described him as 'a man of remarkable life and learning, full of the grace of the Holy Spirit', commending the abbey for its learning and its faithfulness to monastic tradition. Before the Norman Conquest, some 64 English churches bore a dedication in Botulph's name. Three of these were rebuilt by Christopher Wren in the city of London after the Great Fire of 1666. [17 June, R.]

Bray, Thomas (1658–1730): this country priest from the Welsh borders published his *Catechetical Lectures* in four volumes, and attracted the attention of the bishop of London, who was concerned to strengthen the Anglican presence in the American colonies. Bray was appointed Commissioner for Maryland, and there he realized that the key was to establish parish libraries. This was the origin of the Society for the Propagation of Christian Knowledge (S.P.C.K.), now a major Anglican publishing house. He recruited missionaries and sent them out with boxes of books, and a Great Library was established in Annapolis. When the English clergy complained that they too needed books, he revived the concept of rural deaneries, which had fallen into disuse, and advocated that each should have its own theological library. Bray also founded the Society for the Propagation of the Gospel (S.P.G.) with the aid of four philanthropists. It received a Royal Charter in 1700, and went on to become a worldwide missionary society long after the American colonies had declared their independence. Bray became rector of St Botulph's Aldgate in 1708, and devoted the rest of his life to training clergy for the mission field and founding libraries. [15 February, A.]

Briant, Alexander (1556–81): after the arrival in England of the first two Jesuit members of the pope's English Mission, *Edmund Campion and Ralph Sherwin, attempts were made to round up other priests who were still practising the Roman Rite. One of them was Alexander Briant, a young secular priest from Somerset. He had studied at Douai and had carried out a secret mission in the West Country. He was tortured to make him reveal the whereabouts of the Jesuits, but he refused to do so, even though, according to the rack-master, he was 'racked more than any of the rest'. When he was in prison he asked if he might be admitted to the Society of Jesuits, and he is celebrated as one of their martyrs. He was tried in Westminster Hall on an indictment of treason and was sentenced to death. He was executed at Tyburn with Campion and Sherwin. [1 December, R.]

Bridget of Sweden (1302–73) was the wife of a Swedish nobleman at a time when Sweden was a Catholic kingdom. They had eight children. On his early death, she founded a monastery at Vadstena on Lake Vattern, and then went to Rome, where she worked for the return of the pope from exile in Avignon. She spent seventeen years in Rome, experiencing visions, exhorting, prophesying and praying for the city to return to its former ecclesiastical glory. She joined the poet Petrarch in urging Pope Urban V to return, and issued many doom-laden prophecies when he withdrew. She visited Santiago de Compostela and Jerusalem, foretelling the destruction of the Holy Roman Empire. She is remembered for her holy life of prayer rather than for her visions and prophecies. [23 July, A. R.]

Brigid of Kildare (c. 452–524) otherwise Bridget or Bride, is the foremost woman saint in Ireland, and patron of Ireland second only to St Patrick. She was abbess of the great monastery at Kildare and, like *Hilda at Whitby, headed a double monastery of both men and women. Her fame was so great that it was said that she was consecrated a bishop, though there is no evidence for this claim. Many stories of kindness and mercy are associated with her, and some extravagant legends grew up round her name, in which she is sometimes confused with the Druidic goddess Brigg, the Viking goddess Brigantia, and even the *Blessed Virgin Mary; but there seems no doubt that she was a real and much-loved person. St Bride's church, Fleet Street, known as 'the journalists' church', is dedicated in her name. [1 February, A. R.]

Budoc (sixth century) is a Celtic saint known to us through place-names, and chronicles from the ninth century onwards. The place-names include Budeaux, Budoc Vean and Budock Water in Cornwall, St Budeaux in Devon and Saint-Brieuc in Brittany. A chronicle written about 900 says that he was abbot of Youghal and archbishop of Dol. He is referred to in the Chronicle of Dol, and the town of Plourin in Brittany claims his shrine. There are many fantastic legends about Budoc (including one that he was born in a barrel) but there is a good deal of local history and antiquarian evidence to establish his historical existence. [8 December, R.]

Bunyan, John (1628–88) was a Bedfordshire tinker who went from village to village mending pots and pans, and probably farm implements. He learned to read and write, but probably his only reading matter was the Bible. He experienced a shattering religious conversion, and joined the Bedford Meeting of Dissenters, where he discovered that he had a gift for words, and began to preach and to write pamphlets. After the Restoration of Charles II, he was arrested as being 'a dangerous and notorious Dissenter'. His friends would have given sureties for him, but he refused to give up preaching, and was sent to the county gaol, where he remained from 1660 to 1672. During that time, he wrote *Grace Abounding*, an autobiography, and then embarked on *Pilgrim's Progress*. He had doubts about publishing this, because it was fiction, but a Bedford bookseller had it printed and sold it for eighteen pence a copy. Bunyan's allegory of the Christian's journey through life, written in the English of the King James (Authorized) Version of the Bible, has become a classic of religious writing. The second part of *Pilgrim's Progress*, *The Life and Death of Mr Badman* and *The Holy War* were all written after his release from prison. He died in 1688, the year in which the accession of William and Mary finally brought toleration for the Dissenters. [30 August, A.]

Butler, Joseph (1692–1752) was born into a Dissenting family, but he conformed to the Anglican Church. He was ordained and became a noted preacher. He refused many offers of ecclesiastical promotion – including, it is said, the archbishopric of Canterbury – but became bishop of Bristol and dean of St Paul's before accepting the bishopric of Durham. There he took no part in politics, but devoted himself to his *Analogy of Religion: natural and revealed*, which was reckoned to be the greatest theological work of the period. This was a scholarly exposition of natural theology and ethical principles, firmly opposed to the emotional 'enthusiasm' which characterized the Wesleys. Butler was a High Churchman and sometimes accused of 'Romish practices', but he is now recognized as one of the principal exponents of Anglicanism in a period when, as he contended, the Church was failing to state its position. [16 June, A.]

Butler, Josephine (1828–1906): Mrs Butler, the wife of the clerical headmaster of Liverpool College, worked with the full and active support of her husband and her sons to overturn the Contagious Diseases Acts of 1866. These Acts, which had gone through Parliament with very little public discussion, set up a system for the control of prostitutes similar to that which Napoleon had introduced in Europe. Women were subject to arbitrary arrest by plain-clothes police and forced to undergo regular medical inspections to prevent the spread of venereal disease. They had no right of appeal. Josephine Butler attacked the Victorian double standard, contending that the women needed education and employment to take them out of prostitution, and that a system which tacitly accepted that men would use prostitutes and punished only the women was unjust. The campaign was initially greeted with public shock and horror, since Victorian ladies were expected to ignore such unpleasant subjects; but energetic pressure-group tactics, including public prayer-meetings, a petition signed by a quarter of a million women and another signed by 1,500 Anglican clergy, brought success. The special police were disbanded, and the Contagious Diseases Acts were repealed. Mrs

Butler took her campaign to Europe, influencing Pope Leo XIII to issue an encyclical against legalized brothels, supporting *Catherine Booth in her work to help young prostitutes, and opposing the white slave trade. [30 May, A.]

Cabrini, Frances (1850–1917): Francesca Saverio Cabrini, a diminutive school teacher from Tuscany, was named for *Francis Xavier, and determined to follow him into the mission field in spite of her limited education and poor health. The ecclesiastical authorities thought mission work unsuitable for women, but she persisted, building up a group of women prepared to work hard and humbly in hazardous conditions until they were finally approved as the Missionary Sisters of the Sacred Heart. She had hoped to go to China, but when she finally secured an audience with Pope Leo XIII in 1887, his verdict was 'Not to the East, but to the West'. Italian immigrants were crowding into the growing cities of North America, living in their thousands in insanitary tenements, and working in the factories and foundries. Mother Cabrini and her Sisters went into the 'Little Italies' of New York, Pittsburgh, Denver, San Francisco and many other cities, seeking out the helpless and the degenerate, and, as offers of help flowed in, founding schools and hospitals. She organized new foundations and training programmes, schools, foundling homes, hostels and colleges. She founded the first of the Columbus Hospitals in New York in 1892, five hundred years after her fellow-countryman Christopher Columbus reached the Americas. She visited Sing Sing, and addressed the Italian prisoners as 'My good friends'. She remained firmly Italian. She never learned to speak fluent English and worked only with Roman Catholics, though she respected the efforts of the Salvation Army. She became a naturalized American in 1907 because by corporation law the properties of her many establishments had to be in American hands, and she is known as America's 'first citizen saint'. There is a statue to her in St Peter's basilica in Rome. [R. 22 December].

Caedmon (680) was a herdsman on the estate of *Hilda's monastery at Whitby who discovered – according to *Bede, in a vision – that he had the gift of poetry and song. Instructed to 'Sing about the creation of all things', he did so to remarkable effect. The Abbess Hilda 'was delighted that God had given such grace to the man'. He became a monk, and was taught the Scriptures. Then, 'like one of the clean animals that chews the cud', he turned it into 'melodious verse'. He sang of the creation, of Adam and Eve, of the exodus into Egypt and the return to the Promised Land, of the Incarnation, the Crucifixion, the Resurrection and the coming of the Holy Spirit, and much more. Unfortunately, little of his poetry has survived. Many poems which were later attributed to him were not of his authorship, but his impact on his contemporaries was so great that he is generally rated as 'the father of English sacred poetry'. [11 February, R.]

Calvin, Jean (1509–64): the son of a wealthy French Catholic family, Calvin studied in Paris, Orleans and Bourges, and, after an intense conversion experience, joined the Protestant reformers. He had to leave France, and wrote his *Institutes of the Christian Religion* (1536) in Basle. He argued that only two sacraments were necessary to salvation, baptism and 'the Holy Supper'; that Holy Communion was no more than a memorial; and that only the elect would be saved. This uncompromising predestinarianism became a hallmark of his movement. In 1536, he went to Geneva, where he drew up laws for this Protestant canton, which set up a theocratic administration. Denying God was punishable by imprisonment or flogging. Church festivals were abolished. Citizens were fined for non-attendance at church, and rowdy behaviour, including singing bawdy songs and 'provocative dances', was banned. Calvin's work had a strong and lasting influence on the Scottish Presbyterians, led by John Knox; on the English Puritans of the seventeenth century; and on the Dutch Reformed Church. [26 May, A.]

Campion, Edmund (c. 1540–81): Campion was a young man of great promise in Elizabethan England, a junior fellow at Oxford whose learning and talents in oratory earned him the patronage of the queen herself. Cecil, the queen's minister, called him 'one of the diamonds of England'; but increasing doubts about the Elizabethan Settlement led him to Douai and then to Rome, where he became a Jesuit. In 1579, Pope Gregory III excommunicated Elizabeth I, and declared her deposed. Soon after, he initiated the English Mission to re-convert England to Roman Catholicism, and Campion was one of the first two missioners to be sent. Filled with a sense of high adventure, he went in disguise, hid in country houses, and often narrowly missed arrest. He wrote a challenge to the Privy Council, *Campion's Brag*, stating that it was his task 'to cry alarm spiritual against foul vice and proud ignorance'. He followed it with a Latin treatise, *Decem Rationes*, printed in secret. He was captured in 1581 and taken to the Tower of London in bonds, labelled 'Campion, the seditious Jesuit'. There the earls of Bedford and Leicester pleaded with him to accept the Anglican Settlement, but he refused. He was repeatedly tortured on the rack, but remained firm in his beliefs. He conducted his own defence in court, protesting his loyalty to the queen, and insisting that his only offence was his allegiance to the pope – a distinction which the court did not recognize. He was condemned for treason and executed at Tyburn with *Alexander Briant and Ralph Sherwin. [1 December, R.]

Caradoc (1124) was a harpist at the court of Rhys ap Twdyr, a prince in South Wales. He left the court and became a monk at Landaff. Most of his life was spent as a hermit, first in Gower and later on an island off the coast of Pembrokeshire. There he acquired a great reputation for sanctity, but the threat from Viking raiders forced him and his few companions to move again, this time to St Ismael's cell (now St Issell's at Haraldston). He was buried in St David's cathedral at his own request; and part of his shrine still stands there. His twelfth-century biographer, Geraldus Cambrensis, made energetic attempts to have Caradoc canonized, but many saints of this period were not officially recognized by Vatican procedure. The biography has been lost, but there is an account of his life in the *Iterarium* of Geraldus Cambrensis. [13 April, R.]

Carlile, Wilson (1847–1942): the founder of the Church Army was the son of a London merchant. He entered his family's silk firm at the age of thirteen. This gave him an unusual education: he learned negotiation and business management, and became fluent in French and German through his trips to the Continent. He inherited the family business, but lost his fortune in the severe depression of 1873. After a period of illness, he turned to religion.

Though his family were Congregationalists, he was confirmed in the Church of England, and trained at St John's College, Highbury, before being ordained. As a curate at the fashionable church of St Mary's, Kensington, he felt that he was out of touch with the working classes, and he began to hold open-air meetings, where his preaching drew thousands. Attempts to incorporate the Salvation Army into the Church of England had failed: Wilson Carlile set up an Anglican version, the Church Army, which would work alongside it, caring for the homeless and prisoners. The Church Army Training College in Oxford was founded in 1884 to train lay evangelists, and the organization became the largest lay society in the Church of England. [26 September, A.]

Catherine of Alexandria (early fourth century) attracted much devotion in medieval England, and there are many stained glass representations of her. She is represented among the twenty-two virgins in the mosaics of San Apollinare Nuovo in Ravenna, and is one of the Fourteen Holy Helpers of the Rhine Valley. She is said to have been a girl of noble birth who refused to marry the emperor Maxentius, disputed her Christian faith with fifty philosophers, and was tortured by being broken on a wheel before she was executed. The story has some familiar legendary elements, but also distinctive features: it is unusual to hear of a girl disputing with fifty philosophers; and the 'Catherine wheel' became a motif for medieval artists, and the origin of the firework of the same name. Her story was probably brought back to England by the Crusaders. [24 or 25 November, A. R. O.]

Catherine of Genoa (1447–1510), a member of the Guelph family of northern Italy, was married for dynastic reasons to a Ghibelline during a temporary break in the long-running hostilities between the two noble and wealthy families. It was an unhappy and childless marriage. Her husband, Giuliano Adorno, was repeatedly unfaithful and wildly extravagant. After a crisis in their affairs, Catherine persuaded him to change his way of life. They moved to a small house in the grounds of the Pammatone Hospital, and began to serve the sick poor at their own expense, without pay. The Pammatone was a hospital of last resort – many of the patients were lepers, and all were incurable. Catherine, who led an intense spiritual life with visionary experiences, had little contact with the Church apart from her daily attendance at Mass – usually in a distant church where her presence would not be noticed. Giuliano became a Francisan Tertiary. It was only after his death in 1497 that Catherine returned to confession and spiritual direction. She became the administrator for the women's side of the Pammatone, and dictated her major works, the *Vita*, the *Purgatorio* and the *Dialogues*, to her 'spiritual sons', two of the group of noble Genovese who became her disciples. Baron von Hügel and other writers on the mystics have devoted much effort to analysing the reasons for Catherine's long alienation from the clergy, but it seems likely that the answer lies in Giuliano's behaviour rather than hers. As a loyal wife, she could not make a confession which involved his actions. [15 September, R.]

Catherine of Siena (1347–82), was the twenty-third child of Giacomo Benincasa, a prosperous dyer, and his wife Lapa. She was one of twins, and her twin died. Possibly this engendered a sense of guilt. She was much attracted to the Dominicans, whose house was almost opposite hers in the Street of the Dyers, and she tried to emulate the friars in asceticism, depriving herself of sleep and practising penitential exer-

cises. She may have been anorexic. She had a very strong pictorial imagination, and her vivid visions reflect her spiritual struggles. After the 'Spiritual Espousal', which took place on Shrove Tuesday 1367, she became the symbolic 'Bride of Christ'. She turned her energies outwards, serving the poor, visiting prisoners, and nursing lepers and plague victims. She learned to read, teaching herself from an ABC, studied the Scriptures, the Divine Office and the works of the Early Fathers, and became a wise woman to whom many turned for counsel. She wrote many letters to people in authority, including Pope Gregory XI; she told him it was his duty to return to Rome from exile in Avignon. Her *Dialogues* are a spiritual classic. She died at the age of thirty-three after a long illness. [29 April, A. R.]

Cavell, Edith (1865–1915) was the daughter of a Norfolk vicar. She became a qualified nurse at the London Hospital, and went to Brussels to assist in setting up nurse training on the English pattern. She became the matron of the Berkendael Institute in 1907, and continued to run it as a Red

Cross hospital when German troops invaded Belgium in 1914. She helped Allied soldiers, cut off in the retreat, to escape, and on 3 August 1915 she was arrested. Despite the efforts of the American embassy to secure her release (America was a neutral power), she was court-martialled, condemned to death, and executed by a firing squad. In England, this was regarded as an atrocity. There are considerable doubts whether her execution was legal under international law. The point at issue was whether she had *attempted* to secure the escape of Allied soldiers – a comparatively minor offence – or whether she had enabled them to return to active service. The trial took place in German, with only a French interpreter, and she may have been confused by language difficulties – or by nine weeks of solitary confinement when even the American embassy officials were unable to visit her. She is commemorated as an example of Christian charity and humanity, and her statue stands to the north of London's Trafalgar Square. [12 October, A.]

Cecilia (? third century): the legend is that she was an early Christian martyr who was married against her will, refused to consummate the marriage, and converted her husband. They both refused to sacrifice to the Roman gods, and were martyred. However, none of the fourth-century writers on virgin saints, such as *Ambrose, *Jerome or *Pope Damasus I, mentions her. The church of St Cecilia-in-Trastevere is said to have been built on the site of her martyrdom, but it is now thought to have been founded by a Roman widow named Cecilia, and excavations suggest that the original buildings on the site were a house and a tannery. Possibly the martyr and the foundress bore the same name; possibly the legend of the saint was later grafted on to the

church dedication. The splendid life-sized marble statue which dominates the church dates from 1599. Cecilia's

status as the patron saint of music dates from a fifth-century biography which describes how she sang to the Lord, consecrating herself to virginity, as the organ played during her wedding. [22 November, A. R. O.]

Cedd (664) was the brother of *Chad, and with him a pupil in *Aidan's Celtic monastery school at Lindisfarne. He was sent as a missionary monk first to the kingdom of Mercia, and later to the land of the East Saxons, where he became bishop of a new diocese centred on monasteries at Tilbury and Bradwell-on-Sea. When he was offered land for a monastery in Northumbria, he chose a remote site at Lastingham (now in North Yorkshire). He was an interpreter at the Synod of Whitby, and *Bede says that he was convinced by the debates that the Celtic Church should adopt the Latin Rite. He died of the plague soon afterwards at Lastingham. [26 October, A. R.]

Ceolfrith (716) was a learned monk, trained at Ripon in *Wilfrid's tradition, who followed *Benedict Biscop as prior of the monastery at Wearmouth. He became abbot of the twin foundation at Jarrow, and finally abbot of both communities. The young *Bede was one of his pupils, and much attached to him. At one point in their early days at Jarrow, a plague killed most of the choir monks. Ceolfrith trained Bede personally, inspiring him with the desire to be a scholar. Bede, in return, wrote a biography which expresses his debt to his abbot. [25 September, R.]

Chad (672), a Lindisfarne monk, succeeded his brother *Cedd as abbot of Lastingham. During *Wilfrid's long absence in Gaul after his consecration as bishop of Northumbria, King Oswin of Northumbria asked Chad to take his place, and sent him to be consecrated at Canterbury. Wilfrid returned, alleged that Chad's consecration was invalid, and retired to Ripon. Chad said that he had no desire to be a bishop, and retired to Lastingham. The situation was finally resolved by *Theodore of Tarsus, archbishop of Canterbury. He confirmed Wilfrid as bishop of a much reduced diocese, and sent Chad to Mercia, where King Wulfhere had asked for a bishop. Chad spent three years in Mercia, founding monasteries and churches in what later became the diocese of Lichfield, before his death. *Bede describes his holy life and his virtues in some detail. [2 March (or 26 October), A. R.]

Chanel, Peter (1803–41): Pierre Louis-Marie Chanel was a member of the Society of Mary, or Marists, who were mission priests. After some years spent serving in a parish and teaching in the seminary at Belley, he was sent in 1836 'to preach the Gospel in the islands of the Pacific Ocean'. His superiors appear to have had little idea of what this would involve, and his preparation was negligible. He landed on the island of Futuna, where unscrupulous traders had exploited the Polynesian population and abused the women. Resentment against the Europeans, traders and missionaries alike, made the work difficult. In 1841, the son of the king of Futuna asked to be baptized, and the king reacted by ordering all the missionaries to be killed. Peter, who refused to leave, was clubbed to death. A year later the king died, and the whole island became Christian. Peter is regarded as the protomartyr of Oceania. [28 April, A. R.]

Charles I (1600–49), king of Great Britain and Ireland, was executed in Whitehall on 30 January 1649 after the defeat of his forces in the English Civil War. The eldest surviving son of James I, he had encountered growing difficulties during his reign due to the opposition of a Puritan-dominated parliament, the fact that his wife, Henrietta Maria of France, was a practising Roman Catholic, his efforts to raise money through taxation, and his own tendencies to absolutist government. His supporters sacrificed their property and often their lives to put down Oliver Cromwell's forces, but he was captured, imprisoned and tried at Westminster. His enemies called him a tyrant, a traitor, and an enemy of the people. He was a devout Churchman and an upholder of episcopacy in England – though he thought this a lost cause in Scotland. He died bravely, maintaining to the last that 'a king cannot be tried by any superior jurisdiction' and that 'A sovereign and a people are clean different things.' His execution still arouses passionate debate – not least because both sides, King and Parliament, appealed to Christian principles. [30 January, A.]

Chisholm, Caroline (1808–77): Caroline Chisholm first visited New South Wales on leave with her husband, an Indian Army officer. They were appalled at the plight of the women arriving in what was still predominantly a convict colony – some were the wives of men who had served their sentences, some were looking for work or for husbands. The hostel earlier set up by *Elizabeth Fry for such women stood empty, and there was general indifference among the settlers – from the Governor down. Caroline began a campaign to improve the women's living conditions. In all, some 11,000 women were settled and 600 families reunited. When the Chisholms returned to England in 1846 she besieged the Home Office, the Colonial Office and the immigration authorities to set up an information service for prospective colonists, to improve conditions on immigrant ships, and to establish agencies for settlement in the colony. In her day, she was as famous in England as *Florence Nightingale. *Lord Shaftesbury and Charles Dickens were among her many supporters. After a further period of nearly twenty years working in Australia, the Chisholms retired to England, where Caroline was awarded a civil list pension. [16 May, A.]

Christina of Markyate (c. 1097–1161) was the daughter of wealthy Saxon nobles. When she was about sixteen her parents took her to St Albans to visit the shrine of the martyr. She made a private vow of virginity, scratching a cross on the abbey door as a token of her intent; but she was married to a young Saxon nobleman against her will, and refused to consummate the marriage. After a long period in which she was locked up, threatened, starved and beaten, she managed to make her escape with the help of a Saxon hermit, Eadwin, and was hidden by another hermit and an anchoress near Markyate, some miles north of St Albans. Appeals to church authorities

proved fruitless, but Eadwin went to the archbishop of Canterbury, who ruled that a prior commitment to celibacy was an obstacle to marriage, and that the marriage was null and void. Christina became an anchoress. Her brother became a monk at St Albans abbey, and the abbey was her spiritual centre. She gave wise counsel to the abbot, embroidered a mitre and a pair of sandals for Hadrian IV, the only English pope (who had been educated at St Albans), and she was probably the first owner of the St Albans Psalter, which contains references to her family and to virgin saints. [5 December, R.]

Clare of Assisi (1194–1253) was a member of the wealthy Offreduccio family, and her male relatives pressed her to make a dynastic marriage for their benefit. When she left home in 1212 to begin a women's branch of the Franciscan Order, they pursued her to the Benedictine nunnery where Francis and his friars had found shelter for her, and tried to drag her out by physical force. Her widowed mother, two of her sisters and her aunt joined her, with several other women from noble families, and they formed a small community at San Damiano, where Francis appointed Clare as abbess. The nuns did not long have the support of the Franciscan friars, for the pope ordered the friars to keep away, and tried to impose the Benedictine Rule on the nuns, which would have kept them within the enclosure. Clare insisted that they must live in poverty, like the friars, and be free to beg and minister to the poor of the district. She redrafted her Rule many times for successive popes, but it was not until she was near death in 1253 that Pope Innocent III accepted her Rule and came to give her Absolution, saying, 'Would to God that I had as little need of it.' The 'Poor Clares' became the first unenclosed religious Order for women, and Clare was the first foundress to draw up her own Rule. [11 August, A. R.]

Clement of Rome (c. 101) was probably fourth in line of the bishops of Rome, following *Peter, *Linus and Cletus. He is the first of Peter's successors of whom we have definite knowledge, and he is said to have

assumed the office in the year 91. He was certainly alive at the time of the martyrdom of Peter and *Paul. His letter to the Corinthians, written about 95–8, is regarded by scholars as genuine, and provides details of this period not to be found elsewhere. The letter is regarded as the first attempt by a bishop of Rome to order the affairs of another church. He is thought to have been martyred in the time of the Emperor Trajan, being deported to the Crimea and then thrown into the sea with an anchor tied round his neck. The ninth-century Slav missionaries *Cyril and *Methodius claimed to have found his remains with the anchor still attached, and took them to Rome, where they rest in the church of San Clemente. Church dedications to St Clement are common all over Europe: there are forty-three in England, including St Clement Dane's in London, which has an anchor as its symbol. [23 November, A. R. O.]

Clitherow, Margaret (1556–86) was the daughter of a wax chandler or candle-maker in York. The family was Catholic: the Protestants had no use for candles. In 1571, she married John Clitherow, a butcher, who was also a Catholic, though not inclined to risk his life for an outward show of resistance to the Elizabethan Settlement. Margaret came under the influence of Father John Mush, who encouraged her to hide Catholic priests, to keep a 'priest's hole' between her house and the next, and to teach the children Catholic doctrine. He also encouraged her in thoughts of martyrdom. In 1586 the Clitherows' house in the Shambles, the street of the butchers, was raided by the Sheriff of York and his men. A Flemish boy revealed the secret room, and Margaret was arrested. At her trial, she refused to give evidence, saying that she did not recognize the standing of the court. This enabled her to avoid implicating other people: she probably knew the whole Catholic network in the area. At this time, lay Catholics did not usually receive the death sentence; but the penalty for refusing to plead was the ancient and barbarous one of the *peine forte et dure* – crushing with heavy weights. The judge pleaded with her to remember her children (she was thought to be pregnant again) but she continued to refuse, and even joked about her coming execution. The executioners were relatively merciful, piling on all the stones at once instead of leaving her to linger for days. She died within fifteen minutes. John Mush's *True Report of the Life and Death of Mrs Margaret Clitherow* gives a very vivid picture of this tragic death. [25 March, R.]

Clothilde (c. 474–545) was the wife of Clovis, king of the Salian Franks. She was a Christian, he was a pagan warrior. When their first son was born, she insisted on his baptism – and when the child died, there were murmurs at court of sorcery and magic. Their

second son was the child who survived a birth in the forest through the prayers of *Leonard of Noblac; but when he was baptized and became ill, Clovis's wrath began to mount. The child lived – and Clovis, impressed by his wife's steadfast adherence to her faith under attack, took instruction from *Bishop Remigius of Rheims. He listened with near-incredulity to the story of Christ's betrayal and crucifixion, and wished that he and his 'trusty Franks' had been there to defeat Caiaphas and Pilate. He was baptized in a magnificent ceremony in Rheims cathedral, clothed in white, in the light of thousands of candles and among clouds of incense, in 496. Three thousand Franks followed suit. The fifteen hundredth anniversary of this great occasion, which marked the conversion of Gaul, was celebrated in Rheims cathedral in 1996. Clothilde outlived Clovis by thirty-four years, living quietly at Tours, where she eventually died 'full of days and of good works'. [3 June, R.]

Colman of Lindisfarne (?672 or 676): there are at least five Colmans celebrated in the Celtic Church, but Colman, third bishop-abbot of Lindisfarne, following *Aidan and Finan, has

a distinctive history. He had been in office for three years when the Synod of Whitby took place in 664: Aidan had died in 651, and Finan in 661. Like his predecessors, he was a monk of Iona, and he was the chief defender of the Celtic Rite at the synod. When the decision went against him, he resigned his bishopric and went back to Iona, taking with him all the Irish monks and some thirty English monks. They established a new community at Inishboffin in Galway; but *Bede tells how disputes arose between the English and Irish monks, because the Irish 'went off to wander on their own around places they knew' in the summer, leaving the English to gather the harvest. Colman bought land at a place named Mugeo on the Irish mainland for the English, where they established a community which became known as 'Mayo of the Saxons'. Bede praised their austerity and their canonical government, and *Alcuin praised their learning, which 'shone . . . among a very barbarous people'. [18 February, R.]

Columba (c. 521–97) is known as one of the Twelve Apostles of Erin. He was descended from two Irish royal houses, and studied in famous monastic schools, receiving a bardic training in Irish poetry and literature. When he became a priest, his family gave him a fort at Daire Calgaich (Daire or Derry, later Londonderry to the English), where he established his first monastery. He spent fifteen years preaching and founding monasteries in Ireland, including the monastery at Kells. After a tribal war in which his family was involved he had to leave Ireland. He and twelve kinsmen left in a wicker coracle covered with hide, and arrived at the island of Iona at Pentecost. From there they evangelized the Picts, undertaking missions to Inverness, Ardnamurchan, Skye, Kintyre, Loch

Ness and Lochaber. He is often credited with having evangelized the whole of Pictland, but it is likely that some of this work was carried out by his successors. *Adamnán, a later bishop of Iona, describes his fasting and vigils, his labours for the monasteries of Scotland, and his learning, saying that he had 'joy in the Holy Spirit in his inmost heart'. *Bede says that his monks were distinguished for their purity of life, their love of God, and their loyalty to the monastic Rule. [9 June, A. R.]

Columbanus (c. 543–615) came from Leinster and became a monk, first in an Irish monastery, where he studied under a disciple of *Finnian, and then in the great monastery at Bangor. He is said to have been exceptionally well educated, and he probably taught there. About the year 590, he went to Gaul as a missionary with twelve companions. Religious life in Gaul was at a low ebb, and he founded monasteries, first at Annegray in the Vosges, then at Luxeuil, and at Fontes or Fontaine. He established the austere and severely penitential Celtic Rule – and the much-disputed Celtic date of Easter, which had by that time been abandoned in England, and had never been known in Gaul. He did not ask Gaul to accept it: he simply pleaded for tolerance so that his monks could follow their own traditions; but there were repeated altercations with the bishops of Gaul, and conflicts with the royal family of Burgundy. Eventually Columbanus and those of his original monks who were still with him were forced to leave. They worked for a time in what is now German-speaking Switzerland, between Zurich and Bregenz, but a war between the local kingdoms meant that they had to move again. By this time, Columbanus was seventy years of age. He and his monks crossed the Alps and

went to Milan. The king of the Lombards gave them some land at Bobbio, where they made a final foundation. Columbanus died there. His monastery at Luxeuil survived, and later adopted the gentler Benedictine Rule. Despite the many hazards and conflicts of his missionary years, Columbanus is considered to be the most influential of the Irish missionaries to the continent of Europe. Of his writings, the Rule and some letters and poems, all written in enviable Latin style, are still accessible. [21 November, R.]

Cooper, Anthony Ashley, seventh Earl of Shaftesbury (1801–85): first as Lord Ashley, and from 1851, when he succeeded his father to the title, as Lord Shaftesbury, this Victorian aristocrat devoted his life to two causes: the relief of suffering and the Evangelical wing of the Church of England. He entered parliament at the age of twenty-five, and campaigned for social reform – in the mines, factories and lunatic asylums, in public health, and for the 'climbing boys' or young chimney-sweeps. His burden of public work involved fact-finding commissions, writing long and detailed memoranda, drafting legislation, parliamentary speeches, and chairmanship of regulatory bodies set up under new Acts of Parliament. He was also very active in the voluntary social services, particularly those for children. This tireless devotion to the needs of the poor and oppressed sprang from his religious convictions. He supported the foundation of the S.P.C.K. and the Y.M.C.A., chaired the Lord's Day Observance Society, and became the virtual leader of the Evangelical movement in parliament. When Lord Palmerston became Prime Minister in 1855, he turned to Shaftesbury for advice on ecclesiastical appointments; and in the ensuing ten years, Shaftesbury was responsible for the appointment of five archbishops, twenty bishops and thirteen cathedral deans – all of his own Evangelical persuasion. These appointments were roundly condemned by *Dr Pusey and the Anglo-Catholic wing of the Church. But Shaftesbury's reputation rests less on his ventures into the tricky waters of ecclesiastical appointment than on his unique and whole-hearted contribution to many kinds of social reform. [1 October, A.]

Cranmer, Thomas (1489–1556) was a quiet Cambridge scholar recruited by Henry VIII as one of a team of theologians who were to find a way of annulling his marriage to Catherine of Aragon. His own views inclined towards Lutheranism, and on a diplomatic mission to Germany he met and married the daughter of a Lutheran theologian. He became archbishop of Canterbury in 1532. He was president of Convocation when it declared the royal marriage null and void, conducted Anne Boleyn's coronation, and stood as godfather to her daughter Elizabeth. His main work was in reforming the English Church, and supervising the preparation of the Great Bible (a combination of the translations of Miles Coverdale and *William Tyndale), and the first Book of Common Prayer in English. Many of the collects are Cranmer's own work. When Mary Tudor succeeded to the throne, he refused to escape, believing in the validity of the reforms which he had initiated. He was imprisoned in Oxford, ceremonially stripped of his office, condemned as a heretic, and subjected to great psychological pressure over two years to force him to recant. Two days after he finally gave in, he was led out for execution. Instead of repeating his recantation, he firmly stated his belief in the Reformation. He

was burned at the stake, thrusting the hand which had signed his recantation into the flames first. [21 March, A.]

Crispin and Crispinian (c. 305): there are three separate strands of tradition about these two saints, who are thought to have been martyred in

the persecutions of Maximian or Diocletian. One is that they were Roman noblemen who died in Rome. The second is that they were missionaries who went to Gaul and earned their living as shoemakers in Soissons until they were reported to the authorities there. *Gregory of Tours wrote about them at the end of the fourth century, and *Eligius of Noyon, who was a goldsmith, enriched their shrine at Soissons. The third is that they fled Gaul and settled in a house on the site of the present Swan Inn at Faversham. They have an altar in Faversham church. It seems likely that relics were taken to both Soissons and Faversham, and the stories tying them to these localities developed from local devotion or the promotion of pilgrimages. If Henry V did not actually invoke 'Crispin Crispian' before the battle of Agincourt, he does so with great effect in Shakespeare's play. [25 October, A. R.]

Crispina of Theveste (304): there are three special reasons for commemorating Crispina: she was a martyr of the Church in North Africa, of which we have only very scanty records; she conducted a very able defence in court, of which something like a transcript survives; and *Augustine mentions her as a celebrated martyr, whom he compares to *Agnes and the virgin martyrs of Rome, though she was a married woman with children. She was brought before the proconsul Anulinus at Theveste (now Tabessa) and cross-examined by him. The dialogue between them is sharp and compelling: it may have been edited by a later hand, but it records the stand of a very courageous woman. The proconsul threatens to have her beheaded for refusing to worship the gods of Rome, and she retorts: 'Thank God for that. I should certainly lose my head if I took to worshipping them . . . My God, who was and who is, willed that I be born. He brought me to salvation through the waters of baptism. And he is with me to stay my soul from committing the sacrilege you require.' She was executed, and there was a basilica at Theveste which may have contained her shrine. [5 December, R.]

Curé d'Ars: see Vianney

Cuthbert (687) was at Lindisfarne a generation after the Synod of Whitby, and became so celebrated for his holiness and wisdom that both the Scots and the Irish have claimed him as one of their own. He probably came from the Lammermuir Hills on the Scottish border, and was a monk at Melrose abbey, trained in the Celtic Rite. He went on long missionary journeys in the neighbourhood, sometimes for a month at a time, talking to the villagers, and trying to win them away from superstition and squalor. He accepted the Latin Rite after Whitby, and after Colman had taken his party back to Iona, he was sent to Lindisfarne to help to bring the monastery into conformity. He kept his Celtic simplicity, and after twelve years he felt called to the solitary life. He became a hermit on the remote island of Farne, where he could be in close communion with God and nature, and face his own spiritual struggles with the elements. He was there for some years, but when *Theodore of Tarsus became archbishop of Canterbury and set about reorganizing the Church, he was called back to Lindisfarne as bishop. It is said that he left his island retreat in tears. After two years, he developed a mortal illness, and he went back to Farne to die. Durham cathedral has his shrine, which is still a place of pilgrimage. [20 March, A. R.]

Cyprian of Carthage (c. 200–258) was of Roman stock, and studied law and rhetoric before he became a Christian and was ordained. In 248 he became bishop of Carthage. During the persecutions of the Emperor Decian he went into exile, but he wrote a series of pastoral letters to his people, many of which are still extant. When the persecutions were over, he returned and had to deal with the *Lapsi* – Christians who had complied with the demand that they should worship the Roman gods, or who had purchased false certificates to indicate that they had done so. Cyprian dealt with a potentially divisive situation by ruling that they should undergo penances, but might be readmitted to the Church after a suitable interval. In the later persecutions of the Emperor Decian, he again went into exile for a time but returned to Carthage, believing that he must himself give witness. He was martyred in 258. [15 September, A. 16 September, R. O.]

Cyril of Alexandria (376–444) was the patriarch of Alexandria from 412 until his death, and was noted for his adherence to the principles of the Council of Nicaea and the writings of the Early Fathers. He upheld the doctrine that the Virgin Mary was not only *Christotokous*, Christ-bearing, but also *Theotokous*, God-bearing. He is held in high regard in the Eastern Orthodox Church, but some Western commentators have emphasized his rigidity, which caused divisions in the Church. As assistant to his uncle, the previous patriarch, he took part in the persecution of *John of Damascus; as patriarch, he was responsible for convening the Council of Ephesus, which condemned patriarch Nestorius of Constantinople and led to the creation of a separate Nestorian Church. He was also instrumental in having the Jews driven out of Alexandria. [27 June, A. R. O.]

Cyril of Jerusalem (c. 315–86) became bishop of Jerusalem in 350. His episcopate lasted for thirty-five years, and he was destined to spend fifteen of them in exile, since the bitter divisions caused by Arian's supporters led to his deposition on three separate occasions. He used his time out of office to prepare his *Catechetical Instructions*, a valuable source of material on liturgy and Christian teaching in the fourth century. He is also credited with the drafting of the Holy Week liturgy, elements of which are still in use in both the Eastern and Western Churches. As a boy of about thirteen, he is said to have witnessed *Helena's discovery of the True Cross. [18 March, A. R. O.]

Cyril (c. 827–69) and **Methodius** (c. 815–84): these two brothers, born in Thessalonika, had remarkable linguistic skills. Cyril was a scholar priest from Constantinople who led a mission to the Ukraine, and invented what is now known as Cyrillic script for the Slavonic language, which then had no written form. He began to translate the Bible. Methodius was for a time the governor of a Slav colony in the Eastern Empire. In 862, in response to a request from the Christian duke of Moravia, who wanted links with the Eastern Empire to prevent domination by Frankish or Germanic powers, the two were sent to his territories, where they came into conflict with Western missionaries from Bavaria. Relations between the Eastern and the Western Churches were already very strained, but Pope Hadrian II supported Cyril and Methodius rather than the Bavarian bishops. They were summoned to Rome, where Hadrian ordained Methodius, who was still a layman; and the brothers' Slavonic liturgy was celebrated in churches in Rome. Cyril died in Rome, but Methodius lived for nearly a quarter of a century longer. He continued Cyril's work on the Slavonic Bible, compiled a book of Byzantine ecclesiastical and civil law, and worked in Moravia, facing further difficult conflicts with the Bavarian bishops. He died in what is now the Czech Republic, and the brothers are regarded as patrons of ecumenism between East and West. [14 February, A. R. O.]

Damasus I (384), the 'Spanish Pope', was the son of a priest who officiated at the church of San Lorenzo in Rome. His election as pope in 366 was marked by bitter disputes and violence in the streets of the city. The charioteers and the grave-diggers in the catacombs came out to support him, and about 150 people were killed in affrays. Once confirmed in office, Damasus lived in considerable magnificence, and entertained the noble families of Rome lavishly. In 380, both the Eastern and the Western emperors proclaimed

Christianity as the official religion of the Empire, and the public worship of the old Roman gods ceased. Damasus initiated drainage and construction work in the catacombs, making it possible for groups of pilgrims to visit, and he devoted himself to the restoration of the shrines of the martyrs. He composed inscriptions for many, some of which are still extant. *Jerome, who was the papal secretary for three years, advised him that he was 'the successor of the Fisherman' and 'the rock on which the Church is built'. Damasus was the first pope to speak of Rome as 'the apostolic see'. He wrote in one epigram that 'though the East sent the apostles, yet because of their martyrdom, Rome has acquired a superior right to claim them as citizens'. He virtually created the Vatican administrative system, sending formal rulings to the other bishops rather than the pastoral advice they had received from his predecessors, and setting up a papal archive. A Ghirlandaio fresco in the Sistine Chapel shows him wearing the papal tiara. [11 December, R.]

Danes: Martyrs under the Danes (ninth century): Norse raiders of this period often exhibited a special fury against monasteries, smashing their altars and sacred vessels, and putting the monks to the sword. Among those commemorated are two monks of Chertsey abbey, Abbot Hedda of Peterborough, Abbot Theodore and monks of Croyland abbey, and monks of Thorney. They are listed in many older collections of the lives of English saints. See also *Edmund of East Anglia. [10 April, R.]

David of Scotland (1085–1153) was the youngest of the three sons of *Margaret of Scotland and Malcolm Canmore. He was only eight years old when his parents died, and he was brought up at the court of Henry I of England, whose queen was David's sister. He succeeded his brothers Edgar and Alexander as king of Scotland, kept friendly relations with England, where he held a number of baronies, and supported Henry I's daughter, the Empress Matilda, in her struggle against Stephen of Blois for the English throne. In Scotland, he founded five bishoprics and many monasteries and churches, and encouraged closer links with Rome. *Aelred of Rievaulx, who was his close friend and confidant, wrote an encomium praising the quality of his spiritual life, his chastity and his generous alms-giving. [24 May, R.]

David of Wales (? 520 – 589) is the patron of Wales. His mother, Non or Nonna, is commemorated as a saint in Cornwall and Brittany, and his father is said to have been a member of a princely family of Ceredigion (Cardigan). The earliest account of his life is that of Rhugyfarch, son of Bishop Julien of St David's, written about 1090, and based on oral tradition. According to this, David was born in Pembrokeshire, became a priest, studied under a Welsh scholar-monk named Paulinus, and founded the monastery at Mynyw (Menevia), where he became both abbot and bishop. The régime was a very strict one, based on the ascetic practices of the Desert Fathers (see *Antony), and the monastery became a great centre of learning. Rhugyfarch's claims that David became archbishop of Wales by common consent, and that he travelled to the Holy Land, where he was consecrated by the patriarch of Jerusalem, may be unfounded: at the time when he wrote, soon after the Norman Conquest, the Welsh Church was trying to maintain its independence from Canterbury; but he may have travelled to Brittany and Cornwall, and monks from these Celtic lands came to study at Menevia. His cult was approved by Pope Callistus II in 1120, and two pilgrimages to St David's were reckoned to be equal in merit to a pilgrimage to Rome. 'Taffy' as a name for Welshmen comes from the Welsh spelling of his name, Dafydd, but there is no satisfactory explanation of how the tradition arose of wearing a leek or a daffodil on his feast day. [A. R. 1 March.]

Deiniol (?584): his name is a Welsh form of Daniel, and he was the founder of two great monasteries, Bangor Fawr on the Menai Straits and Bangor Iscoed in Clwyd. According to Bede, there were so many monks at Bangor Iscoed that they were divided into seven sections, each with no less than 300, and the monastery was the most famous in Britain. Deiniol was regarded as the first bishop of Bangor. The most famous dedication to him is that of St Deiniol's, Hawarden, where W. E. Gladstone's great library is still available to readers. [11 September, R.]

Denys of Paris (c. 250), patron of Paris, is said by *Gregory of Tours to have been born in Italy. He was sent with five other missionaries to convert the Gauls. He and two companions, Rusticus and Eleutherius, set up a church on an island in the Seine, but were seized and beheaded. They were buried at the place called Saint-Denis, and the abbey that was raised round their shrine became the coronation-place and burial-place of French kings. This story was complicated in the ninth century by Abbot Hilduin of Saint-Denis, who claimed to identify Denys with Dionysius the Areopagite (Acts 17:13–34), and also with the fifth-century Neo-Platonist writer Pseudo-Dionysius. The highly fanciful *Legends of Denys* were a result of combining these three separate personalities. [9 October, A. R.]

Dominic (1170–1221) was the founder of the Order of Preachers, otherwise known as the Dominicans or Black Friars. He was born at Calruega in Spain, and became an Augustinian friar. In 1203 he accompanied the Bishop of Osma to the Languedoc, where the Cathars or Albigenses had been declared heretics. The Dominicans started as a small band of special preachers whose task it was to convert them. The Cathars were put down with great ferocity by a military crusade led by Simon de Montfort after the fall of Toulouse in 1214; but the Dominicans developed into a new Order – mendicants who combined a simple way of life with theological scholarship. They were officially approved as Friars Preachers in 1217, and the movement spread throughout Christendom. *Thomas Aquinas was a Dominican. [8 August, A. R.]

Donne, John (1572–1631): this Elizabethan poet, lawyer and theologian, was brought up as a staunch Catholic. Born in an age of religious turmoil, appalled by the ferocity displayed to both Catholic and Protestant martyrs, and excited by the implications of the discoveries of Copernicus, Galileo and Columbus, he followed a long and painful intellectual journey in poverty before he was ordained as a priest of the Church of England at the age of forty-three. He proved to be an outstanding preacher, and a powerful apologist for the Anglican position. He became dean of St Paul's in 1621. His poetry – many commentators rank him as the greatest of the metaphysical poets – uniquely sets the expression of love between a man and a woman in the context of God's creative activity in the universe. [31 March, A.]

Drexel, Katharine (1858–1955): this American benefactress was proclaimed a saint of the Roman Catholic Church in January 2000. Her grandfather, Francis Martin Drexel, was the founder of Drexel's Bank in Philadelphia, and she inherited great wealth. Brought up as a member of a powerful and influential family, she abandoned the life of a young socialite to become a nun, training in the convent of the Sisters of Mary in Pittsburgh. On the suggestion of Pope Leo XIII, she founded her own Order, the Sisters of the Blessed Sacrament, devoted to bringing Christianity to the American Indians and Negroes. She travelled indefatigably through the West and South of the United States, founding schools and orphanages. She went into Indian territory not long after Sitting Bull had finally laid down his war pipe, and in Texas she was threatened by the Ku Klux Klan. She founded Xavier College in the coloured quarter of New Orleans, and saw it grow into Xavier University, the first American university for non-whites. She lived to the age of ninety-seven. An obituary in the *New York Times* recorded that she 'gave her money as cheerfully as she gave her life'. [3 March, R.]

Dunstan (c. 909–88) was appointed abbot of Glastonbury by King Edmund of Wessex and was given land for his monastery. Though there were religious houses for women in Wessex, this appears to have been the first for men in the Anglo-Saxon period. Exiled by Edmund's successor, Dunstan spent two years in continental monasteries and learned about the Benedictine Rule. On his return to Wessex, he was appointed successively bishop of Worcester, bishop of London and, in 960, archbishop of Canterbury. Together with *Oswald, bishop of Worcester and Aethelwold, bishop of Winchester, he is credited with a remarkable revival of monastic life in southern England. The liturgical service which Dunstan devised for the coronation of Edgar at Bath abbey in 973 is still used, almost in its entirety, for the coronation of British monarchs. [19 May, A. R.]

Eata (686) was one of the first twelve boys taught by *Adrian at Lindisfarne. He entered the monastery at Melrose and became abbot. There he trained *Cuthbert, who was greatly devoted to him. After the Synod of Whitby, Eata accepted the Latin Rite and became prior of Lindisfarne, and in 678, bishop of Bernicia, the northern half of Northumbria. When *Theodore of Tarsus, archbishop of Canterbury, reorganized the northern dioceses, he became bishop of Hexham, while Cuthbert became bishop of Lindisfarne. He died a year later, and was buried at Hexham. *Bede calls him 'a gentle man, and greatly revered'. [26 October, R.]

Edmund of Abingdon (c. 1175–1240) studied in Oxford and Paris, and taught Divinity at Oxford in the Scholastic tradition. St Edmund's College, long known as 'Teddy Hall', commemorates his name. He became treasurer of Salisbury cathedral and was a noted public preacher. Pope Gregory IX nominated him as archbishop of Canterbury in 1233. He exerted a beneficent influence over the young king, Henry III, and became involved in power struggles with his former guardian and regent, Hubert de Burgh. Edmund's diplomacy averted the threat of civil war. He had some notable conflicts with the papal legate, resisting attempts to limit his authority as metropolitan. He died at Pontigny, and was buried there. [16 November, A. R.]

Edmund of East Anglia (841–70) was a young king who led his troops into battle with the Viking invaders (see *Martyrs under the Danes). He

was defeated by a tribal chief named Ingvar, who offered to let him rule as a vassal under Danish suzerainty. Edmund refused twice, and he and his men were pursued by the Danes. He was ritually tortured and finally beheaded. There is some debate as to where his martyrdom took place (both Norfolk and Suffolk claim him), but he was buried at the place now known as Bury St Edmunds. More than sixty English churches are dedicated in his name. He became a national hero, a model of holiness, courage and resistance to foreign invasion. In the Wilton Diptych (now in the National Gallery) he appears with Edward the Confessor as a sponsor of the young Edward II, presenting him to the Virgin and Child. [20 November, A. R.]

Edwin of Northumbria (584–633) received the Roman emissary *Paulinus as escort to his Kentish bride, and after much thought and discussion, was converted by him. The entire royal household, including his thirteen-year-old relative *Hilda of Whitby was baptized with him. He built the first (wooden) church on the site of the Roman legionary headquarters in

York, where York Minster now stands. King Edwin was defeated and killed at the battle of Hatfield Chase in 633 by the ferocious Penda of Mercia and his ally Cadwalla of Wales. A year later, *Oswald defeated and killed Cadwalla, regaining the kingdom and bringing in *Aidan and Celtic monks from Iona. [12 October, R.]

Edward the Confessor (?1004–66), son of Ethelred 'the Unready', was taken to Normandy by his mother, Emma, after Ethelred's death in 1016. Though Emma subsequently returned to England to make a dynastic marriage with Canute, Edward stayed with his uncle, Duke Robert of Normandy, for twenty-five years before he was called

back to England as king. His title of 'the Confessor' probably refers to his Christian witness. He was a man of great piety who endowed a number of monasteries. Though tradition has made him a defender of the rights of the Anglo-Saxons, he was strongly pro-Norman, bringing in many Norman knights and clerics, and strengthening links with the papacy. When he had to make his death-bed choice between his Saxon brother-in-law Harold Godwinson and his cousin William of Normandy, it is likely that he favoured William, though the Saxon barons pressed for Harold to be his successor. Edward died on 5 January 1066, and

Harold took the throne for rather less than a year, before he was defeated by the Normans. Edward was buried in the abbey church of St Peter at Westminster, one of his own foundations, which he had chosen as the place of coronation and burial for English monarchs. [13 October, A. R.]

Elfleda (653–715), niece of *Hilda of Whitby, was an infant when her father, Oswy of Northumbria, offered to consecrate her to the religious life if he defeated Penda of Mercia. He was victorious, and the child was put in Hilda's care. Elfleda was a scholar and a woman of intelligence. She was a friend of both *Wilfrid and *Cuthbert, and she seems to have played a considerable part in reconciling their views at the Synod of Whitby. She became abbess of Whitby in about 704. During her time as abbess, the monastery had an excellent reputation for scholarship, and produced the earliest life of *Gregory the Great. [8 February, R.]

Elizabeth of Hungary (1207–31): Elizabeth's short life fell into three periods: her childhood in Christian Hungary, as the daughter of King

Andrew II; her marriage to the Landgrave Ludwig of Thuringia, which proved a love match, and brought her three children by the time she was twenty; and her melancholy widowhood after Ludwig's death. Her infant son became the landgrave, under male guardianship. Her two daughters were placed in nunneries, and she was left under the direction of a former inquisitor, Conrad of Marburg, who treated her with great harshness and severity. She died at the age of twenty-four, and the memory of this gentle, maltreated princess was preserved in Germany until the Reformation. Her shrine at Marburg was a place of pilgrimage until a Lutheran landgrave had it destroyed. [18 November, A. 17 November, R. O.]

Eloi (Eligius, c. 588–660) was a goldsmith at the court of the Frankish king Clotaire II. He was given gold and precious stones to make a throne, and finding that there was too much

material for one, made two. Clotaire admired both his workmanship and his honesty, and made him Master of the Mint at Marseilles. Some coins of this period bear his portrait. He made many famous reliquaries, including those of *Denys and *Genevieve in Paris, and *Crispin and Crispinian at Soissons. He became wealthy and influential, but when he was in his fifties, he asked to be relieved of his duties. The king gave him land for a monastery at Solignac, and there he retired with a group of disciples. He was called out of his retreat, probably in 641, when the people

35

of Noyon elected him bishop by popular acclaim. He was as good a pastor as he had been a goldsmith, carrying out missions in Flanders, and preaching powerfully against the superstitions, many of Greek or Roman origin, which were still common. His sermons provide the best account we have of the teaching and practices of the Church in Frankish territory at this time. He worked with the regent, *Queen Bathildis, to free slaves, many of them captives of war: Romans, Britons, Moors and Saxons. He was bishop of Noyon for nineteen years, and became one of the most popular saints in western Europe. Chaucer's Prioress swears 'by Saint Loy'. [1 December, R.]

Ephrem of Syria (c. 306–73), also called Efrem or Ephraim, is known in the Eastern Church as 'the Harp of the Holy Ghost'. He was born in Nisibia in Mesopotamia, where he became head of the cathedral school. When the city was ceded to Persia and the Christians left, he retired to a cave near Edessa, where he acquired great respect and influence for his holy and abstemious life. When there was a famine in Edessa in 372–3, the wealthy men of the city entrusted him with money and supplies to relieve the starving population, and he organized a relief service for the sick. He died only a month later. Ephrem became a deacon, but it is not clear whether he was ever ordained priest. In his cave, he wrote prolifically: his texts against the Gnostics were famous, and his Nisibian hymns are still sung in Syrian churches. He is thought to have invented organized hymn-singing as part of worship. His meditations on the Gospels show great devotion and poetic power. He wrote in Syriac. Some of his works were translated into Greek, but it was not until 1730 that they were translated into

Latin and became widely known in the Western Church. [9 June, A. R. O.]

Epiphanius of Salamis (c. 310–403) was born in Palestine, and became abbot of the monastery at Eleutheropolis. He is known in the Eastern Church as 'the oracle of Palestine' and is commemorated as one of the Fathers of the Church. He stood up fearlessly against imperial persecution, and his powerful writings challenged the heresies of his day. In 367 he became bishop of Salamis and metropolitan of Cyprus. It is said that he became very headstrong and outspoken in his old age, but if the dates are right, he lived to ninety-three, and towards the end, he must have known that his time was short. [12 May, R. O.]

Eskil (c. 1080) was a monk of Glastonbury who accompanied *Sigfrid on his mission to Scandinavia. While Sigfrid worked in Norway, Eskil moved on to Sweden, where he was consecrated bishop at Strangnäs, near Stockholm. When the Christian king Inge died, he was succeeded by Sweyn the Bloody, who led a violent reaction against the Church and instituted a great festival glorifying the old Norse gods. A pagan altar was set up and sacrifices were prepared. Eskil, seeing that former Christians were taking part, confronted them and pleaded with them to give up their pagan practices. When his plea went unheeded, he called on God for help. There was a violent hailstorm in which the altar and the sacrifices were destroyed. But Sweyn declared that this was sorcery and ordered Eskil to be killed. This martyrdom was remembered: the place where he was buried is still called Eskilstuna. [12 June, R.]

Ethelbert of Kent (560–615) married Bertha, daughter of Charibert of Paris, who was a Christian, agreeing that she and her court should be free to practise their faith. *Pope Gregory the Great sent *Augustine, later of Canterbury, on his English mission to Ethelbert's court in 597. Ethelbert's first reaction was hesitant, but he became the first Anglo-Saxon king to be converted to Christianity. Pope Gregory sent him a letter and gifts in 601. Ethelbert gave Augustine land in Canterbury, and built the monastery of St Peter and St Paul for him. He also influenced Sabert, king of the East Saxons, whose jurisdiction extended to London (then exclusively north of the Thames), and founded the first church on the site of St Paul's cathedral. Ethelbert introduced a code of law in his kingdom, and reigned peacefully for fifty-six years. A candle was kept burning in front of his tomb in Canterbury cathedral until the time of the Reformation. [24 February, R.]

Ethelburga of Barking (c. 675) was the sister of Bishop Earconwald of London, who was appointed to the see by *Theodore of Tarsus. There is a tradition that they were members of the royal family of the East Saxons. Earconwald built two monasteries, one for himself at Chertsey, and a double monastery at Barking for Ethelburga: as abbess, she had oversight of both the men's and the women's community. He also sent for a French prioress to instruct her in the Benedictine tradition, which she followed. Little more is known about her apart from *Bede's comment that 'she always bore herself in a manner worthy of her brother the bishop, upright of life and constantly planning for her community'. [11 October, A. 12 October, R.]

Etheldreda of Ely (679) was popularly known as St Audrey in medieval times. The word 'tawdry' came from comments on the poor quality of goods

sold at the fair on her feast day; but it also indicates how popular the fair was, and how widely her feast was kept. A daughter of King Anna of the East Saxons, she sought the religious life, but was forced into two dynastic marriages. The first was to a prince in the Fen country who died soon after the wedding, and left her the Isle of Ely, then surrounded by swamps and marshes. The second was to Egfrid, the son of King Oswy, who was a boy of fifteen. Neither marriage was consummated. When Egfrid wanted Ethelburga to live with him as his wife, she pleaded a prior commitment to virginity, and appealed to *Wilfrid, who was then archbishop of York. Wilfrid ruled that she should be allowed to enter a convent, and after her novitiate she built a double monastery at Ely which she ruled as abbess. She was greatly respected, and scenes from her life are carved on the walls of the Lantern Tower in Ely cathedral. [23 June, A. R.]

Ethelwold of Winchester (984) was a monk of Glastonbury, and became prior when *Dunstan was abbot. About 954 he became abbot of Abingdon, where he revived a great monastery which had fallen into a sorry state, and instituted the Benedictine Rule. In 963, after Dunstan became archbishop of Canterbury, King Edgar approved Ethelwold's appointment as bishop of Winchester, the royal capital of Wessex. He embarked on monastic reforms, dismissing the lax canons of Winchester and replacing them with monks from Abingdon – a policy which led to protests and the nickname of 'Boanerges' (son of thunder). Together with Dunstan and *Oswald of York, he worked to bring about a revival of monastic life in England, and reformed some thirty monasteries, while founding others. He is said to have translated the Rule of St Benedict into Anglo-Saxon. [1 August, R.]

Faringdon, Hugh (1539) was, together with *Richard Whiting and *John Beche, one of the Three Abbots martyred on the orders of Henry VIII at the time of the dissolution of the monasteries. He became abbot of Reading in 1520, and was strongly opposed to Lutheran doctrines when they reached England, calling the Protestants 'heretics and knaves'. He was on good personal terms with Henry VIII, who often saw him when the court was at Windsor, and called him 'my own abbot'. When the question of the king's divorce arose, he went as far as he could to keep his monarch's favour: he signed the petition to the Pope for the annulment of Henry's marriage to Catherine of Aragon, accepted the royal supremacy, and the king's subsequent marriages to Anne Boleyn and Jane Seymour. No doubt he wanted to preserve his monastery as well as his head; but when the dissolution of the greater monasteries began, he was driven to resistance. In 1539, he was arrested and charged with treason. On the scaffold outside the gateway to his abbey, he spoke out clearly for the supremacy of the pope, and he was executed together with two priests. [1 December, R.]

Felicity: see **Perpetua and Felicity**

Felix of Dunwich (648) was a Burgundian bishop who volunteered to undertake a mission to the East Angles. He carried out a mission in what are now the counties of Cambridgeshire, Suffolk and Norfolk, and founded a monastery at Soham. As a priest of the Latin Church, he preceded *Augustine of Canterbury by about 150 years, and was reputedly on good terms with the

Celtic clergy to the north of his missionary area. Little knowledge has survived of his ministry, which was apparently extensive. The area was later overrun by Viking invaders, and his episcopal seat, Dunwich, is now covered by the sea as a result of coastal erosion. [8 March, A. R.]

Ferard, Elizabeth (1883) is commemorated as the first deaconess of the Church of England. Bishop Tait of London sent her to Kaiserswerth, the Lutheran deaconess institution where *Florence Nightingale had studied nursing. The Tractarians, led by *Dr Pusey, were initiating Anglo-Catholic religious communities for women, and the bishop evidently wanted a Protestant model for women's work in the Church. Miss Ferard and her companions started a community (without formal religious vows or claims to ecclesiastical status) in the King's Cross area of London, as the Community of St Andrew. They carried out a variety of works, mainly serving women and children, in this poor district, within the parish structure and under the direction of the clergy. In July 1862, Miss Ferard received the bishop's licence as the first deaconess. The Community later moved to Notting Hill. [18 July, A.]

Ferrar, Nicholas (1592–1637) was a wealthy and influential man, the secretary of the powerful Virginia Company (until James I revoked its licence in 1624 and made its extensive properties in North America a colony). During a plague epidemic, Nicholas took his mother, his brother, and sister and their families to the dilapidated manor of Little Gidding in Huntingdonshire, where he founded a unique Christian community on Puritan lines. This devout community, remote from the affairs of the world, drew *George

Herbert and *Isaac Watts, among others, to share its pattern of worship and its structured way of life. Some of their works (which they printed themselves) are now in the British Library. The community was wrongly suspected of Roman Catholic practices and was raided by Puritan troops in 1646, ten years after the founder's death. Nothing remains except the church which inspired T. S. Eliot's poem in *The Four Quartets*. [4 December, A.]

Finnian of Clonard (549) was a founder of monasteries and a bishop who was known as 'the Teacher of the Saints of Ireland'. He was born and educated in Leinster, trained in the monasteries of Wales in the tradition of *David, and was abbot of the great monastery at Clonard, where he is reputed to have had three thousand disciples. It was a centre of learning, particularly for biblical studies, and a missionary centre: Finnian sent his monks out with a Gospel-book, a crozier and a reliquary, round which they were enjoined to build a church or a monastery. Over the centuries, the monastery suffered from the repeated attacks of the Danes, and later of the Normans. In the thirteenth century, what remained of the monastery at Clonard was taken over by Augustinian canons. The Irish documents relating to Finnian have been translated into Latin and English, and have attracted a considerable interest from scholars. The *Penitential of Finnian*, now firmly attributed to him, demonstrates the breadth of his scholarship, since it includes elements from older Welsh and Irish penitentials, and from the writings of Latin scholars such as *Jerome and John Cassian. [12 December, R.]

Fisher, John (1469–1535): bishop, cardinal and martyr under Henry VIII,

Fisher is commemorated on the same day as his contemporary and fellow-martyr, Thomas More. He was the most influential theologian in England. As vice-chancellor of the University of Cambridge, he founded Christ's College and St John's College, built up the university library, and introduced the study of Greek and Hebrew in accordance with the New Learning of the Renaissance period. Henry VIII made him bishop of Rochester: he refused wealthier sees, and combined painstaking attention to his pastoral duties with continuing scholarship. He was regarded as the chief defender of the Church against Lutheranism, preaching powerful sermons and writing a rebuttal of Luther's propositions in four weighty volumes. Inevitably, he became the leader of the movement against Henry VIII's split with Rome – and a marked man, suffering harassment from Thomas Cromwell's men and several attempts on his life. He accepted the Act of Supremacy with the proviso, 'so far as the law of Christ allows'; but when Pope Paul III refused to agree to the annulment of the king's marriage to Catherine of Aragon, he obeyed the pope. In 1534, he was arrested on a charge of treason and sent to the Tower of London. Pope Paul III sent him a cardinal's hat, and the king swore that he should not have a head to put it on. Weak and emaciated, he was executed on Tower Hill on 22 June 1535. [6 July, A. 22 June, R.]

Fortunatus, Venantius (c. 535–605): this cultured Roman poet and scholar nearly lost his eyesight in his late twenties, and he attributed his recovery from blindness to the miraculous intervention of *Martin of Tours. When he left Ravenna to make a pilgrimage to Tours, the Lombard invasion of northern Italy was already imminent, and he never returned. On his journey across France, he stayed in noble houses and thanked his hosts with flattering and elaborate poems in the Roman manner, but when he reached Tours, he was not at home in the somewhat uncouth society of the Franks. He found a refuge in Poitiers, where Queen Radegund had founded the monastery of the Holy Cross. He became chaplain to the queen and her cultured nuns, who appreciated his wit and his learning. They entertained him royally, and he repaid them with charming letters, poems and shrewd advice on political matters; but this rather worldly cleric also developed a deep and genuine spirituality. He is the author of some great liturgical hymns, including 'The royal banners forward go' and 'Sing, my tongue, the glorious telling'. Some of his hymns are based on the rhythms of the songs sung by the Roman legionaries on the march. He also wrote a number of lives of the saints. When he was sixty-nine, the people of Poitiers elected him bishop. He took on his new pastoral tasks with great zeal, but he died within a year of his consecration. [14 December, R. O.]

Foster: see **Vedast**

Foucauld, Charles de (1858–1916): this unusual and gifted French aristocrat undertook military service with the Chasseurs d'Afrique, and subsequently explored Morocco, travelling in disguise as a poor Jew to parts then inaccessible to Christians, and publishing two scholarly books on his discoveries. He became a Trappist monk, but was released from the Order to find a life of even greater silence and solitude. After some three years in the Holy Land, he went back to Africa as an anchorite, living in the Sahara Desert near a French garrison in austerity and humility. He worked with the Tuaregs, not attempting to convert

them to his own Catholic faith, but preaching natural law, the commandments of the God who is worshipped by Christians and Muslims alike, and works of charity. He spoke their language fluently, and completed a French-Tuareg dictionary and a translation of Tuareg poems. He was much loved and respected by the tribesmen. His death came about during World War I, when the Turks stirred up hatred against the French, and he was shot by a fanatic. [1 December, A. R.]

Fox, George (1624–91): the son of Puritan parents, Fox left home at the age of twenty-one to find the answer to the religious questions which dominated his life. He came to the conclusion that 'being bred in Oxford and Cambridge did not qualify a man to be a minister of Christ'; and that God did not dwell in temples made with hands. Together with other 'Friends of Truth', he became convinced that the True Light illuminated all who sought it, without the need for clergy, churches or formal prayers. They refused to bear arms, pay tithes or swear oaths. They interrupted services in what they called 'steeple-houses' and refused to doff their hats to people in authority. The Friends were called 'Quakers' because they shook with the force of the Spirit. They faced considerable persecution from the landed gentry, clergy and magistrates in the provinces. They were charged with sedition, riot and other offences, and they survived beatings and repeated imprisonment for their convictions. Many went abroad. George Fox travelled to the English colonies in North America and the West Indies and on the Continent to preach to a growing movement. After the passing of the Toleration Act in 1689, these peaceful people were able to worship freely in England. George Fox's *Journal*, which describes the stormy early period of the Society of Friends, has become a classic of the movement for religious toleration. [13 January, A.]

Francis of Assisi (1181–1226), the son of a prosperous merchant of that city, dramatically renounced his heritage in order to follow a simple life of poverty and chastity outside the framework of the monastic system. He founded the Friars Minor (now the Society of St Francis), who took literally Christ's injunction to travel and preach the Gospel without money or baggage (Matt. 10:5–20). In a violent and venial society much given to worldly values, the movement grew rapidly and spread to other parts of Christendom. Francis was no revolutionary: he always worked within the framework of the Church, with the consent of the pope and the bishops, and he gained their support and cooperation. His respect for the priesthood was so great that he refused to become a priest himself, remaining a deacon, and he left the management of his Order to others. His church at San Damiano became the centre of the Franciscan movement. He encouraged *Clare of Assisi to found a parallel Order for women, and started a Third Order (tertiaries) for lay people willing to commit themselves to a rule of life. [4 October, A. R.]

Francis de Sales (1567–1622): more than half a century after *Jean Calvin's Protestant reforms, Francis was appointed by the Roman Catholic Church as the provost of Geneva. The title was an empty one, for the city of Geneva was still a Protestant theocratic state. In the mountainous rural areas, the scattered population was neglected by both Protestants and Catholics, and had tended to give up religious observance altogether. Francis trav-

elled through the district, regardless of wolves and bands of outlaws, reopening churches and finding priests to serve them. When Henri IV offered him a wealthy bishopric in France, he said that he had a poor wife already, and he could not desert her for a rich one. He became bishop of Geneva, resident in Annecy, in 1602, and it is as 'Monsieur de Genève' that he is remembered. A gentle and sensitive priest, he became renowned as a spiritual director, and many of his pastoral letters survive. His treatises, *On the Love of God* and the *Introduction to a Devout Life*, have become classics. [24 January, A. R.]

Francis Xavier: see **Xavier**

Frideswide (c. 680–727): the little that is known historically about Frideswide establishes that she was the daughter of a sub-king on the northern borders of Wessex, and that she was the first abbess of the double monastery at Oxford. Her church was set on fire, and most of its records destroyed, in 1002. Her shrine is known to have been a place of pilgrimage in the eleventh century, and her monastery was refounded as an Augustinian house of canons after the Norman Conquest. In the early fifteenth century, she was adopted as the patron of the University of Oxford. Cardinal Wolsey suppressed the monastery to provide revenues for Cardinal College (now Christ Church), which was built on the same site. The church became the cathedral church of the Oxford diocese. It was desecrated in 1558 by Protestant reformers who mixed Frideswide's bones with those of the wife of a Zwinglian theologian in order to suppress her cult. Part of the shrine has now been reconstructed. [19 October, A. R.]

Fry, Elizabeth (1780–1845): the wife of a Quaker banker, Elizabeth Fry visited Newgate prison, and was appalled at the condition of the women and their children, 'reduced to the state of wild beasts'. After facing much official opposition, she succeeded in starting a school for the children, and organized sewing groups for the women, whom she described as 'harmless and kind'. She pressed for the appointment of a matron, and for separate women's prisons with women staff. She visited and organized the convict ships which took women prisoners to the colonies, insisting that they should have decent conditions. Her many other reforms included a night shelter for the homeless in London, and the first training establishment for nurses. Elizabeth bore eleven children, and managed her large household with the dignity and Christian commitment which she brought to her public work. She is commemorated as a pioneer of early nineteenth-century social reform. [12 October, A.]

Gardiner, Allen (1794–1852): after the final defeat of Napoleon, the British Navy was cut back, and Allen Gardiner, a lieutenant of deep Evangelical conviction, turned to mission work, having seen the need for it in many parts of the world. He set up a mission station in Zulu territory in southern Africa, and worked in the islands of the Indian archipelago. In 1851 he led a small party, including a surgeon, a carpenter and a catechist, in a mission to Tierra del Fuego, on the southernmost tip of South America. It seems that they were totally unprepared for the climate or the task of converting the local people. They endured repeated storms and bitter cold. The Fuegans would not listen to them, and stole their supplies. They awaited further supplies, but these were delayed in the Falklands for want of transport, and the whole party died of starvation. Their journals were recovered, and it is thought that Allen Gardiner was the last to die, on 6 January 1852. This heroic and ill-fated expedition was widely reported in the English press. Later a missionary ship was named *The Allen Gardiner*, and his son became a missionary in Patagonia. [6 September, A.]

Genevieve of Paris (c. 500) is the patroness of Paris. She became a dedicated virgin at the age of fifteen, on

the death of her parents. Germanus of Auxerre blessed her as a child, and later sent her blessed bread as a token of his esteem for her work. She lived with her godmother in Paris, practising austerity and charity. When Paris was besieged and suffering from famine, she made an expedition by river along the Seine to Troyes with an armed band to secure provisions. She seems to have encountered great hostility – perhaps from the merchant classes who benefited from the scarcity of food. She inspired the people of Paris to build a church in honour of *Denys, and in 451 she led a campaign of prayer and fasting to avert the threat of attack by Attila the Hun. Many miracles were attributed to her, and she was invoked by the people of

Paris during times of crisis or national disaster. Her shrine was desecrated during the French Revolution, and the Panthéon, now the national mausoleum, was built on the site. There are many representations of her, including frescoes in the Panthéon (1877). [3 January, R. O.]

George (c. 304), patron of England, was probably martyred at Lydda, now Lod in Israel, during the persecutions of Diocletian. Pilgrims visited his tomb at Lydda in the fifth century, and a monastery in Jerusalem bore his name. His martyrdom was known in England in Anglo-Saxon times, and a fresh devotion to him was brought back by the Crusaders after the First Crusade. A vision of St George and St Demetrius was said to have resulted in the defeat of the Saracen army at the time of the siege of Antioch. He became the patron of soldiers, and Richard I is said to have placed his army under St George's special protection. Whether Henry V cried 'God for England, Harry and St George!' as he does in Shakespeare's play is not certain, but it is a fact that after the battle of Agincourt, St George's commemoration was raised to the status of a major feast. Edward III made George the patron of the Order of the Garter, and St George's Chapel, Windsor, is dedicated in his name. He had become an honorary Englishman. It was probably inevitable that a legend should develop that he had visited England from Ireland, and this seems to be the origin of the name 'St George's Channel' for the Irish Sea. George's cult came to embody the ideal of Christian chivalry. Though he did not, as far as we know, slay a dragon and rescue a maiden (there are various interpretations of this legend), he is also a patron of Russia, Venice, Genoa, Portugal, Aragon and Lithuania, he is one of the Fourteen Holy Helpers of medieval European tradition, and he is even mentioned in Islamic tradition. [23 April, A. R. O.]

George Mtasmindeli (1014–66): the curious name of this Orthodox saint means 'George of the Black Mountain'. He is also known as 'George the Athonite' (a reference to his connection with Mount Athos, where he was ordained and spent some time as abbot of Ivoron) and 'George the Hagiorite'. He became the disciple of another Georgian monk, George the Recluse, who urged him to use his excellent Greek education in translating Greek texts for the benefit of the Georgian (Iberian) Church. He translated the Old Testament, the New Testament and many of the works of the early Fathers of the Church. Though he refused to become a bishop, he did much to reform the Georgian Church and to defend it against the claims of the patriarch of Antioch. When Georgia was threatened by Turkish invasion, he set out for Mount Athos with twenty-four orphans whom he had taught Latin and Greek, intending that they should enter the monastery. He died on the way at Constantinople. The Georgian Church recognizes him as a Doctor of the Church. [27 June, R. O.]

Gildas (c. 500–570), known as 'the Wise', was a monk of the monastery of Llanilltyd in South Wales, and probably a pupil of *Illtud. An outstanding figure in Welsh monastic life, he also had connections with the Irish Church. *Finnian of Clonard was one of his pupils. For some years he was a hermit on Flatholm, an island in the Bristol Channel now off the coast of Weston-super-Mare, and it was here that he wrote his *De excidio Britanniae*, a powerful work about the failings of British rulers and clergy, prophesying doom at the hands of the heathen Saxons who were ravaging the coast. Historians have found this work, with its mixture of theology and denunciation, a fascinating source of speculation about the state of southern Britain about the time of the battle of Mount Badon – whether or not the battle involved the legendary King Arthur. It is the only contemporary British account of this period in the Dark Ages. Gildas probably exaggerated the effect of the invasions of Wessex in his day: he may have personally witnessed the siege of Pevensey, which was particularly barbarous. He became an abbot, and was commemorated in a number of Anglo-Saxon martyrologies. [29 January, R.]

Gilbert of Sempringham (c. 1083–1189) was a priest who founded a religious community on the estate in Lancashire which he inherited from his father. This began with seven devout young women who were professed as nuns. He later added lay sisters and lay brothers. The sisters followed the Benedictine Rule, the brothers the Cistercian Rule, and when he added priests, they were Augustinian canons. The Order, which was approved by Pope Eugenius III as the Sempringham Order, was thus an amalgam of three distinct monastic traditions. Other houses were set up in Lincolnshire and Yorkshire, and Gilbert travelled between them, helping in such tasks as carpentry or copying manuscripts. He was a quiet and modest superior, who led a very austere life. The Order became known as the Gilbertines, and when *Archbishop Thomas Becket had to escape the wrath of Henry II in 1163, he took shelter in their houses, and went disguised as a lay brother before escaping to the Continent. The king eventually pardoned Gilbert, and the Order continued to grow. By the time

of the dissolution of the monasteries, there were twenty-five monasteries in England and one in Scotland. The Order died out, but it is remembered as the only distinctively English Order in the history of Latin monasticism. [4 February, A. R.]

Giles of Provence (eighth century) was a hermit who lived in a wild and uninhabited area of Provence, near the mouth of the River Rhône, not far from

Marseilles. It is thought that he was a Greek from Athens. Later, others seeking seclusion from the world joined him, and the hermitage became a monastery. In the Middle Ages the monastery became a well-known pilgrimage centre. Pilgrims from England and northern Europe on their way to Jerusalem or Rome often sailed from Marseilles, which was a major port. Giles had a reputation as a healer, and in time became the patron of lepers. Because lepers were not allowed to enter medieval towns, there were often leper settlements outside the walls of a town, and a church built for the lepers frequently had a dedication to St Giles. Some 162 medieval churches were dedicated in his name, including the cathedral in Edinburgh and St Giles, Cripplegate, in London. His name is often attached to junctions, because he was also the patron saint of blacksmiths and smithies, which were usually sited at crossroads. St Giles's Fair is still celebrated annually in Winchester and Oxford. [1 September, A. R.]

Gilmore, Isabella (1842–1925): Isabella, a younger sister of William Morris, married a naval officer. When her husband died, she determined to become a hospital nurse. Though she encountered great opposition from her family, she worked at Guy's Hospital, which served a slum district of London, until the bishop of Rochester asked her to begin the work of deaconesses in his diocese. Women's work for the Church of England was developing rapidly, usually in the form of the revived women's Orders introduced by the Tractarians, and the bishop wanted to develop a form of service more appropriate to the average parish. Mrs Gilmore became a deaconess in 1887 at the age of 45. She trained many deaconesses, including head deaconesses for at least seven other dioceses, in work which specialized in parish visiting and groups for women and children, often in very poor parishes with many problems. Her paper on 'Deaconesses, their Qualifications and Status' (1908) claimed that the deaconess was the female equivalent of a deacon, bearing 'life-long character', but this claim was firmly denied by the Lambeth Conference of 1930, in which the bishops resolved that deaconesses were 'outside the historic Orders of the Ministry – supplementary and complementary to them'. A bas-relief in Southwark Cathedral commemorates her pioneer work. [16 April, A.]

Godric of Finchale (c. 1070–1170) led a roving life as a young man. He was born of a peasant family in Norfolk, became a pedlar in Lincolnshire, and then traded in Flanders and Denmark. He became so prosperous that he

was able to buy a half-share in one ship and a quarter-share in another, becoming captain of the second. Some sources identify him with the 'English pirate' named Godric who took Baldwin I, king of Jerusalem, to Jaffa in 1102. He is known to have made three pilgrimages to Jerusalem, and to have visited Rome and Compostela. When he gave up his seafaring life, he sold all his goods and renounced the world. He was over forty when he settled at Finchale on the River Weare, on the site now occupied by Finchale Priory. He accused himself of fraud and impurity in his worldly life, and led a penitential existence, living on roots and berries until he learned how to grow his own vegetables. He was to spend sixty years at Finchale. After some time, he was offered a rule of life and confraternity with the monks of Durham. He was also visited by *Aelred of Rievaulx and Robert of Newminster. He became celebrated as a wise counsellor and a healer, and wrote hymns in Middle English, some of which survive in a fourteenth-century manuscript in the British Library. Many legends became attached to his name in his later years. [21 May, R.]

Gore, Charles (1853–1932): Gore was an Oxford scholar who was appointed vice-principal of Cuddesdon theological college at the age of twenty-seven. A Christian Socialist in the tradition of F. D. Maurice, and a moderate Anglo-Catholic, he went on to become the first principal of Pusey House, Oxford, before founding the Community of the Resurrection in 1887. This is a community of Anglican priests committed to celibacy, regular prayer and simplicity of life, with annually renewable vows. In *The Sermon on the Mount* (1896) and *The Body of Christ* (1901), Gore expressed new theological views of the Person of

Christ based on higher criticism which would be unexceptionable today, but which drew bitter attacks from extreme Anglo-Catholics and extreme Protestants. He became bishop of Worcester in 1902, and was instrumental in the creation of the diocese of Birmingham, becoming its first bishop in 1905. This diocese suited his industrial radicalism. In 1911 he became bishop of Oxford. He retired in 1919 at the age of sixty-six, to become involved in a number of movements for world peace, industrial order and Church unity, and in the foundation of the Industrial Christian Fellowship. From this period in his life came a series of major theological works culminating in *A New Commentary on Holy Scripture* (1928), known to successive generations of theological students as 'Gore's Commentary'. [17 January, A.]

Gregory of Nazianzus (329–90) was the friend and colleague of *Basil the Great. The two were students together in Athens, and later both lived as hermits near the River Pontus; but Basil went on to help Bishop Eusebius of Caesarea in his struggle against the Arians, while Gregory returned home to assist his father, the bishop of Nazianzus. Basil became bishop of Caesarea, and Gregory followed his father as bishop of Nazianzus. Later he spent five years in contemplative solitude, and became patriarch of Constantinople, preaching a moving sermon on Basil's ministry at the latter's funeral. He is celebrated with Basil as one of the Fathers of the Eastern Church. [2 January, A. R. O.]

Gregory of Nyssa (c. 330–95) was a younger brother of *Basil the Great, and was taught the faith in his youth by his elder sister, *Macrina the Younger. He became bishop of Nyssa in 371.

Basil, Gregory of Nazianzus and Gregory of Nyssa are known collectively as 'the three Cappadocian Fathers', and Gregory of Nyssa is widely regarded as the most philosophical and speculative of the three. His writings on Arianism and his *Life of Moses* are highly regarded. In *On the Soul and Resurrection*, otherwise known as the *Macriniae*, he describes how he visited his sister after Basil's death, and how, though she was near death herself, she helped him to deal with his distress and gave him a greater understanding of death and the hope of resurrection. Of all the members of this remarkable family, Gregory speaks most clearly of their family affection and the strength of their Christian beliefs. [19 July, A. 19 March, R. O.]

Gregory of Tours (539–94) was born in the Auvergne, and became bishop of Tours in 573. In the wars and intrigues of Merovingian Gaul, he had to deal with four different rulers capable of violent and unstable behaviour. He was not afraid to confront them when necessary, offering sanctuary to those they persecuted. He ably defended the rights of the Church, and undertook a number of diplomatic missions in the cause of peace. He rebuilt and enlarged the cathedral at Tours, which had been destroyed by fire, restored churches, and was widely renowned for his administrative abilities and his works of charity. His great work is his ten-volume *History of the Franks,* as valuable a source for the ecclesiastical history of sixth-century Gaul as *Bede is for the history of Anglo-Saxon England. Among his other writings are seven volumes on the lives of the saints, a book on the lives of the Desert Fathers, and one on the Offices of the Church. He encouraged devotion to the *Virgin Mary at a time when this was widely disregarded. He was buried in his cathedral at Tours, and his shrine became a place of pilgrimage; but it was destroyed by the Vikings in the ninth century. It was restored, only to be destroyed again by the Huguenots in the sixteenth century. [17 November, R. O.]

Gregory the Enlightener, (c. 260–330), otherwise known as Gregory the Illuminator, is the patron saint of Armenia. Christianity reached Armenia at some time in the second or third century, and was probably brought by missionaries from Syria or Persia. At that time, Armenia was under Persian domination. There are many legends, some of them of dubious validity; but Gregory is said to have been the son of a prince, brought up in exile, and educated and baptized in Caesarea. When he was able to return to his own country, he made, many converts. For a time, he suffered persecution from the ruler, Tiridates, but he was freed from prison and was able to convert his persecutor. Christianity was recognized as the state religion. Gregory was consecrated in Caesarea in 314, and returned to Armenia with Greek and Syrian missionaries to set up a clergy school and found churches and monasteries, before spending his last days as a hermit. [30 September, O.]

Gregory the Great (c. 540–604) was a Roman, the son of a senator, who inherited great wealth. In 373 he became prefect of Rome, but he soon turned against the intrigues of high office. He sold all his estates and founded seven monasteries, entering that of St Andrew's on the Coelian Hill himself. It was during his period as abbot that he is reputed to have seen flaxen-haired slaves in the market.

Having established that they were Angles, he determined on a mission to England. It is said that he intended to lead the mission himself, but in 591, he became Pope Gregory I. He took a group of monks from St Andrew's with him to the Vatican, and continued to live a monastic life during his pontificate. Though *Augustine of Canterbury went to England in his place, Gregory planned the mission himself, and sent Augustine detailed instructions on how it was to proceed. *Bede describes Gregory as 'the apostle of the English'. There was much for him to do in Italy, as the country suffered from floods, famine and the advancing Lombard hordes. Gregory was a prodigious writer. Many of his pastoral letters of instruction and guidance survive, together with pastoral and exegetical works for the use of the clergy, forty *Homilies on the Gospels*, four books of *Dialogues*, and biblical commentaries. [3 September, A. R.]

Gregory the Thaumaturge (c. 213–70), or 'wonder-worker', was greatly revered by the Cappadocian Fathers (see *Basil, *Gregory of Nazianzus, *Gregory of Nyssa). He came from an earlier period in the history of the Church in Asia Minor, when there were still intermittent persecutions, and Christians were few in number. He was born in Pontus and educated in Caesarea, where he studied law and rhetoric. He became a Christian under the influence of Origen, and became bishop of Pontus at a time when there were said to be only seventeen Christians in the town. Through his preaching and healing ministry he attracted converts, and was soon able to build a church. Macrina the Elder, grandmother of Basil, Gregory of Nyssa and *Macrina the

Younger, learned from his preaching, and passed her Christian knowledge on to her children and grandchildren. Gregory the Thaumaturge had to face many dangers and difficulties – the persecutions of Decius in 250, when he had to retire into the desert for a time; a plague epidemic; and an invasion by the Goths. Before he died, he asked that his burial place might be obscure and not specially marked. Basil later commended Gregory the Thaumaturge's great reverence, his simplicity and his resistance to anger and bitterness, while Gregory of Nyssa composed a panegyric on his life which is still extant. [30 September, R. O.]

Hadrian of Canterbury (710)

came from the Church in North Africa. and was abbot of the monastery of Nerida, near Naples. When asked by Pope Vitalian to go to England to reconcile the Celtic and Latin factions in the Church after the Synod of Whitby, he declined, saying that he was neither worthy nor suitable, but recommended one of his monks, the Greek *Theodore of Tarsus. The pope agreed, on condition that Hadrian would accompany Theodore and support him. Theodore was consecrated archbishop of Canterbury, and they travelled from Rome to England together, visiting many monasteries on the way. Theodore appointed Hadrian abbot of St Peter's at Canterbury. For over forty years, Hadrian directed a celebrated school of learning attended by students from all over the British Isles, including a number of future bishops and abbots. It is a pleasant sidelight on his character to know that the miracles later attributed to him were concerned with helping boys who were in trouble with their teachers. [9 January, R.]

Hannington, James (1847–85):

Bishop Hannington's memorial is prominent in the Anglican cathedral in Kampala, Uganda. He volunteered for work with the Church Missionary Society after hearing of the death of two missionaries in Central Africa, and undertook a gruelling journey overland from Zanzibar to Lake Victoria and the source of the Nile in Buganda, the southern part of Uganda. When he returned to London, he addressed many missionary meetings, and he was appointed the first bishop of Equatorial Africa at the age of thirty-six. In January 1885 he arrived at Mombasa with a small party, and attempted to reach his base near the source of the Nile by travelling due west through Masai country. Neither he nor the British authorities knew two key factors: that the friendly *kabaka* (king) of Buganda had died, and his successor, Mwanga, was both vicious and anti-Christian; and that the Masai country was Buganda's 'back door', closed to Westerners. When his way was blocked by hostile tribesmen, he sent the other missionaries in the party back, and went on alone with African porters. He was seized by Mwanga's men near the end of his journey, at Ukassa, and after several weeks of imprisonment, he was shot. The deaths of the *Martyrs of Uganda took place in the following year. [29 October, A.]

Helena (Helen, Elena, c. 250–330)

was the mother of the Roman Emperor Constantine. Legends which say that she was English, and the daughter of King Coel, originated with Geoffrey of Monmouth in the fourteenth century, and can be discounted. She was born in Drepanum, now Hersek, in Asia Minor, of Greek stock, and is thought to have been the daughter of an innkeeper. She married Constantius, then a Roman general on active service. Bede says that she was his concubine, but presumably means only that it was not a Christian marriage. Constantius consistently regarded Constantine, their only child, as his eldest son and heir. When Constantine followed his father as Roman Emperor, he called his mother to Rome, and did her great honour, later proclaiming her Augusta or Empress. Helena became a Christian in 312, and it was probably through her influence that Constantine made many magnificent gifts to the Church, ordered the construction of the first basilica of St Peter in Rome, and personally chaired the Council of Nicaea in 324–5. In 328 he sent Helena to the Holy Land (at the age of about seventy-eight) with a letter to the archbishop of Jerusalem, ordering him to undertake excavations to find the True Cross. Several historians of the period tell the story of how she was present at the discovery of the Cross, and how she sent three of the nails back to Constantine, who wore one in his helmet, and the other two on his horse's bit and bridle. Her tomb is in the church of Santa Croce in Rome. [21 May, A. O. 18 May, R. 18 August, O.]

Helier (sixth century) is said to have come from Tongres in Belgium. He became a monk and went to Jersey to live as a hermit. He lived in a cave above the town which now bears his name, leading a life of prayer and fasting, and preaching the Gospel to the people. He was killed either by pirates or robbers whom he was attempting to convert, and ranks as Jersey's first saint and first martyr. [16 July, R.]

Herbert, George (1593–1633): the son of a celebrated London hostess, Magdalene Herbert, and the younger brother of Lord Herbert of Cherbury,

George Herbert became University Orator at Cambridge, and hoped for preferment under the patronage of King James I; but on James's death in 1625, he lost his prospect of worldly success, and in the following year he became rector of the country parish of Bemerton in Wiltshire. Among his friends were *John Donne, Isaac Walton, *Lancelot Andrewes and *Nicholas Ferrar. He ministered to his congregation with a deep devotion which is reflected in his poems. These were not published during his lifetime, but were collected after his death by Nicholas Ferrar, and transcribed at Little Gidding. They include some of the finest metaphysical poems of his era, which suggest that he spent many hours in his quiet country church in meditation. Among them are 'Easter Wings' and 'Redemption', and some hymns which are now well-known, such as 'Teach me, my God and King' and 'Let all the world in every corner sing'. His ministry at Bemerton lasted only three years: he died of consumption at the age of forty, but he is remembered as an exemplary Anglican priest in an age of religious turmoil. [27 February, A.]

Hilary of Poitiers (c. 315–65) was born in Poitiers of a Romano-Gallic family. He had a classical education, and became a public orator, but after extensive study he was inspired by the Prologue to St John's Gospel, which brought together the classical Greek idea of the *Logos* (the Word) and Christian belief: 'The Word was with God at the beginning, and through him all things came to be.' Hilary became bishop of Poitiers by popular demand in 350, and took a stand against the Arians, who were supported by the Emperor Constantius. He was exiled to Asia Minor for four years, but during this time he produced his greatest works, the treatise on the Trinity and that on Synods. In 361, he returned to Poitiers. He was joined by *Martin of Tours, who later became his successor. Hilary was highly praised by *Jerome and *Augustine of Hippo, who both call him 'the Athanasius of the West'. His feast day is traditionally the first day of the spring term (known as the Hilary term) in the law courts and the older universities. [13 January, A. R.]

Hilda of Whitby (614–80) was baptized with *King Edwin of Northumbria's household in 627. When she was thirty, she decided to join her sister at the royal monastery of Chelles in France; but *Aidan of Lindisfarne persuaded her to stay in England. After a period of seclusion, she became abbess of a small monastery at Heruten (Hartlepool), and later abbess of the double monastery of Streanashalch (now referred to by its more manageable Danish name, Whitby). Hilda was the superior of both monks and nuns, and responsible for the management of a large estate with many labourers and craftsmen. One of them was *Caedmon, the herdsman-poet. She established a regular pattern of monastic life, and built up a remarkable library of manuscripts. Five of her monks, including *Wilfrid of Ripon, became bishops. Her energy and wisdom were highly regarded. When, in 664, the question of whether the English Church should follow the Celtic or the Latin Rite was to be decided, King Oswy met the bishops and clergy at Hilda's great monastery, where the Synod of Whitby was held. We are largely dependent on *Bede for a near-contemporary account of Hilda's life. The abbey and the library at Whitby were destroyed during the Danish invasions of the tenth century. [19 November, A. R.]

Hildegard of Bingen (1098–1179) was the prioress of a Benedictine monastery for women in the Rhine Valley. It was a house of prayer, study and music for learned maidens. She dictated her visions to a monk named Volmar, who had his abbot's permission to act as her scribe. Among her remarkable writings are *Scivias* (an abbreviation of *Nosce vias Domini* or 'Know the ways of the Lord'), *The Book of Divine Works* and *The Book of Life's Merits*. Many of her images are of Platonic absolutes – Reason, Justice, Chastity, Divine Wisdom. She wrote many letters of counsel and advice to people in authority, including four popes. She warned Pope Anastasius IV against the abuse of power, and sent a similar letter to Henry II of England shortly before the murder of *Thomas Becket. Hildegard was also a gifted poet who has been compared to Dante or Blake: many of her poems were dedicated to saints and martyrs. But she is probably best known today for her church music, which is widely available on compact discs and cassettes. She composed seventy-seven pieces to echo the celestial harmonies, many of them with dissonances and passages in a minor key which appeal to modern ears. [17 September, A. R.]

Hill, Octavia (1838–1912): the artist John Ruskin helped the young Octavia, whose family had been left in poverty, by suggesting that she might manage three run-down properties which he owned. These slum properties – she never used the word – were rented out, often a room at a time, to poor families. She introduced a new principle: the reciprocal duties of landlord and tenant. She repaired the properties, and she expected the tenants to look after them. Frequently she sat down with the tenants and showed them how to budget their slender resources. From these small beginnings, her work grew. Ruskin put more houses under her management, *Samuel and *Henrietta Barnett invited her to take over properties in Whitechapel, and the Ecclesiastical Commissioners asked her to manage their properties in Deptford and Southwark. Training centres in Housing Management were set up in Southwark, Leeds, Liverpool and Manchester, and the system spread to Germany, Holland and the United States. She was instrumental in getting many London squares opened to the public; she was also an advocate of open spaces and green belts round the cities, and a founder member of the National Trust. She sat on two Royal Commissions (on Housing and on the Poor Laws) but avoided public speaking. She lived very modestly, and refused a suggestion that she might be buried in Westminster Abbey. [13 August, A.]

Holy Helpers: the Fourteen Holy Helpers were a group of saints collectively venerated in the Rhineland from the fourteenth century. The cult spread to Sweden, Hungary and other parts of Germany. In the sixteenth century, it was a target for the Lutheran reformers, and it was discouraged by the Council of Trent. However, it was revived in Swabia and Bavaria, where elaborate monuments to these saints can be found in Baroque churches. The Fourteen, in alphabetical order, are Acacius, Barbara, Blaise, *Catherine of Alexandria, Christopher, Cyricus, *Denys, Erasmus, Eustace, *George, *Giles, *Margaret of Antioch, Pantaleon and *Vitus. They come from a variety of countries and historical periods. There is no obvious link between them, and some of them are now thought to be legendary rather than based on historical characters. A representation of the Fourteen by Lucas Cranach is in Hampton Court. [8 August, R.]

Holy Innocents (first century): the Gospel according to Matthew tells how, when Jesus Christ was born, King Herod commanded that all the male children in Bethlehem under two years of age should be killed (Matt. 2:1–12, 16–23). The Holy Family escaped to Egypt, but lamentations arose in Bethlehem as the massacre was carried out. The parallel with Pharaoh's slaying of the first-born of Israel (Exod. 1:13–22) is a strong one. The babies killed in Bethlehem are known as the Holy Innocents, or the Holy Children – martyred in infancy in place of the Christ-Child. They are mentioned in many of the works of the Early Fathers, and Bede wrote a long poem to them. Their festival was formerly known as Childermas. At the time when the massacre occurred, Bethlehem was only a village, and modern scholars think that probably the number of babies involved would not have been large. Some very small stone sarcophagi lodged in the wall of a cave close to that of the Nativity, of which ten or twelve can be seen, are said to be their tombs. [28 December, A. R. O.]

Hooker, Richard (1553–1600): this Elizabethan theologian, born in Exeter, held the influential post of Master of the Temple. Despairing of the religious controversies of his day, he retired to a country living near Salisbury, later moving to Bishopsbourne, near Canterbury. He devoted his time to writing *Ecclesiastical Polity*, a massive eight-volume work remarkable for its moderation and its defence of the position of the Anglican Church. While he did not accept the jurisdiction of the pope, he refuted the Protestant view that the Scriptures contained all that was necessary for salvation, arguing that natural law and reason were also sources of religious insight and understanding. He insisted that the Church of England was in continuity with the historical Church, defended the doctrine of the Apostolic Succession and the institution of episcopacy, and maintained a devotion to the 'holy mysteries' of the Eucharist. The work, a classic of theological exposition and literary style, was written to offer a bridge of reconciliation with Rome. It was well received in the Vatican, and it is said that Pope Clement VIII was much impressed with it, saying that it contained 'seeds of eternity'; but in England, religious controversies were too violent for any kind of settlement. Hooker despaired, and concluded that his only recourse was to 'pray for the peace of Jerusalem'. *Ecclesiastical Polity* has continued to influence Anglican thought through the succeeding centuries. [3 November, A.]

Hugh of Lincoln (c. 1140–1200), born at Avalon in south-eastern France, became a monk at the remote and mountainous monastery of La Grande Chartreuse, renowned for its austerity

and silence. After some ten years, he was sent to England to set up the first Carthusian house in Somerset: the establishment of this religious house was one of the penalties enjoined on

King Henry II after the murder of *Thomas Becket in 1171. Henry II came to respect Hugh's spirituality and intelligence, and in 1186 nominated him as bishop of Lincoln. Hugh accepted only on condition that he was allowed to maintain his obedience to the abbot of La Grande Chartreuse. In view of Becket's fate, he had no desire to become the king's man. He found the diocese in a very poor state: the office of bishop had been vacant for eighteen years, and Henry II had appropriated the income. Morale was low in the diocese, and the cathedral had been devastated by an earthquake. Hugh commenced the rebuilding of the cathedral, and often helped the builders himself. He made Lincoln a centre of learning which bore comparison with Paris, and inspired the clergy and people. He became the champion of the oppressed, righting injustices, providing settlements for lepers (there were many lepers in England after the Crusades) and defending the Jewish communities, which were often subject to persecution. On one occasion, he faced a mob alone and unarmed. Hugh advised three very difficult Angevin monarchs – Henry II, Richard I and John, and succeeded in staying on good terms with all three, though he was not afraid to speak out when he thought they were acting unjustly. He died in London after making a pilgrimage to Becket's shrine. [17 November, A. R.]

Ia and Ives (dates unknown) are often confused, which may be why they long shared a feast day. Ia, otherwise known as Hya or Ives, is the patron saint of St Ives in Cornwall. She was an Irish virgin who settled at St Ives, and persuaded Dinan, lord of Cornwall, to build a church there. The legends surrounding her life are recorded by Canon G. H. Doble in his *Cornish Saints*. Ives or Yves is the patron saint of St Ives in Huntingdon, and it has been conjectured that he was a Persian bishop. His body was one of four discovered in the year 1001. It had been buried with episcopal insignia, which suggested that he had come from outside Europe, and had ended his days as a hermit, since a European bishop's relics would have been translated back to his see. A peasant's dream and a miraculous spring added to the mystery, and a monastery was founded on the site, the unknown wandering bishop becoming the centre of a local cult. [Ia: now 4 August, R.; Ives: 24 April, R.]

Ignatius of Antioch (c. 37–107): according to tradition, Ignatius was a disciple of *John the Evangelist. Antioch was one of the great cities of the ancient Mediterranean world, and both *Paul and *Peter preached there. Ignatius became bishop of Antioch in the year 69, and was martyred during the persecutions of Trajan (98–117). Though nothing definite is known about his life and work until the time of his arrest, he wrote seven letters to other churches while he was being taken to Rome under guard. He urges the churches to work together, and describes the Eucharist as 'the medicine of immortality', the Christian's way to eternal life through Jesus Christ. These letters are of great importance, giving insight into the theology of the early Church. Ignatius was prepared for martyrdom, and when Christians at Rome came out to meet him, he begged them not to stand in the way of his going to the Lord. He was taken to the Colosseum and was thrown to the lions, dying very quickly. Though there has been some discussion about the authorship of three of his letters, most scholars now believe them all to be genuine. [17 October, A. R. O.]

Ignatius of Loyola (1491–1556) was the son of a Basque nobleman. One of his legs was shattered by a cannon ball at the siege of Pamplona in a war with the French. In a long and painful period of convalescence, he turned to reading the life of Christ and the lives of the saints. When he could walk again, he spent a year in penance as a hermit near the abbey of Montserrat. It was during this time that he wrote the first draft of his *Spiritual Exercises* – a drill manual for the Christian life. He undertook a pilgrimage to Jerusalem with the intention of converting the Saracens, but was deterred by the Franciscans who guarded the holy places: they had seen other missionaries, including some of their own number, die in similar attempts. Back in Europe, Ignatius was imprisoned for a time on suspicion of heresy, but managed to convince the authorities of his orthodoxy. He went to the University of Paris, where he studied Latin, philosophy and theology, and graduated as a Master of Arts. He gathered round him a small group of fellow spirits, including another Basque, *Francis Xavier. They set out on a mission to the Holy Land, but had to return when war was declared on the Turks, and it was Xavier who finally pioneered the missions to the East. Ignatius built up his organization on military lines, demanding total and unquestioning obedience from his priests, and a readiness for martyrdom. It received papal approval as the Society of Jesus in 1540. By the time Ignatius died in 1556, there were over a thousand Jesuits working in Europe, and a number, led by *Edmund Campion and Ralph Sherwin, took part in the 'English Mission' during the reign of Elizabeth I. [31 July, A. R.]

Illtud (Illtyd, Hildutus) (early sixth century), was the founder and abbot of the monastery of Llanilltud at the place now known as Llantwit Major in Glamorgan. He is thought to have been a disciple of Germanus of Auxerre, and was renowned as the most learned Briton of his age. The monastery housed hundreds of monk-scholars, many of whom became missionaries. Illtud's life is recorded by Samson of Dol, who is thought to have been one of his monks. Though this account contains many improbable marvels and legendary attributions (including one that he was a cousin of King Arthur), it is clear that Illtud was an outstanding figure of considerable influence. Many churches in Wales are dedicated in his name. [6 November, R.]

Irenaeus (c. 125–202) was of Greek stock, born in Asia Minor. In his youth, he sat at the feet of *Polycarp, bishop of Smyrna, who had known *John the Evangelist and 'others who had seen the Lord'. Through Irenaeus; this tradition of personal contact with the apostles was passed to Gaul, where Irenaeus settled after studying in Rome under *Justin Martyr. Lugdonum, now Lyons, was a major trading centre with the East, and a Christian community was already established there. Irenaeus became part of the household of Bishop Pothinus, and in 177 he was entrusted with an important mission to Rome. He was there when the terrible persecutions later in that year led to the death of Pothinus and the other Martyrs of Lyons. Irenaeus returned to become bishop of Lyons and to rebuild the work of the Church. He proved a worthy successor. He learned the local language and went out with his priests to evangelize the people of the Rhône Valley. He wrote in defence of the faith against the unsound doctrines which were then circulating. His *Adversus Haereses* ('Against Heresies') contrasts the teachings of the apostles with those of the Gnostics, who combined Neo-Platonism with superstition and secret cults. Tertullian writes that Irenaeus was 'a curious explorer of all kinds of learning', and Irenaeus referred to his work as 'stripping the fox' – exposing the beliefs of the Gnostics as false. Irenaeus is commemorated as a master of Christian apologetics, and a direct transmitter of the faith of the apostles. His shrine at Lyons was destroyed by Calvinists in 1562. [28 June, A. R. O.]

Ithamar (c. 660) was the first Anglo-Saxon bishop in the Latin Church. He became bishop of Rochester in 644, being consecrated by Honorius, the third archbishop of Canterbury. Ithamar succeeded *Paulinus. He was said to be a man of great learning. *Bede records that Ithamar consecrated Deusdedit, a West Saxon, as the fourth archbishop of Canterbury, and that Deusdedit in turn consecrated Damian, a West Saxon, on Ithamar's death. It appears that these events were part of a plan for naturalization in which Anglo-Saxons were intended to take over the leadership of the English Church from the original Roman missionaries. [10 June, R.]

Jacopo da Todi (c. 1230–1306): this wealthy Umbrian had a harsh father and a disturbed childhood. He became a wild and violent student, often engaged in drunken street brawls, and a self-indulgent adult, much given to ostentatious display. He went through a long period of intense and violent grief after the death of his young and devout wife, in which he took to religious mortification in forms which were bizarre even by the standards of the fourteenth century. The Franciscans brought him back to reason: after some hesitation, they admitted him to their Order, where he gravitated towards the *Zelanti* (Zealots), the strict group who practised extreme forms of mortification very different from the gentle spirituality of *Francis of Assisi. He became involved in the disputed election of Pope Boniface VIII, and spent five years in prison for his savage satires on the pope. Loaded with chains in a dark and evil-smelling cell, he began to write poetry of great spirituality and lyricism in his own Umbrian dialect. After his release from prison, these were published as the *Laude*. His poems were sung in the streets and the market-places of Umbria. Eventually they were translated into Latin, and became widely known. There is a biography by *Evelyn Underhill, and a memorial in the church of San Fortunato at Todi, erected in 1906. [25 December, R.]

James the Deacon (late seventh century): when *Paulinus returned to southern England after the death of *King Edwin of Northumbria in 633, James was the only cleric of the Latin Rite who remained in the north of England. He had come over to England with Paulinus, and so was probably an Italian from one of the Roman monasteries. He had settled near Catterick in North Yorkshire, and had escaped the sack of York. A year later, *Oswald of Northumbria won back the throne, and brought *Aidan and the Celtic monks from Iona; but James continued to preach and baptize in the wilds of Swaledale according to the Latin Rite. He kept the Latin date of Easter, baptized in the chilly waters of the Swale, and sang Gregorian chant. He seems to have been the only chanter in the north of England until *Wilfrid and *Benedict Biscop brought chanters from Rome many years later. As an old man, James was present at the Synod of Whitby, and saw the Latin Rite re-

adopted by the Northumbrian Church. [11 October, A. R.]

James the Great (44): the apostles James and *John, the sons of Zebedee, were called by Christ as they mended their fishing nets by the Sea of Galilee

(Matt. 4:21–22). James was a leader among the twelve apostles: he was present at most of the major events in the earthly life of Christ, and headed the Church in Jerusalem in the early days of the Church, both when *Peter was in prison and when he undertook his missionary journeys. He was the leader of the Jewish Christians, while Peter was the first to see the importance of taking the faith to the Gentiles. The very ancient *Liturgy of James*, in Aramaic, reputedly dates from his ministry. James was the first of the apostles to die, being killed on the orders of Herod Agrippa (Acts 12:2). The cult of St James (Santiago) in Compostela in northern Spain was a medieval rallying point for Christians against the Moors. As far as can be established, James never visited Spain, and was not buried there, though there is historical evidence that relics were taken to Compostela from Jerusalem in the ninth century. The three great medieval pilgrimages were to Rome, to Jerusalem and to Compostela, and the feast of St James is still kept in Compostela with great ceremony, attended by many pilgrims who walk the traditional routes with his emblems, the staff and the scallop-shell. [25 July, A. R. O.]

James the Less (first century): this James, sometimes known as James the Younger, was also an apostle, and is identified in the Gospels as the son of Alphaeus. He is usually associated with *Philip the Apostle, and they share a feast day. He has been identified with James 'the brother of the Lord' whom *Paul refers to as the leader of the Church in Jerusalem (Gal. 1:19). The Letter to the Galatians was written some years after the death of *James the Great. Some writers have speculated that references to the brothers and sisters of Jesus may refer to an earlier marriage by *Joseph, and that he was a widower when he married the *Virgin Mary. Others hold that James was a cousin of Jesus rather than a blood-brother. [1 May, A. 3 May, R. O.]

Janani Luwum see **Luwum**

Japan, Martyrs of: *Francis Xavier is said to have made a thousand converts in Japan. By 1587 there were about 15,000. Franciscan and Jesuit missionaries had arrived in force, many of them learning the language, training indigenous priests and catechists, and respecting Japanese cultural institutions. But Japan entered into a period of acute suspicion of Western imperialism, and the emperor Hideyoshi decreed the expulsion of all the foreign missionaries. In 1597, the first of the martyrdoms of Nagasaki took place, when twenty-five Christians, both missionaries and Japanese, were mutilated, bound to crosses and killed by sword thrusts. There were repeated outbursts of persecution: in 1617, a hundred Christians were executed between Nagasaki and Omura; in 1622,

twenty-two missionaries were killed by being burned over a slow fire, while thirty Japanese converts were beheaded. From 1623, all Japanese were forced to declare their religious allegiance once a year, and those suspected of being Christians were made to trample on a tile bearing the image of the Virgin and Child. In 1637–8, there was a revolt in Nagasaki. A massacre followed in which thousands of Christians – Europeans and Japanese – were killed. Japan barred its ports against Europeans, and it was not until the Meiji Restoration of 1865, over two hundred years later, that the missionaries were able to return. They found families in the Nagasaki district who still knew Latin and Portuguese phrases, and who had preserved relics of the martyrs. Though Christianity is not a majority religion in Japan, it is still strong in the Nagasaki area. [6 February, A. R.]

Jebb, Eglantine (1876–1928): a Cambridge graduate of thirty-six, Eglantine Jebb went out to Macedonia in 1912 to distribute relief to thousands of refugees after the Balkan War of that year. At the end of World War I, she was involved in the work of the Fight the Famine Council, and became the honorary secretary of the Save the Children Fund. As a result of her energetic campaigning, Save the Children International was established in 1923, with offices in Geneva. She compiled the Declaration of Geneva – a first statement of the rights of all children to physical, mental and spiritual development. This was adopted by the League of Nations, and became the basis of later human rights declarations and conventions. She continued to work, ever more intensively, to meet the needs of sick and starving children in Russia, the Balkans, Africa, India and China. Under her leadership, the

Save the Children Fund fed and housed child refugees, and set up schools, hospitals and homes for disabled children. Her life was a very strenuous one, and she died at the age of 52. A model village named Xheba (Jebb) was founded in Albania in her memory. [17 December, A.]

Jerome (Eusebius Hieronymus Sophronius) (c. 342–420) was born in Aquileia in Dalmatia. He studied in Rome, travelled widely, visited the Holy Land, and lived as a hermit in the desert for five years. He was ordained priest in Antioch, and studied theology under *Gregory of Nazianzus. His ambition was to complete a new translation of the entire Bible in Latin from Greek and Hebrew texts. Though there were partial translations in existence, they were often derived from other translations, and frequently inaccurate and slipshod. Jerome's scholarship was meticulous, and *Pope Damasus I commissioned his life-work. Jerome became the pope's secretary for the last three years of his pontificate. His knowledge of Rome's heritage from the time of the martyrs was encyclopaedic, and he was able to advise on projects to open up the catacombs and create shrines. Jerome became very influential in the Vatican, and might have succeeded Damasus as pope; but his overbearing and sarcastic manner made him much resented. Slaves were bribed to make unfounded allegations against him, and when Siricius was elected pope, Jerome had to leave Italy. He went to Bethlehem and settled in a cave close by the cave of the Nativity, where he worked on his biblical translations and commentaries with the help of scribes and copyists. The wealthy Roman lady *Paula endowed a monastery in Bethlehem. Jerome became the abbot, and was able to continue his work there until his death. His translation of the Bible forms the basis of the Vulgate. Jerome also wrote lives of the saints, and compiled the first full Calendar of saints, known as the *Hieronymianum*. He is generally regarded as the most scholarly of the four Latin Doctors of the Church. [30 September, A. R. O.]

Joachim is the traditional name of the father of the *Virgin Mary, husband of *Anne. Their names are recorded in the *Gospel of James*, written about 170–80, and the most famous of the apocryphal writings. According to this source, the couple were childless: Joachim went into the desert to pray, while Anne remained at home, beseeching God for a child. They learned in visions that their prayers were being answered. There is a celebrated painting by Albrecht Dürer showing their rejoicing at the Golden Gate of Jerusalem. This story, which has biblical parallels in the Old Testament stories of the birth of Isaac and Samuel, has not been accepted by the Church as having a proven historical basis, but it indicates the love and respect which the early Church bore for the parents of the mother of Jesus. Unusually in Jewish tradition, it is Joachim, not Anne, who is thought to be sterile, and the rejoicing is not for a first-born son, but for a daughter. [26 July, A. 9 September, R. O.]

Joan of Arc (Jeanne d'Arc, 1412–31): the story of the Maid of France, born at Domrémy, who heard the voices of *Margaret of Antioch and *Catherine of Alexandria, and inspired the Dauphin to fight against the English, is very well known. She wore armour, rallied the troops, and saw the Dauphin crowned at Saint-Denys. Subsequently she was captured, tried, and sentenced to be burned at the stake. A number of books, plays and films have repeated the story. George Bernard Shaw's *St Joan* is based on the transcript of her trial, which is still in print. Jeanne is the second patron of France (next in importance to *Denys), and her courage, her commitment and the injustice of her condemnation and execution have long been a source of pride to the French and of guilt to the English. The historical basis is more doubtful. The Orléanists in France have long maintained that the legend of the *Pucelle* who would save France was politically inspired rather than miraculous. Her recognition by the Roman Catholic Church was long delayed: she was finally beatified in 1910 and canonized in 1920. She is recognized as a saint, but not a martyr, being commemorated as a virgin who endured persecution and death for her strong religious faith. [30 May, A. R.]

John XXIII (1881–1963) was thought to be a 'caretaker pope' when he was elected in 1958 at the age of seventy-seven in a very difficult election (the College of Cardinals went to twelve ballots). The five years of his pontificate turned out to be momentous ones for the Roman Catholic Church. Born Angelo Guiseppe Roncalli of a peasant family from Sotto il Monte, near Bergamo, he was to open the floodgates of reform. He broke with tradition by leaving the Vatican, increased the number of cardinals, and proposed an ecumenical council to renew the religious life of the Church, bringing its teaching and organization up to date, and seeking closer unity with other Christian Churches. He issued a papal encyclical, *Pacem in terris* (Peace on Earth) advocating reconciliation with the Eastern Orthodox Church. During his pontificate, the Secretariat for Promoting Christian Unity was set up, the Roman Catholic Church was for the first time represented at the meetings of the World Council of Churches, and relations with the Anglican and Lutheran Churches were greatly improved. The Second Vatican Council, which Pope John attributed to the direct inspiration of the Holy Spirit, met from 1962 to 1965. Although he died after the first session, which took place in October to December 1962, great expectations of change and renewal had been raised throughout the Roman Catholic world, and the reform movement continued under his successor, Pope Paul VI. Services were no longer held in Latin, but in the language of the congregation. The liturgy, the Calendar and many aspects of Church organization were revised, and attitudes to the laity became less authoritarian. These changes were welcome to many Roman Catholics, but alarming to others, who regretted the loss of the structure and discipline they had come to rely on. There has not been another Vatican Council since; and the proclamation of Pope John's beatification in September 2000 was coupled with the beatification of Pope Pius IX, who convoked the First Vatican Council of 1869–70. That Council was of a very different character, resulting chiefly in the formal declaration of papal infallibility: that the pope, speaking *ex cathedra* (with the full weight of his office) cannot be wrong in matters of faith and morals. The result of the double proclamation may be seen as a delicate balance between the old and the new which will reassure conservative Roman Catholics – but it will disappoint the progressives, and many Christians in other Churches to whom the doctrine of papal infallibility is the chief stumbling-block to Christian unity. [R. Date of observance not yet known].

John Chrysostom (347–407): Chrysostom means 'of the Golden

Tongue', and John is known for the beauty and clarity of his preaching and theological writings. He studied at Antioch, became a monk, and after some years as the bishop's assistant, was called to be patriarch of Constantinople. An austere man who lived very simply, he incurred the opposition of the imperial court, particularly that of the empress Eudoxia, when he attacked court morals, extravagance and failure to respect the holy days of the Church. Eudoxia retaliated by having a statue of herself placed outside his cathedral, Hagia Sophia, and by organizing races and games on Good Friday and Holy Saturday. John also attracted the enmity of Theophilus, patriarch of Alexandria, who had been a candidate for the patriarchate of Constantinople, and whom he had denounced as corrupt. Theophilus summoned a council of hostile bishops to condemn John on trumped-up charges. He was condemned in his absence, and exiled. In Constantinople, there were riots in the streets. Hagia Sophia was set on fire, and the Christians were accused of trying to burn it down themselves. One of those who stood trial was the deaconess *Olympias, who wrote to John and sent him money in exile. Seventeen of his letters to Olympias survive: they show the extent of his sufferings as he was harried from place to place, and the enduring quality of his faith and hers under persecution. Frail and exhausted, John died in exile. [13 September, A. R. 13 November, O.]

John of Beverley (721) was educated in the monastic school at Canterbury in the time of *Theodore of Tarsus. He became one of *Hilda's monks at Whitby, where he was distinguished for his learning and his care of the poor. He became bishop of Hexham, and ordained *Bede. In 705, he was appointed bishop of York. Little

is known about his episcopate except for Bede's account. Bede stresses his concern for his people, and his ministry of healing. In his old age, John retired to the monastery which he had founded at Beverley, near York, 'to end his days in a manner pleasing to God'. *Julian of Norwich writes of John at some length in her *Revelations*, referring to him as 'a full high saint in heaven . . . a worthy servant of God, greatly God-loving and dreading'. Henry V invoked John's protection before the battle of Agincourt, which was fought on his feast-day. John's shrine at Beverley was a well-known place of pilgrimage before the Reformation. [7 May, R.]

John of Bridlington (1379): his name was coupled with that of *John of Beverley in Henry V's invocation before Agincourt. This John was born at Thwing, near Bridlington, studied at Oxford, and became a canon in the Augustinian monastery at Bridlington. When his brother monks wished to elect him prior in 1360, he tried to avoid the office, but was constrained to accept it. He was prior for seventeen years, during which he was renowned for his wisdom, his mildness, and the depth of his prayer life. John of Bridlington's cult was widespread in the Middle Ages: he is featured in medieval stained-glass windows in churches at Morley (Derbyshire) and Ludlow (Shropshire) and in the Beauchamp Chapel at Warwick. [21 October, R.]

John of Damascus (c. 676–749) was of Greek stock, and of a Christian family. His father held an important hereditary post at the court of the Caliph, which John inherited. At this time, not long after the death of Mohammed, the followers of Islam recognized Christ as a prophet (though they believed that Mohammed was a greater one), and Christians were not persecuted. When a new and less tolerant Caliph came to power, John gave away his considerable property, and went to Mar Saba, the monastery founded by Sabas near Jerusalem. There he spent the rest of his very long life in meditation and writing. At Mar Saba, he was beyond the reach of the Caliph, and he was also outside the jurisdiction of the Eastern Empire, where the Iconcoclasts were smashing pictures and statues of Christ, the *Virgin Mary and the saints. John wrote three treatises against the Iconoclasts, arguing that holy images should be respected, because they represented the Church Triumphant, and were models for Christians to live by. Images of the crucified and risen Christ, and of the Virgin Mary, were particularly to be honoured. His greatest work is *De Fide Orthodoxa* (On the Orthodox Faith), a powerful and often lyrical account of the Creation, the Incarnation and the theology of the sacraments. [4 December, A. R. O.]

John of the Cross Juan de Yepes y Alvarez (1542–91) became a Carmelite friar after a poverty-stricken childhood. He studied at the University of Salamanca, and was ordained in 1567. *Teresa of Avila, who had founded a reformed Carmelite house for women, had permission from the Spanish ecclesiastical authorities to found a parallel movement for men, and John was one of the first two friars she chose. When in 1571 Teresa became prioress of the house at Avila, she sent for John to be the spiritual director and confessor. The new movement was much resented by the unreformed Carmelites (Carmelites of the Observance). On two occasions, they captured John and went to extreme lengths to force him to renounce the new movement. He was shut up in solitary confinement in a tiny cell in the Carmelite priory in Toledo, flogged, half-starved, and told that his immortal soul was in danger. In 1577, after over eight months of captivity, he succeeded in escaping, taking with him the poems he had written in his darkest hours. When the reform movement was established, John wrote more poems, remarkable in their vivid imagery of light and darkness, of suffering and sublime love, of the soul searching for Christ. He went on to take heavy administrative responsibilities, setting up new priories, training priests and nuns, and writing his major prose commentaries, *The Ascent of Mount Carmel, The Dark Night of the Soul, The Spiritual Canticle* and *The Living Flame of Love*. The Vatican named him as a Doctor of the Church Universal in 1926. [14 December, A. R.].

John the Baptist (first century): the Gospel according to Luke tells in detail the story of John's conception, and his mother Elizabeth's meeting with the

*Virgin Mary, when 'the child in her womb leapt for joy' (Luke 1:44). John is the forerunner of Christ: he came out of the wilderness preaching repentance, baptizing in the River Jordan, proclaiming the coming of the Messiah; and Jesus came to him for baptism. He was cast into prison, and

Herod was induced to sentence him to death by beheading as a result of the scheming of Herodias and her daughter Salome. John has two festivals: his birth is commemorated on 24 June, and his death on 29 August. Traditionally, the date of his birth – unlike that of other saints – has taken precedence, on the grounds that he 'met' Christ before his birth, and was born without sin. John is frequently shown in medieval paintings and stained glass windows as a shaggy and unkempt figure, from the days when he lived in the wilderness on locusts and wild honey. Many churches have been dedicated in his name. He was patron of the Knights Hospitallers, a military Order based at Rhodes and later Malta, who guarded pilgrims on their way to Jerusalem. Their property was sequestered in 1540. An Anglican revival in 1831 led to the foundation of the St John Ambulance organization. [Birth: 24 June; Beheading/Passion: 29 August, A. R. O.]

John the Evangelist (c. 100) is traditionally held to be the apostle John, son of Zebedee and brother of *James the Great, 'the disciple whom Jesus loved' in the Gospel according to John, the author of that Gospel, and also the author of three New Testament Letters and the Revelation to John. Christ called James and John as they were mending their nets on the shores of Lake Galilee, and they were nicknamed *Boanerges* ('Sons of Thunder') in reference to their ardent but impulsive natures. If John is the writer of the Fourth Gospel, it is understandable that he refers to himself only as 'the other disciple' or 'the disciple whom Jesus loved'. This disciple was close to Jesus at the Last Supper, and asked who would betray him; with *Peter, he followed Jesus after his arrest, and heard Peter's denials; the *Virgin Mary was commended to his care from the

Cross – 'Son, behold thy mother'; and when *Mary Magdalene said that she had seen the risen Lord, he ran to the empty tomb – faster than Peter, but

waiting to let the older disciple enter first. He was witness to two Resurrection appearances – in the upper room, and on the shores of the sea of Tiberias, and the rumour went out among the disciples that he would not die, but would live until Christ came in glory. We know that John had a very long life. *Irenaeus was told by *Polycarp of Smyrna that he lived at Ephesus until the time of the Emperor Trajan (98–117). He seems to have outlived all the other apostles, and he is the only one of whom it is certain that he did not die a martyr. It is established that the Fourth Gospel was written early in the second century, or earlier. Most scholars have concluded that the Gospel is based on John's teaching, but that scribes or collaborators probably developed it into a coherent narrative. The authorship of the Revelation and the Letters is more doubtful, and has been much disputed. John's symbol is the eagle, representing the fourth of the living creatures about the throne of God. In medieval painting, he usually appears as a young man with red hair – perhaps a reference to his impetuous nature. He is the patron of theologians. [27 December, A. R. O.]

John Wyclif: see Wyclif

Johnson, Samuel (1709–84): Dr Johnson, author, critic, man of letters and lexicographer, was the son of a bookseller, and books were his passion. He was born in Lichfield, and though he had to leave Oxford when his father's business failed, his erudition was immense. After some years of contributing to such publications as *The Gentleman's Magazine, The Rambler* and *The Idler*, he embarked on his plan for a massive dictionary of the English language. It took him eight years, and its publication in 1755 made him famous. He also wrote an eight-volume life of Shakespeare, and ten volumes on the lives of the poets. We are indebted to James Boswell's *Life of Johnson* for a remarkable portrait of this strange man – his ponderous manner, his wit and humour, his strange gesticulations, his untidiness, his fits of melancholy and his affection for his cat Hodge. He was a High Tory and a High Churchman, and wrote many prayers and sermons for the clergy. His church was St Clement Dane's in Fleet Street, and he was a strong defender of the Church of England and the Book of Common Prayer. Despite his political views, he was kind to humble people, carrying his black servant on his back when the man was sick, speaking out against slavery, and the rigours of a still barbarous criminal law, and pressing pennies into the hands of sleeping children in the street. Dr Johnson's solid, rounded prose belongs to another age, but the memory of his unique personality is enduring. He is buried in Westminster Abbey. [13 December, A.]

Joseph of Arimathea (first century): Joseph was a rich man and a disciple of Jesus, 'waiting expectantly for the kingdom of God'. After the Crucifixion, he went to Pontius Pilate and asked for the body of Jesus, having it interred with reverence in an empty rock-tomb, probably prepared for himself and his family. By the time Jesus died, it was nearly sunset, and the Sabbath was about to begin. Burials could not take place on the Sabbath, so it was necessary to move quickly. Luke tells us that Joseph was a member of the Council (the Sanhedrin) and had not voted against Jesus, and John says that he had kept his discipleship secret 'for fear of the Jews'. John also adds that Nicodemus, the Pharisee who had visited Jesus secretly by night and held a long discussion with him on the kingdom of God (John 3:1–20), went with Joseph, bringing myrrh and aloes for the burial. Joseph became the subject of many legends. In the apocryphal fourth-century *Gospel of Nicodemus*, he is said to have been imprisoned by the Jews and miraculously released. In the Holy Grail legends, he is said to have collected Christ's blood in a cup at the Crucifixion. This cup became a sacred object much celebrated in medieval literature, art and music. The legend that Joseph of Arimathea came to England and planted his staff, which flowered as the holy thorn of Glastonbury, does not appear to have been known until 1400, when a monk-chronicler named John of Glastonbury associated both Joseph and King Arthur with the monastery, probably to increase its prestige among pilgrims. [31 August, R. O.]

Joseph of Nazareth (first century): Joseph the carpenter is the husband of the *Virgin Mary, and the adoptive father of Jesus. The Gospel according to Matthew specifies his genealogy in detail (fourteen generations from Abraham to David, and fourteen from David to Joseph), because it had been prophesied that the Messiah would be of the house of David. A just man, he was not willing to expose Mary to public shame when he found that she was expecting a child. When he learned in a dream that the child was to be born of the Holy Spirit, he took on the role of protector to both mother and baby. He was present at the nativity, and took them both down to Egypt to escape Herod's persecution. They lived in Nazareth, and went regularly every year to Jerusalem to celebrate the feast of the Passover until Jesus was twelve. He and Mary sought the boy anxiously among the crowds, to find him sitting among the teachers in the temple. After that, Joseph disappears from the Gospel narratives. At the time of the Crucifixion, Mary was evidently a widow. She was committed to the care of *John, who would act as a son to her. Traditionally, Joseph had been seen as an elderly man at the time of the birth of Jesus, but he must have been strong enough to support his family and to make the repeated journeys up to Jerusalem. Some scholars have speculated that Mary may have been his second wife. There was no tradition of celibacy in Judaism, and most men married young. If that was the case, the references to Jesus's 'brothers and sisters' (Matt. 13:55) may be to step-brothers and step-sisters, the children of an earlier marriage. A devotion to Joseph developed in the Western Church in the sixteenth century, and he is the patron of manual workers and the fathers of families. [19 March, A. R. O.]

Jude the Apostle (first century) is named as 'Judas, not Iscariot' (John 14:22). He is usually identified with Thaddeus, who occurs in the lists of the apostles (Matt. 10:3; Mark 3:18), and is thought to be the author of the Letter of Jude. He is bracketed together with *Simon the Zealot in Western Calen-

dars, though they have separate feast days in the East. They are both thought to have undertaken a mission in Persia, and to have been martyred on the same day. In recent times, Jude has become popular as the patron of lost causes, and 'Grateful thanks to St Jude' has become a well-known phrase. The reason is said to be that, because of the similarity of his name to that of Judas Iscariot, Jude was the last of the twelve apostles to be invoked in time of need, and he was only asked to favour the most desperate and hopeless of causes. [28 October, A. R. O.]

Julian of Norwich (1342–?1413) was an anchoress who took her name from St Julian's church in Norwich, a Benedictine foundation which belonged to the nuns of Carrow. She must have been a nun who was granted the special privilege of living in seclusion from the world in a cell attached to the church. She lived a life of constant prayer, and had a number of visions which she recorded with unusual clarity and detail. On 8 May 1373, when she was 'thirty and a half', she was ill and in pain. She prayed that she might see Christ's Passion, and had fifteen visions between four o'clock and nine o'clock in the morning. She saw Christ suffering on the Cross; and our Lady, 'a simple maid and meek'. And God showed her a little thing, like a hazel-nut, which represented everything that was made; and she was assured that 'it lasteth, and ever shall, for God loveth it'. She understands that God is in all things, and is assured that 'All shall be well and all shall be well and all manner of thing shall be well.' Julian's book, *The Revelations of Divine Love*, has become a classic in the mystical tradition. She says that she was fully awake at the time – these were not dreams – and, unlike such fourteenth-century mystics as *Richard

Rolle and *Walter Hilton, she has no theories about the mystical life: she simply reports an experience of great spiritual intensity, and gives thanks for it. There is a Julian shrine at her church in Norwich. [8 May, A. R.]

Juliana of Mount Cornillon (1195–1258) was an orphan, brought up by the nuns of Amescoeur, near Liège. At the age of sixteen, she had one vision, many times repeated: she saw the moon in full splendour, but with a dark stain on one side. The explanation came to her in sleep: the moon represented the Church, and the stain was the lack of a special day for celebrating the gift of Christ's body and blood in the Eucharist. A canon of St Martin's church, John of Lausanne, consulted his ecclesiastical superiors, and they took the view that there was no reason why such a festival should not be instituted. Juliana was 'mocked at, hooted at, scorned by all'. On one occasion, an excited mob broke into the convent, violating the enclosure, but she escaped. The persecution continued. The feast of Corpus Christi was contemptuously dismissed as 'a women's feast', and it was not until Jacques Pantaleon, formerly bishop of Cambrai, became Pope Urban IV, that it was fully recognized by a papal Bull of 1264. The present office for Corpus Christi in the Roman Catholic Church is a compilation from several writers, including *Thomas Aquinas. The Anglican Church has a 'day of thanksgiving for the Institution of Holy Communion'. [Juliana: 5 April, R.]

Julius and Aaron (?third or fourth century): *Bede mentions these two men immediately after his account of the martyrdom of *Alban, and says that they were martyred in the City of Legions, tentatively identified as Caerleon-upon-Usk. Giraldus Cam-brensis, writing in the twelfth century, mentions dedications to them in and around Caerleon, but nothing more is known of them. [3 July, R.]

Justin Martyr (c. 100–165) was a Greek philosopher born in Samaria, and a searcher after truth. He tried in turn the claims of the Stoics, the Peripatetics, the Pythagoreans and the Platonists, but none of these satisfied him. Then, while walking on the beach, he met 'a venerable old man' who told him about Christianity. This was the answer to his quest. He taught Christian apologetics in Ephesus and later in Rome, where he set up his own philosophy school, opposing the confusing claims of Gnostics, those who worshipped the Greek and Roman gods and the many religious cults of the Middle East. He excelled at sharp intellectual debate, and incurred considerable enmity from his opponents. During the persecutions of the reign of Marcus Aurelius he was arrested. He refused to sacrifice to the Roman gods, and was beheaded. Justin was the first philosopher of note to bring together the insights of Aristotle and Plato with those of Judaeo-Christian beliefs. He saw the Incarnation not as a break with history, but as the fulfilment of history. His views profoundly influenced later Christian writers such as *Augustine of Hippo and *Thomas Aquinas. Justin is also an excellent and reliable witness to the religious practices of the early Church. He visited Bethlehem and Calvary, and described the rites of Baptism and the Eucharist in detail. [1 June, A. R. O.]

Keble, John (1792–1866) was a friend and colleague of *John Henry Newman. Both were Fellows of Oriel College, Oxford. Keble's Assize Sermon of 14 July 1833 is usually taken as the starting-point of the Tractarian movement. Unlike his colleagues, Newman, and *Pusey, Keble was of a retiring nature and avoided public life. He refused ecclesiastical preferment in order to assist his father, the vicar of Fairford, Gloucestershire, and later moved to be vicar of Hurley, near Winchester. He remained at Hurley for thirty years, content to be a good parish priest. His intense spirituality was expressed in his poems, some of which, like 'New every morning', have become well-known hymns. Keble was a High Churchman of what was then a very old and partially forgotten school of churchmanship, with a strong personal attachment to the memory of *Charles I. He took little part in the theological debates of his own day. After his death, a subscription was raised to build an Oxford college in his memory. The architecture of Keble College perhaps owes more to the Victorian splendours of the Tractarian movement than to the shy and retiring contemplative it commemorates. [14 July, A.]

Ken, Thomas (1637–1711) has gone down in history less as a champion of the Anglican Church than as the bishop who temporarily ruffled Charles II by 'refusing Nelly a lodging'. Nell Gwyn was forced to accept the hospitality of the dean instead; but the easy-going monarch did not hold a permanent grudge, cheerfully assenting to Ken's appointment as bishop of Bath only a year or two later. The determination to live by his principles which had led Ken to refuse to house a royal mistress was evident again in 1687, when James II attempted to repeal the Test Acts (which imposed civil disabilities on Roman Catholics and Dissenters), and Habeas Corpus. Ken was one of the bishops who refused to accept this exercise of the royal prerogative, and he was imprisoned in the Tower of London. The flight of James and the accession of William III and Mary II in 1688 freed them; but Ken felt unable to take the oath of allegiance to the new monarchs, because he had sworn an oath of allegiance to James. It was a very difficult period in which to have a conscience as keen as his. He became a 'non-juring bishop'. The archbishop of Canterbury, seven bishops, four hundred clergy and nearly all the bishops and clergy of Scotland refused to take the oath, and were deprived of their offices. Ken, who spent the rest of his life at the home of his friend and protector Lord Weymouth at Longleat, was the author of several well-known Anglican hymns, including 'Awake my soul, and with the sun' and 'Glory to thee, my God, this night'. [8 June, A.]

Kentigern (Mungo) (c. 518–603): many legends have clustered around Kentigern's name. He was said to have been the son of a Scottish princess who refused to reveal the name of her lover, and was thrown from the top of a cliff on the southern side of the Firth of Forth. She and her child survived, and the child was brought up by a monk, Serf or Servanus, who called him Mungo or 'darling'. Accounts of his ministry have a stronger historical basis. He became a Celtic monk so much honoured in the Strathclyde region that the people asked for him to be their bishop, and he was consecrated from Ireland. He is said to have met *Columba, who died in 597, and to have exchanged croziers with him. He certainly lived well into his eighties, though the date of his death is not certain. St Mungo's cathedral in Glasgow commemorates him as the first bishop of Glasgow. [13 January, A. R.]

King, Edward (1829–1910): despite poor health which interrupted his education, Edward King's spirituality and pastoral gifts were so marked that he became principal of Cuddesdon Theological College. He was appointed Regius Professor of Pastoral Theology at Oxford in 1873, and bishop of Lincoln in 1885, largely due to the influence of W. E. Gladstone as prime minister. Bishop King's spiritual model was *Francis de Sales. A moderate Anglo-Catholic, he was attacked in 1858 by the ultra-Protestant Church Association and accused of 'ritual acts contrary to the Prayer Book'. These were that he celebrated Holy Communion in the eastward position (facing Jerusalem) instead of from the north end of the altar, as the Evangelicals did; that he had lighted candles on the altar; that he mixed water with wine in the chalice; that he allowed the Agnus Dei to be sung in Latin; and that he used the sign of the Cross in blessing. He faced an ecclesiastical court consisting of Archbishop E. F. Benson and six bishops, all convinced Low Churchmen. The trial took four years, and caused him much pain and humiliation. Many High Churchmen came to his support, and subscriptions were raised to pay his legal costs. The final verdict was that his practices were acceptable, except for the eastward position and the sign of the Cross (both of which continued to be used by many clergy). This was the last of a series of litigious actions against 'ritualism' in the Victorian Church. [8 March, A. R.]

Kivebulaya, Apolo (1933): Apolo was probably born in the late 1870s. He was a boy living in a Ugandan village north of Lake Victoria when *Bishop Hannington and the *Uganda Martyrs were killed in 1885 and 1886. He was seized from home by a band of Moslem soldiers and forced to join them for a time, but in the upheaval following the rebellion of 1888, he managed to escape, and joined a group of Christians travelling through the bush. He came under the influence of a Scottish missionary-engineer known as 'Mackay of the Great Lakes', and carried out his own mission in the dense forests to the west of Uganda. He made his way to Boga, on the borders of the Congo near the Mountains of the Moon, where he built a small thatched church and exerted such an influence over the tribes that he was able to stop cattle-raiding (a frequent cause of tribal warfare), free slaves, and put down the opium trade. In 1903, he was ordained. He built a school, trained catechists, and went out into the forests to contact the Pygmy people of the area. He learned their language, translated the Gospel according to Mark for them, and brought Anglican missionaries to meet them. Apolo worked in the Boga area for over thirty years, and on his death, the Church Missionary Society took over his work in what had become a strong Christian community. [30 May, A.]

Kolbe, Maximilian (1894–1941): this Polish Franciscan grew up near Lodz when Poland was under Russian domination. He studied in Rome, was ordained in 1919, and after some time teaching Church history, developed a small religious community which produced weekly and daily newspapers through which Catholic principles and Polish patriotism were circulated to an oppressed people. Father Kolbe went to Japan, where he established a community in Nagasaki, and returned to Poland as prior of a community of eight hundred friars at Niepokalanow. When Germany invaded Poland in 1939, he continued to publish without regard for the views of the invaders, and organized a refugee camp for the thousands of displaced Poles and Jews in the area. In May 1941, he and four other friars were arrested by the Gestapo and sent to the concentration camp at Auschwitz. When he ministered to his fellow-prisoners, he was beaten and made to shovel manure. In August of that year, a prisoner from his block escaped. The prisoners were paraded, and ten were selected to die by slow starvation as a reprisal. When one cried out that he had a wife and children, Father Kolbe stepped forward and took his place. In the death-hut, he ministered unflinchingly to the dying men, and was one of the four still alive a fortnight later. They were executed by lethal injection. This story of extreme brutality and extreme heroism became one of the rallying-points for the Polish Resistance. It was a fellow-Pole, Pope John Paul II, who promulgated Father Kolbe's canonization in 1982. [14 August, A. R.]

Kopuria, Ini (1945) was baptized by the Melanesian Mission. His unusual Christian name is not Melanesian, but that of a Christian king of Dorset. He went to a mission school, and became a police officer in Guadalcanal. After a serious illness, he spent much time in meditation, and with the permission of the bishop, became an evangelist in the remote islands of Melanesia. Others came to join him, and he formed the Melanesian Brotherhood, established in 1935. Members took temporary vows and worked in groups of eight. The numbers grew to 1,500. There was also an Order of Companions – men and women who met for prayer and undertook works of charity. This indigenous movement was not without its critics among the European missionaries, but Ini was a charismatic leader and a gifted evangelist among his own people. The movement was shattered when Japan entered World War II and invaded the islands. The mission centre was burned, and some of the Brothers

were shot. Ini escaped, but returned to Melanesia to build up the work again when the Japanese were driven out by the American forces. He died in June 1945, shortly before the final Japanese defeat. [6 June, A.]

Lanfranc (1005–89) was William the Conqueror's choice as his archbishop of Canterbury after the Norman Conquest of England. An Italian from Pavia, he was abbot of Bec and then of William's own foundation, St Stephen's, at Caen. He was a brilliant administrator with an extensive knowledge of ecclesiastical and civil law. He had no desire to come to England, regarding the Anglo-Saxon Church as backward and insufficiently in touch with Rome; but on William's insistence, he accepted the office and proceeded to overhaul the Church in conformance with Norman principles. Norman bishops and cathedral deans replaced Saxons, monasteries were given Norman abbots and priors, and the Benedictine Rule was tightened. New dioceses were formed to take account of population movements, courts of ecclesiastical jurisdiction were set up, and a commission went round the country, changing church dedications to honour saints in the Roman Calendar rather than Anglo-Saxon ones. After his death, a cult developed in Pavia and at Bec-Hellouin in Normandy – but not in Canterbury, where his innovations were much resented. Lanfranc's treatise *On the Body and Blood of Our Lord* is regarded as a precursor of the doctrine of transubstantiation. [28 May, A. R.]

La Salle, John Baptist de (1651–1719): this French priest came from a wealthy family, and had a comfortable post as a canon of Rheims when he was asked to help in setting up schools in the city for poor boys. He was horrified

Latimer, Hugh

at the poor quality of the teachers, saying that he ranked them below his own servants, and 'the thought of living with them was unbearable'; but after much prayer, he was moved to form a community with twelve teachers as 'Brothers of the Christian Schools'. In 1684 he resigned his canonry and gave away his inheritance, so that they might start on equal terms. In 1694, he and twelve brothers took perpetual vows, dedicating themselves to teaching the poor. They were to be 'ambassadors of Christ to the young'. Despite difficulties, some caused by the opposition of clergy who ran fee-paying schools, and some by the early deaths which resulted from the Brothers' very poor living conditions, the movement spread. Its distinctive characteristic was that it was an Order of teachers, not of clergy: no priest might join the community, and no member of the community might be ordained. This is still the case, and there are now some 20,000 members in many countries, known as Christian Brothers or Salesian Brothers, whose vocation is to teaching rather than pastoral ministry. [7 April, R.]

Latimer, Hugh (c. 1485–1555): 'old Father Latimer' was arraigned with *Thomas Cranmer and *Nicholas Ridley in the reign of Mary Tudor. He had seen many changes in the Church in the days of Henry VIII and Edward VI, and had come to believe that the Scriptures should be available in English for the ordinary people, and that the Catholic Church was in need of reform. As bishop of Worcester, he worked hard to reform a run-down diocese where many clergy did not even own a Bible or New Testament, and he preached against 'purgatory pick-pockets' and 'mass priests' who offered salvation for cash. He was too Protestant for Henry VIII, and had to

resign from his bishopric after helping a Protestant to escape to the Continent. By the time Mary Tudor came to the throne, he was in failing health. Questioned in Latin after his arrest, he said wearily that he had not used the Latin tongue much in the past twenty years. He said that he could not find a Mass in the New Testament, and he believed that the service of Holy Communion was a memorial: 'the bread is still bread, and the wine still wine, for the change is not in the nature but the dignity'. On 15 October 1555, he and Nicholas Ridley were both burned at the stake at what is now the Martyrs' Memorial in Oxford. Cranmer was to follow soon after. Before the fires were lighted, he embraced Ridley, saying, 'Be ye of good cheer, Master Ridley, and play the man. We shall this day light such a candle by God's grace as shall never be put out.' [16 October, A.]

Laud, William (1573–1645) was the leader of the High Church or 'Arminian' party at Oxford, opposed to the Calvinistic practices which were being adopted in the Church of England. His views were close to those of *Charles I, in whose reign he became successively bishop of Bath and Wells, bishop of London and archbishop of Canterbury. As archbishop, he instituted a visitation of the dioceses to ensure conformity in religious observance, and demanded obedience from the clergy. He was particularly opposed for his refusal to ordain men who engaged in itinerant preaching rather than ministering in parishes, and for his insistence that the altar should be removed from the centre of the church and placed at the east end, where it would be a focus for worship. Though his aim was to restore the Catholicity of the Anglican Church, not to rejoin the Roman Catholic Church, he was inevitably drawn into supporting the absolutist rule of Charles I and his minister, Thomas Wentworth, Earl Strafford. When the Puritan-dominated Long Parliament met in 1640, Strafford and Laud were both impeached for treason. Strafford was executed, and Laud spent four years in prison before he also went to the scaffold. [10 January, A.]

Laurence of Canterbury (619) was the second archbishop of Canterbury, following *Augustine. He was one of the first party of monks sent to England by *Pope Gregory the Great. Augustine sent him back to Rome to report on the first phase of the mission, and to seek the pope's guidance on a number of difficult issues, including the functions of a bishop, his relationship with the clergy, his own responsibilities with regard to the 'British' (Celtic) bishops in Wales and the north of England, and detailed matters of Church discipline. He returned in 601 with Gregory's directions, and worked closely with Augustine, who designated him as his own successor. Augustine died in 604. Laurence coordinated the work of the mission in Kent, and attempted to come to terms with the British bishops, but his demand that they should conform to Roman practices, particularly in the matter of the date of Easter (an issue which was clearly seen to be of great importance even at this early stage, sixty years before the Synod of Whitby), created mutual misunderstandings. [2 February, R.]

Laurence of Rome (258) was one of the seven deacons of Rome in the time of Pope Sixtus II, and worked closely with the pope. He was responsible for the care of Church property in the city, and for administering alms to the poor. When the Emperor Valerian persecuted the Christians, Pope Sixtus

and four deacons were arrested and executed in a Roman cemetery. Laurence is said to have been ordered to produce an inventory of Church treasures for the emperor. He sold the sacred vessels and other objects, and gave the money to the poor. Then, surrounded by the blind and halt and lame, he told the prefect of Rome, 'These are my treasures.' He was executed four days after the pope. This story is credible, and his martyrdom is well established. The story of his death on the gridiron, though lending itself to vivid artistic representations, seems to be of medieval invention. As a Roman citizen, he would have been executed by a sword-thrust, not by lengthy torture. [10 August, A. R. O.]

Law, William (1686–1761) was a Fellow of Emmanuel College, Cambridge, when the Elector of Hanover became King George I in 1714. Since he could not in conscience rescind the oath of allegiance which he had sworn to the deposed James II, he resigned his fellowship and became a private tutor, friend and spiritual director to the family of Mr Edward Gibbon, father of the author of *The Decline and Fall of the Roman Empire*. He was ordained in 1728. George I had died in the previous year, and with the accession of George II, the prospect of a Stuart succession must have seemed remote. On Mr Gibbon's death in 1740, Law retired to his native village, King's Cliffe, Northamptonshire, where he devoted himself to study and writing, and to works of charity. He was exceptionally well read in devotional works, including the works of the mystic Jacob Böhme, the Abbé Fénelon, and *Francis de Sales. His most celebrated work is *A Serious Call to a Devout and Holy Life*, which inspired *Dr Johnson and *John Wesley, and is a widely read Christian classic. His deep and genuine piety had a considerable effect on the early Methodist movement, and he has been called 'the true founder of Methodism'. [10 April, A.]

Lazarus (first century), friend of Jesus and brother of *Mary and Martha, was raised from the dead, and the Gospel according to John tells the dramatic story (11:1–44). Jesus came to Bethany four days after Lazarus died, and Martha and Mary made their affirmations of faith. As Jesus gave a great cry of 'Lazarus, come out', the dead man walked out of the tomb, still in his grave-clothes. The chief priests plotted against Lazarus as well as Jesus (John 12:1–2, 9–11) because the raising of Lazarus had caused many people to believe in Jesus. After that, there is no mention of Lazarus or his sisters in the New Testament. There are many apocryphal accounts – that he followed Peter to Syria; that he and his sisters went to Cyprus, where he became bishop of Kition (Larnaca); that the three were put to sea in a leaky boat without oars or a rudder, which carried them to Marseilles, where Lazarus became a bishop and was martyred in the time of the Emperor Domitian. French legends proliferated, and Lazarus of Bethany became confused with the fictional Lazarus, the beggar in the parable of Dives and Lazarus. The *lazarettos* of western Europe derive their name from the beggar who was 'full of sores', not from Lazarus of Bethany, as does the Paris church of Saint-Lazare and the nearby railway station. [29 July, A. R. 17 December, O.]

Leo the Great (461): Pope Leo I was distinguished as a diplomat and a theologian. In a twenty-year pontificate, he negotiated with both Huns and Vandals, raising tribute to keep them from sacking Rome. He advised the monk-theologian John Cassian on his treatise on the Incarnation, which Cassian dedicated to him, and he produced a concise definition of the nature of the person of Christ, known as 'the Tome', which healed a threatened breach between the bishops at the Council of Chalcedon in 451. Leo was an energetic and watchful pope. His letters supporting, advising or reproving bishops in Italy, Gaul, Spain and north Africa, warning them against the doctrinal errors of the day and solving disputes, show a constant care for all the churches, and 143 of them survive. Leo is one of only three popes who are referred to as 'the Great', the other two being *Gregory I and Nicholas I. [10 November, A. R. O.].

Leonard of Noblac (?sixth century) was a Frankish nobleman at the court of Clovis. He entered a monastery and later became a hermit, refusing Clovis's offer of a bishopric. When

Clovis and his queen, *Clothilde, were out hunting near his hermitage, Clothilde suddenly went into labour, and Leonard remained with her, praying until her child was safely born. Clovis gave him the land for the abbey as a thank-offering. The town of Saint-Léonard-de-Noblac, near Limoges, was once the site of his abbey, where Crusaders stayed on their way to Marseilles. It is recorded that Bohémond I, prince of Antioch, visited the abbey in 1103, on his way back from the Holy Land. He had been a prisoner of the Saracens, and gave the abbey a gift of silver chains fashioned on the pattern of those he had worn in captivity. English Crusaders brought home a devotion to Leonard as the patron saint of prisoners. The towns of St Leonards on the Sussex coast and in Roxburgh, and some 117 church dedications in England all bear his name. [6 November, A. R.]

Linus (c. 78) is named as the second bishop of Rome in papal lists, following *Peter. *Irenaeus identifies him with the Linus mentioned in Paul's Second Letter to Timothy (2 Tim. 4:21). He is thought to have been bishop of Rome for about twelve years. For centuries he was assumed to have been martyred, but it has been established that no persecutions took place during his period of office. So little is known about him that his name has been dropped from the Universal Roman Calendar, but he is still mentioned in the Roman Canon of the Mass, immediately after the Apostles *Peter and *Paul. [23 September, R.]

Lowder, Charles Fuge (1820–80): Father Lowder, a parish priest who worked among the poorest sections of society in the London Docks, was much loved by the Anglo-Catholic wing of the Church of England, but was attacked by a rowdy element who objected to High Church practices. His services at the mission church of St George's-in-the-East (where he wore vestments, had two lighted candles on the altar, and intoned the liturgy) were disrupted by hissing and jeering. Cushions and other objects were thrown at the altar, choir-boys were spat upon, and fireworks were set off. In 1859–60, no less than seventy-three

policemen were sent in to keep order, and when they failed to do so, the bishop of London, A. C. Tait, closed the church for two weeks. When it reopened, Anglo-Catholics from all over London came to defend their own, and to keep out the rowdy element. Father Lowder was the founder of the Confraternity of the Blessed Sacrament and one of the founding members of the Society of the Holy Cross. He is remembered in the East End not only for this remarkable confrontation, which gave Anglo-Catholics the freedom to worship in their own way, but also as a devoted priest who ministered to the people of the London slums. [9 September, A.]

Lucius, 'King of Britain': the story of 'King Lucius' is an excellent example of the way in which errors can be compounded in the lives of the saints. *Bede tells us that in the year 156, Lucius, king of Britain, wrote to Pope Eleutherius asking to be made a Christian. Thereafter, 'the British kept the faith as they had received it, pure and in its fullness, in peace and quietness until the time of the Emperor Diocletian.' There was no 'king of Britain' in the year 156. If a local British chief wrote to the pope, the story has escaped mention by any other British authority of the period. Scholars have produced an ingenious explanation: the only king known to have accepted Christianity before the end of the second century is Abgar (or Lucius) of Edessa, and Edessa was latinized in documents as 'Britum Edessenorum'. A monk-copyist may have substituted 'Britannia' for 'Britum'; but from Bede's time on, the English stories about Lucius multiplied. In the Welsh chronicles, he became 'Lleufer Mawr' (Great Splendour). William of Malmesbury repeats the story of the mission, and Geoffrey of Monmouth, a highly imaginative chronicler, tells how the entire country was converted, the *flamens* and *archflamens* of Roman rites being replaced by Christian bishops and archbishops, the archbishops being based in London, York and Llandaff. Continental legends make Lucius a missionary, a bishop and a martyr, and one says that he was baptized by the *Apostle Timothy. But if there was a real Lucius in Britain, the truth about him has disappeared under layers of surmise and invention. [3 December, R.]

Lucy (304) is one of the most famous of the early virgin martyrs. A fourth-century inscription in Syracuse (Sicily) records the death of a girl named Euskia on Lucy's feast day, which indicates that she was honoured by the Church soon after the Edict of Milan (314) gave Christians the freedom to worship publicly. She is thought to have been martyred during the persecutions of the Emperor Diocletian. Nothing definite is known about the circumstances of her death, though there have been many legendary accounts. She is one of the twenty-two virgins (with *Agnes, Agatha and *Cecilia) shown on the sixth-century Byzantine mosaic in the church of San Apollinare Nuovo in Ravenna. Many medieval artists, including Titian and Fra Angelico, portrayed her as a typical virgin saint. Her name suggests light and purity, and the song 'Santa Lucia' refers to her. The customary celebration of her feast day in Sweden (occurring near the winter solstice, when there are few hours of light) is a celebration of virginity, in which young girls dressed in white and crowned with lighted candles process to church. [13 December, A. R. O.]

Luke the Evangelist (first century) is the author both of the Gospel according to Luke, and of the Acts of the Apostles, which have striking stylistic and linguistic similarities. He is thought to have been a Hellenic Jew.

Paul refers to him as 'the beloved physician' (Col. 4:14), and he writes in the good classical Greek of an educated man. Early tradition says that he came from Antioch. He makes it clear in the prologue to his Gospel that he was not an eye-witness to the earthly life of Jesus, but that he has talked to many of those who were close to him, and is concerned to set down an orderly account of the whole story, 'after investigating everything carefully from the very first'. He clearly joined the apostles at a fairly early stage in their ministry. He is the only one of the four Evangelists who tells in detail the stories of the Annunciation and the Visitation to Elizabeth, which he must have heard either from the Virgin Mary herself, or from a group of women who knew her. In the second part of the Acts of the Apostles, when he is dealing with the missionary journeys of Paul and his companions, he switches from 'they' to 'we', and gives what is evidently a first-hand account based on diary jottings. He was with Paul in Macedonia (Acts 16:10) and Troas (20:6), and set sail with him for Italy (27:1–28:15). He ends his account in Rome, when Paul, having been for two years in prison, is free to preach and teach, ending before the death of Peter and Paul, which is thought to have taken place about the year 65. We do not know whether he also died, or whether he went back to Jerusalem, perhaps leaving the manuscript behind in haste during the period of persecution. Luke is the patron of artists as well as doctors. His symbol as one of the four Evangelists is an ox, and he is depicted in many church paintings, stained-glass windows and mosaics, usually writing or painting. [18 October, A. R. O.]

Lull, Raymond (Ramón Llull, 1232–1316) was born in Palma, in the brief period when Majorca was a kingdom in its own right. He became a page at court, and later marshal and high steward to the king. He was wealthy and well educated. When he was thirty years old, he had a repeated vision of Christ crucified which convinced him that he must devote his life to converting the Moors. There was no conflict between Christians and Moors in Majorca. After a period of prayer and seclusion, he spent nine years in learning Arabic. He wrote prolifically, including theological works and a novel, *Blanquerna*, in which the hero became pope; but in spite of his learning, he could not persuade the Church authorities to take him seriously. He was a great man in Majorca, but he was a layman. He was not under ecclesiastical obedience, and his writing was highly critical of abuses in the Church. He was rebuffed by scholars and churchmen in Rome, Genoa and Paris, and by two popes, to whom he made a direct appeal. The Dominicans refused him, but the Franciscans finally allowed him to become a tertiary (a member of their lay Order). He went three times to North Africa, preaching in the streets of Tunis and Bougie. Twice he was roughly handled, imprisoned and returned to Majorca. On the

third occasion, he was stoned and left for dead. Some Genoese sailors rescued him and took him by ship to Majorca, but he died within sight of Palma harbour. He is buried in the church of San Francisco in Palma. Ramón's writings have been translated into English with his biography, *The Fool of Love*. [29 June, R.]

Luther, Martin (1483–1546) was an Augustinian canon, a theologian and official preacher to the parish church at Wittenberg. When he nailed his ninety-five Theses to the door of the church in protest against the sale of indulgences by Friar Tetzel in 1517, he started a movement which was to take him and much of northern Europe outside the jurisdiction of the Catholic Church. He argued that the merits of Jesus Christ were not a 'treasury' controlled by the papacy for its own purposes, but were freely available to all believers; and that people should be allowed to interpret the Scriptures in their own languages for themselves. The result was a dramatic confrontation with papal authority. At the Diet of Worms in 1521 he was required to reject and abjure all his many books. When he refused, he was excommunicated. Luther escaped imprisonment with the aid of some of the German princes, who had political reasons for rejecting papal control. Subsequently, he married an ex-nun, had a family of five children, and devoted himself to translating the Scriptures into German. *William Tyndale used some of his translations in order to write his own English versions. What had started as a liberating and reforming movement within the Church degenerated in Germany into the Peasants' War, in which monasteries and churches were pillaged and mob rule got out of hand. Luther supported the princes against the mob. The new Protestant theology which developed went far beyond his proposals for reform. Since the Second Vatican Council, Catholic scholars have begun to recognize the strength of Luther's desire to maintain Christian unity, and to remedy abuses in the Church from within rather than creating a major division in its structure. [31 October, A.]

Luwum, Janani (1922–77): a boy from East Acholi in northern Uganda, Janani was educated and trained for the Anglican ministry through the auspices of the Church Missionary Society. His appointment as archbishop of Uganda in 1974 was widely welcomed in his own country and by leaders of the Anglican Communion, who respected his ability to contribute to the work of the world-wide Church while keeping in touch with his African roots and his own people. Idi Amin, the military dictator of Uganda, came to believe that Christians in Uganda were in league with Zionists, whom he regarded as his enemies. In August 1976, the archbishop sent a memorandum to President Amin, telling him that the international community was outraged by the breakdown of law and order in the country. On 5 February 1977, following a period of harassment by the security forces, he was driven to a meeting with the president, and never seen again. It was subsequently announced that he had died in a car crash, but investigation showed these claims to be false, and a report from Tanzania that Idi Amin was personally responsible for shooting him was widely believed. Later in the same month, Amin ordered the massacre of the Langi and Acholi tribes. The horrors of the Amin régime came to an end in 1978, when forces from Tanzania invaded Uganda and drove Amin from power. Janani Luwum, a modern African martyr, is represented on the martyrs' statues on the west front of Westminster Abbey. [17 February, A.]

Macrina the Younger (c. 330–79) was a sister of *Basil of Caesarea and *Gregory of Nyssa. She is known as 'the Younger' because her grandmother Macrina, and her parents Basil the Elder and Emmelia, are recognized as saints in the Eastern Orthodox Church. While Basil was sent to study at the great teaching institutions of the Eastern Mediterranean – Caesarea, Constantinople and Athens – Macrina, the eldest girl of a large family, stayed home to help her mother and grandmother teach the younger children. She was particularly close to Gregory, her junior by some five years. Later, she joined her mother as a consecrated virgin in the community at Pontus on the banks of the River Iris, and became a spiritual director of note. Basil died in 379, and Gregory, then bishop of Nyssa, visited Macrina to share his grief with her. He found her very ill, and herself near death; but she rallied her strength to give him comfort and a renewed hope of the resurrection. His account of their discussions together, known as the *Macriniae*, shows her as a woman of deep piety and theological understanding. He writes of her with great respect, referring to her as 'The Teacher'. Macrina died shortly afterwards. Her story was not known in the West until the eleventh century, when Gregory of Nyssa's life and the *Macriniae* were first translated into Latin. [19 July, A. R. O.]

Marcellus Akimetes (c. 485) is the best-known of the Akimetoi, an Order of Eastern monks committed to singing the Divine Office continually by day and night. Their name means 'the not-resters'. Marcellus was abbot of a community sited on the Bosphorus opposite Constantinople, and ruled his monastery for forty-five years. He was known as a champion of the 'Athanasian' Creed against the many unorthodox views of the Trinity then circulating in Asia Minor. [29 December, R. O.]

Margaret of Antioch is such a shadowy figure that she is thought to be a character of pious fiction, not a real person. There is no sign of an early cult, and Pope Gelasius declared her legend to be apocryphal in the year 494. Nevertheless, her popular appeal has been very wide. Her story was known in England before the Norman Conquest and reinforced by the Crusaders returning from the East. She is one of the Fourteen Holy Helpers of the Rhineland, and Joan of Arc believed that she heard Margaret's voice inspiring her to her mission. More than two hundred churches were dedicated to her in England. Her popularity seems to stem from the promises that the legend attributes to her: that those who invoke her on their death-beds will receive divine protection; that those who dedicate churches or light candles in her name will receive the good things they pray for; and that pregnant women who call upon her will have an easy time in childbirth. [20 July, A. R. O.]

Margaret of Scotland (c. 1046–93) was the sister of Edgar the Atheling, claimant to the throne of England. The two, with their sister Christina, were exiled from England first by Canute, and then, after a period at the court of Edward the Confessor, by William the Conqueror. They fell into the hands of the fearsome Malcolm Canmore (Malcolm III of Scotland) when he was raiding Northumberland. Malcolm protected them for political reasons, and insisted on marrying Margaret. Gently reared and educated in the Benedictine tradition, she had a

remarkable effect on Malcolm and his court. Drunkenness and uncouth behaviour were curbed, debauchery was stopped. Court ladies were treated with respect, and set to ecclesiastical embroidery. Knights were induced to say grace after meals. Malcolm was devoted to Margaret. She taught him to pray, which he did with much perplexity and many groans. Poor people were brought into the palace daily, and king and queen waited on them personally, giving them food and wine. Margaret took Malcolm's gold for alms and ransomed many Norman captives taken by the Scots, sending them back to England. She founded Holy Trinity abbey in Dunfermline, persuaded Malcolm to rebuild the monastery at Iona which had been sacked by Vikings, and reformed the Culdees, the Celtic solitaries who had sadly lapsed since the days of *Oengus. Three of her sons became successively kings of Scotland, and a daughter married Henry I of England. [16 November, A. R.]

Margery Kempe (born c. 1373) is known through her autobiography, *The Book of Margery Kempe*, a unique record of middle-class life and religious practices in the fourteenth century. She was the wife of a burgess of Lynn (now King's Lynn, Norfolk). After she gave birth to her only child, a son, her behaviour became erratic. She saw devils, slandered her husband and her friends, wore extravagant clothes, and tried to run a brewery and a corn mill. When these enterprises failed, she turned to religion, saw many visions, kissed lepers, and cried continually with 'boisterous sobbing'. She persuaded her husband, John, to make a vow of chastity before the bishop of Lincoln, and she made several voyages abroad, including the three great Christian pilgrimages to Rome, Jerusalem and Santiago de Compostela, often without money, and dependent on the charity of those whom she met. She was arrested several times on suspicion of being a Lollard (see *John Wyclif). In England, she defended herself against the ecclesiastical authorities with spirit. She visited *Julian of Norwich, and went to Rome after the death of *Bridget of Sweden to pay honour to her memory. Margery's account of her wandering life is full of vivid detail, and her search for God, through all her physical and psychological difficulties, has all the marks of a genuine spiritual experience. [9 November, A.]

Mark the Evangelist (first century): most biblical scholars assume that Mark, the author of the Second Gospel, is the same person as John

Mark, who accompanied *Paul and *Barnabas on their first mission to Cyprus. There are two references in the Acts of the Apostles to 'John, whose other name was Mark' (Acts 12:12, 25) and one to 'John, who was called Mark' (Acts 15:37). Barnabas was a Greek Cypriot, and John Mark was his cousin. Mark was with Paul in Rome (Col. 4:10) and, according to the fourth-century Bishop Eusebius of Caesarea, after the execution of *Peter and Paul he went to Egypt, where he carried out a mission and became bishop of

Alexandria. Mark's Gospel is the shortest of the four, and the earliest: the Gospels according to both Matthew and Luke draw on it, and John's Gospel is known to have been written last. Mark is thought to have set it down either in Rome about the time of the deaths of Peter and Paul, or in Alexandria about five years later. He has been venerated as a martyr since at least the fourth century, and his shrine in Alexandria was a medieval place of pilgrimage. His emblem, shown in many paintings and other works of art, is the winged lion. He is the patron of Venice: in the ninth century, his relics were taken to that city to avoid desecration by the Turks, and were buried under the high altar of the great church in what became St Mark's Square. The two winged lions on the landing stage nearby are also his symbols. [25 April, A. R. O.]

Maro (c. 423 or 433) was a hermit and teacher who lived near the city of Cyrrhus (now Cyr) in Syria. He lived a life of extreme asceticism in the ruins of an abandoned temple, and gained a reputation as a spiritual counsellor and healer. He was greatly reverenced by *John Chrysostom, who quoted his brief and pithy sayings. After his death, the monastery of Beit-Marum was built round his shrine, and this is said to be the origin of the Maronite communities. Maronites have their own Calendar for the Church's year, beginning in October, and their own liturgy. Maro's name is mentioned in the Canon of their Mass. They separated from the Church (which had not yet divided into East and West) in the seventh century, joined the Western Church at the time of the Crusades, and have remained in communion with the Roman Catholic Church, with their own rites in Syriac. Repeated massacres at the hands of the Turks in the nineteenth and early twentieth centuries greatly reduced their numbers, and many of those who were able to escape went to the United States. They are now comparatively few in number in the Middle East. [14 February, R. O.]

Martin of Tours (c. 316–97) was an army officer and a member of the Imperial Guard when he encountered a

beggar at Amiens, and cut his voluminous cloak in two to give the beggar half. Martin became a disciple of *Bishop Hilary of Poitiers, and lived as a hermit for some years. His reputation for holiness grew so great that others came to join him, and he established a monastery, thought to be the first in France. After Hilary's death, he was elected bishop of Tours by popular acclaim. He continued to live a simple and ascetic life, and became a missionary bishop, travelling through the Loire valley on foot, by donkey, or by small boat. He actively confronted the pagan cults of his time, smashing idols and razing temples; but he argued that heretics should not be put to death, and defended the Priscillians, a group of Gnostics who were tried and executed for sorcery. He founded a number of monasteries. Martin's work was not always appreciated by the other bishops of Gaul, who found him unorthodox and lacking in episcopal dignity; but he was much loved by the people of Tours. The pilgrimage to his shrine at Tours was one of the most popular in the Middle Ages (it lay conveniently on the route from Canterbury to Santiago de Compostela). Churches were dedicated in his name across Europe – including the church at Canterbury which Augustine and his party used when they first reached England. His appearance in some Orthodox Calendars may be due to the fact that the Crusaders took his devotion to the Middle East. [11 November, A. R. O.]

Martin de Porres (1579–1639) was a mulatto – the child of a Spanish grandee in conquered Peru and a freed black slave from Panama. He had his mother's dark colouring. He was apprenticed to a barber-surgeon, and learned herbalism from his mother. He entered a Dominican priory in Lima to serve the brothers as a lay helper, and in time became a member of the Dominican Third Order, acting as barber, surgeon, infirmarian and master of the herb garden. Though there was a law in Peru forbidding the religious Orders from accepting 'Indians, blacks and their descendants', the prior offered him full status as a friar. Martin at first refused, saying that he was unworthy. He suffered greatly from the double stigma of illegitimacy and colour in a rigidly racist society, calling himself 'this dog of a mulatto'; but the Dominicans encouraged him to become a lay brother. Martin's gentleness and healing skills, his love for the poor and for animals, won him many friends, and when he died, Spanish bishops and noblemen attended his funeral. In South America, he is the patron of race relations and social justice. [3 November, A. R.]

Martyn, Henry (1781–1812): when he was a student at Cambridge, Henry

Mary and Martha

Martyn came under the influence of *Charles Simeon, the celebrated Evangelical vicar of Holy Trinity parish. After ordination, he became Simeon's curate for a time, then took a post as chaplain to the East India Company in Bengal, where he took services for Indians, preached to the beggars in the streets, and visited Hindu temples to hold discussions with the Brahmins. He translated the New Testament and the Book of Common Prayer into Hindustani, and went on to translate the New Testament into both Arabic and Farsi, the language of Persia and Afghanistan. He travelled widely, meeting Islamic scholars and debating the basic beliefs of Christians and Moslems. These journeys were taxing for a young man with a delicate constitution, and he died in Armenia at the age of thirty-one from 'consumption' (possibly tuberculosis). His extensive letters and diaries were edited after his death by Bishop Samuel Wilberforce, and were published in 1831. Martyn's New Testament translations in Hindustani and Farsi are in the British Library. [19 October, A.]

Mary and Martha (first century): *Luke sharply differentiates the characters of these two sisters. He tells how Jesus came to the house in Bethany where they lived with their brother *Lazarus. Martha was 'worried and distracted by many tasks', presumably ordering the household and preparing food for the guests. Mary sat at Jesus' feet and listened to him. When Martha asked Jesus to tell Mary to help her, she was told that only one thing was necessary: to listen to the word of God (Luke 10:38–42). The Gospel according to John tells the story of the raising of Lazarus: by the time Jesus arrived in Bethany, Lazarus had already been in the tomb for four days. Active, practical Martha came out to meet Jesus and told him that Lazarus might have lived if he had come more quickly; but she added in faith that she believed God would do whatever Jesus asked. This is the occasion of the tremendous statement, 'I am the resurrection and the life.' When Jesus told the mourners to move the stone, she protested at first that his body would already have begun to decay in the hot climate, but stood silent in awe as Lazarus stumbled into daylight. Quieter, more contemplative Mary stayed at home, grieving with their friends; but she also witnessed the raising of her brother. According to John (11:1–4) Mary was the woman who anointed Jesus' feet with costly ointment, and wiped them with her hair in thanksgiving. The apocryphal stories about Lazarus often include his sisters, who are said to have shared his leaky boat and to have settled with him in Cyprus or in south-eastern France. The Gospels emphasize the strength of the affection between brother and sisters, and two sharply contrasting roles for the women. [29 July, A. R. O.]

Mary Magdalene (first century) was one of a group of women whom Jesus had cured of 'infirmities and evil spirits', and who followed him. Luke, the physician, describes her as one from whom 'seven devils had gone out' (8:2). She stayed close to Jesus during the terrible events of his death and burial. She stood with Mary his mother and Mary Cleophas at the foot of the Cross while he was dying, went with Joseph of Arimathea to beg his body from Pontius Pilate, and sat grieving outside the tomb while the stone was rolled against the entrance. She went back to the tomb early on the day of the Resurrection, bearing spices to anoint Jesus' body, to find that the stone had been moved. She was the first to see the risen Lord, at first mistaking him for the gardener (John 20:12–16). She ran to tell the Apostles, and for this reason she was known in medieval times as 'the apostle to the Apostles'. An Eastern tradition says that she subsequently went to Ephesus with Mary the mother of Jesus and the Apostle John, to care for Mary in her later years. There is nothing in the Gospel stories to justify the later view that Mary of Magdala was a former prostitute. Many medieval paintings and stained-glass windows show her as a repentant harlot; the characterization was dramatic and easy for artists to represent. But modern interpretations of 'devil-possession' in biblical times suggest that she may well have suffered from a form of mental illness or epilepsy before she met Jesus, and was cured. [22 July, A. R. O.]

Mary of Egypt (?344–421): this Mary appears on many stained-glass windows and in medieval Books of Hours. She is identifiable by her long hair, which covers her body, and the three loaves which she carries. There

are two ancient Greek stories about her life, written in the sixth century. She was a child prostitute from Alexandria who found her way to the Holy Land, and after visiting the church of the Holy Sepulchre, became a hermit in the Jordanian desert. A monk encountered her in her old age, gave her his cloak to wear because her clothes had long

rotted away, and administered Holy Communion to her. When he returned, he found her dead, wrapped in the remains of his cloak. The medieval popularity of Mary seems to derive more from her unusual appearance and the dramatic nature of her repentance than from any understanding of the miseries of child prostitution. [1 April, R. O.]

Mary the Virgin, mother of Jesus (first century): what we know of Mary's earthly life comes from the Gospels: the story of the Annunciation, the Visitation to Elizabeth, the Nativity, the Presentation in the Temple, the

Flight into Egypt, and the occasion when she and *Joseph found their son listening to the elders and asking them questions. She asked Jesus to help at the marriage feast of Cana, and the water was turned into wine. She stood by the Cross during his crucifixion, and was commended to *John the Apostle. She was present with the disciples when Matthias was chosen to take the place of Judas. We learn most about her from the Gospel of Luke, who is interested in the women's experience, and from the Gospel of John, who was charged to care for her in later life; but none of the Evangelists attempts to tell her life story. The focus of their narrative is the life, teaching, death and Resurrection of Jesus, and his mother is mentioned only in relation to him. She

Matthew the Evangelist

is an obedient handmaid of the Lord, and a devoted mother. She finds it hard to understand the magnitude of her son's mission, but is faithful to him to death and beyond. In the Middle Ages, Mary became the ideal woman, celebrated in special liturgies and hymns and in every possible form of artistic expression. She became the intercessor for sinful humanity, with many cults and legends attached to her name. In the Eastern Orthodox and Roman Catholic Churches she is regarded as not only *Christotokous*, 'Christ-bearing', but *Theotokous*, 'God-bearing'. The doctrines of the Immaculate Conception (of Mary by her mother *Anne), the Assumption, or bodily reception of Mary into heaven, and the Ever-Virginity of Mary, with many special devotions, exalt her to the status of the Queen of Heaven. Since the sixteenth century, the Anglican and Free Churches have been cautious of over-emphasizing Mary's status, taking the view that the more extreme Marian cults are unscriptural and sometimes involve dubious theology; but the Calendars of the Anglican, Roman Catholic and Orthodox Churches all celebrate the life of the Blessed Virgin – her Birth, the Annunciation and the Visitation as well as the Nativity of the Christ-Child. [Festival of the Blessed Virgin Mary, 15 August, A. Solemnity of the Blessed Virgin Mary, 1 January, R. Annunciation, 25 March, Visitation, 31 May, Birth, 8 September, all A. R. O.]

Matthew the Evangelist (first century): Matthew, otherwise called Levi, was a Jew – and a tax-collector for the Jews' Roman masters, a highly stigmatized occupation. When Jesus called him, he left his tax-booth and followed. He gave a feast at which Jesus met many other 'tax-collectors and sinners', demonstrating that he had not come only to call the righteous, but

to offer salvation to all. This was much resented by the Pharisees. Thereafter, Matthew is named as one of the twelve

apostles (Matt. 10:3; Mark 3:18; Luke 6:15). Scholars generally agree that the Gospel according to St Matthew was the work of this apostle. He is closely associated with Jewish tradition, and is clearly writing for a Jewish readership, starting with a lengthy account of the genealogy of Joseph all the way from Abraham, twenty-eight generations earlier. The Gospel was written in the second half of the first century, during the lifetime of the historical Matthew. It draws in part on the even earlier Gospel of Mark, and on a common source known as 'Q'. There is an ancient tradition that Matthew became a missionary either in Ethiopia or Persia, and that he was martyred. In paintings and stained-glass windows he is often shown wearing spectacles and perusing his account books. [21 September, A. R. O.]

Matthias the Apostle (first century): after the death of Judas, who had betrayed Jesus, Peter told the disciples that they should elect another apostle to take his place among the Twelve and witness to the Resurrection. After they had prayed, Matthias was elected (Acts 1:21–26). There are traditions that he preached in Judaea, and carried out a mission in Cappadocia or Ethiopia or both. He is said to have been martyred, and he is sometimes portrayed in art with an axe or a halberd, suggesting

that he was beheaded. *Helena, mother of Constantine, is said to have sent his relics back to Rome from Jerusalem. [14 May, A. R. O.]

Maurice, Frederick Denison (1805–72) was an Anglican clergyman who worked with Charles Kingsley, the author of *The Water Babies*, to found the Christian Socialist movement. Appalled by the social conditions of Victorian England, they both supported the Chartist movement for electoral reform and worked for the education of the working classes. Their *Tracts for Priests and People* were widely distributed, and Maurice became President of the Society for Promoting Working Men's Associations. When the Working Men's College (later Ruskin College, Oxford) was set up, he became its first principal. Later, he became a professor in the new institution of King's College, London, and helped his sister to establish Queen's College for women. Maurice had his detractors in the academic world, who commented that his scholarship was broad rather than deep; but the task of bringing education to the working classes necessitated a broad approach. He also attracted much hostility from Evangelical and Anglo-Catholic churchmen, because of his comparative indifference to the sectarian issues, and he was dismissed from his Chair at King's because he could not subscribe to a view of hell as eternal damnation. In 1866, Cambridge offered him a Chair of Moral Theology which enabled him to teach his own vision of Christianity as a living faith involved in the world, and he remained there until his death. His writings include *The Kingdom of Christ* (1838) and *What is Revelation?* (1859). He was influential in many social reform movements of his time. [1 April, A.]

Mechtild of Magdeburg (1210–98) went to live in the abbey of Helfta in Saxony in her old age, when her sight was failing. She had lived for thirty years with the Béguines of the Low Countries, a group of devout laywomen who prayed together and ministered to the sick and poor around them. Helfta was a remarkable community where the nuns, under Abbess Gertrude, lived an intense prayer life and worked very closely together, so that the authorship of their works is not easy to assign. Mechtild recorded some of the visions of a younger Gertrude of Helfta, but there is no doubt that her *Revelations: or The Flowing Light of the Godhead* represents her own distinctive visions. Unlike the scholarly nuns of Helfta, she could not write in Latin, because she was 'unlearned'. She wrote in the vernacular of the Low Countries, sometimes in poetry and sometimes in prose, expressing the glory of the created universe and the joy of the interior converse with God. It is possible that she learned about Plotinus and Pseudo-Dionysius, whose thought she seems to echo, from the Helfta nuns. Her writings were translated into Latin by her spiritual director, and are thought to have been read by Dante. She describes a journey into hell which reads very much like an early version of *The Inferno*. [19 November, A. R.]

Melania the Younger (?383–439) and **Pinian** were a very wealthy Roman young married couple who decided to lead a celibate life after the death of their two young children. They freed their slaves and organized a centre of charity and religious observance on their estates near Rome. When the barbarians threatened Rome, they sold off their Italian lands and went first to Sicily and then to North Africa. They settled at Tagaste in Numidia, where *Augustine of Hippo called them 'real lights of the Church'. Melania founded two monasteries, one for men and one for women, and lived a very ascetic life in the women's monastery. In 417 they left North Africa for the Middle East, where, after visiting the monks of the Egyptian deserts, they settled in Jerusalem to lead lives of solitude and contemplation. Melania was a cousin of *Paula, who introduced her to *Jerome, and she became one of his helpers. Jerome referred to her as 'the devout Lady Melanium' and wrote that she was 'eminent among Christians for her true nobility'. After Pinian's death, she founded a community on the Mount of Olives, close to his grave. She refused to act as superior, and continued to live a life of great asceticism and contemplation. Melania has long been honoured in the Byzantine Church, but little was known about her in the West until the publication of a major biography by Cardinal Rampolla in 1905. An English version of her life by Elizabeth A. Clarke (1984) has attracted considerable attention among scholars interested in women saints. [31 December, R. O.]

Methodius of Constantinople (847) was the patriarch of Constantin-

ople, and is often called 'the Confessor' or 'the Great'. His period in office coincided with the second great outbreak of Iconoclasm in the Eastern Church. This movement was influenced by the growth of Islam, which forbade any representation of sacred objects. Crosses were smashed, and statues, pictures and mosaics were destroyed. Methodius, like *John of Damascus before him, argued that such representations were aids to devotion, and that they were necessary to the maintenance of Christian tradition. Methodius was thrown into prison by the Eastern emperor, and his sufferings were extreme. It was seven years before he was released, emaciated and hairless, his skin blanched from living in darkness. But when the next emperor, Theophilus, began to smash images, Methodius courageously attacked emperor-worship, saying that if Christ could not be worshipped with images, the imperial statues and temples should also be destroyed. The old patriarch was flogged and thrown back into prison. When friends rescued him, his jaw was broken. On the death of Theophilus, the empress Theodora stopped the persecution, and Methodius was reinstalled as patriarch, still wearing a bandage to sustain his broken jaw. In his second period of office, which lasted only four years, he convened a synod in Constantinople which reaffirmed the lawfulness of religious pictures and statues; but since that time, icons in the Eastern Church have deliberately been painted in a highly stylized way to prevent the faithful from mistaking the image for the reality. [14 June, R. O.]

Miseki, Bernard (?1860–96) was a young African from Mozambique who offended the local chief. He went to Cape Town and worked at any humble job to earn his living. He came in contact with the Cowley Fathers, the Mission Priests of St John the Evangelist. He went to night school and then became the cleaner for their boarding house. Through their auspices, he was baptized and educated, studying at Zonnebloem College, where black, white and coloured students were taught together. He became an *Umfundisi* or teacher, and volunteered for a mission led by the first bishop of Mashonaland, who took six catechists with him to establish his diocese. Bernard was left to run a mission for a Mashona tribe on Mount Mahopo, where he built a mission hut, said his daily Offices, and taught both the adults and the children. He had a good relationship with the chief, Mangwende, and made a Christian marriage to one of his granddaughters. The bishop, before going on furlough, told Bernard to stay with Mangwende. He did so faithfully, even when the Matabele rising spread to the Mashona. He was warned to leave the area, but stayed at his post. On 18 June 1896 he was killed by three of Mangwende's disaffected sons, who resented his influence with their father and sought power for themselves. His shrine at Theydon, near Marandellas, became a place of pilgrimage, and Bernard Miseki College is named after him. [18 June, A.]

Monica (332–87) was the mother of *Augustine of Hippo, and Augustine writes at length about her and about their relationship in his *Confessions*. She was a Christian, and she agonized over the brilliant son who could not share her faith. He was wayward as a student, was attracted by Manichaeism and had a mistress, by whom he had a son. When he went to teach in Italy, Monica followed. In Milan, where he came under the influence of *Ambrose, she induced him to send his mistress home to Africa, and tried to arrange a wealthy marriage for him. When he finally became a Christian and was baptized by Ambrose, she kept house for him and a group of like-minded friends. She was, Augustine suggests, a very possessive mother. He could not understand her frequent tears and prayers, she could not understand why it took a brilliant scholar so long to become a Christian. Their relationship, compounded of affection and exasperation, was finally resolved in mutual understanding at Ostia, and she died soon after. In his *Confessions*, the mature Augustine pays tribute to the woman who 'brought me to birth in her body, so that I was born into the light of time, and in her heart, so that I was born into the light of eternity'. [27 August, A. R. O.]

Monsell, Harriet (1811–83) was the daughter of an Irish baronet and the wife of a prebendary of Limerick. Her husband contracted tuberculosis, which was then incurable, and when he finally died, she found herself 'alone with God'. She was still under forty. She went to stay with her sister and brother-in-law at Clewer, near Windsor. The vicar, the Revd T. T. Carter, acted as her spiritual director, helping her to find her way through inconsolable grief. He was a Tractarian, and *Dr Pusey was calling for the reestablishment of the religious life for women in the Church of England. Harriet, determined to devote the remainder of her life to Christian service, became the founder and superior of the Community of St John the Baptist at Clewer. As Mother Harriet, she was greatly respected as a wise and practical counsellor. The community extended its work into schools, hospitals and missions, and has made foundations in India and the United States. [26 March, A.]

More, Thomas (1478–1535) stands out in Tudor history as a man of conscience and honour, a Humanist who looked for the reformation of the Church – but from inside, not by schism. He wanted to be a monk, but obeyed his father in entering a legal career. On a diplomatic mission to the Low Countries in 1515, he wrote Part II of *Utopia* ('No place'), an account of a remarkable society in which people lived communally, money was unknown, divorce was allowed (once), and there were women priests. (Part I, written after his return to England, was a searing attack on Henry VIII's justice system.) He wrote in Latin so that his ideas should not lead the common people astray; and commentators have long debated whether the book was an exercise in Catholicism or Communism, or a tongue-in-cheek essay in what would now be called science fiction. More became a member of parliament, under-sheriff of London, and, on the fall of Cardinal Wolsey in 1529, lord chancellor of England. He held the office for three years, enjoying the friendship and confidence of Henry VIII, until the king defied the pope, annulling his marriage to Catherine of Aragon and marrying Anne Boleyn. More resigned his chancellorship and lived with his family in considerable poverty. He refused to take the oath of allegiance to Henry VIII as the head of the Church. After several months in the Tower of London, he was convicted on false evidence and condemned to death. On the scaffold he asked for the prayers of the people, saying that he was the king's good servant, but God's first. The best testimony on More's character comes from the life, *The Mirror of Vertue in Worldly Greatness*, written by his son-in-law, William Roper. Holbein painted More several times, from life. Much of the script of the film *A Man for All Seasons* comes from Roper's book and from the trial transcript. [6 July, A. 22 June, R.]

Mungo: see **Kentigern**

Nathanael: see **Bartholomew**

Neale, John Mason (1818–66) joined the Tractarian movement while he was at Trinity College, Cambridge. He began to work on Byzantine art and the liturgies of the Eastern Orthodox Church, and was spoken of as a coming man in High Church circles; but after a few weeks as vicar of Crawley, Sussex, he resigned his living on the grounds of ill health, and devoted himself to his major work, *The History of the Holy Eastern Church*, which was finally published in five volumes. He became warden of a small almshouse – Sackville College, East Grinstead – where he ministered faithfully to thirty 'poor and aged householders'. The real cause of his resignation from Crawley may have been opposition to his High Church practices – and this was to follow him to East Grinstead, where a hostile bishop accused him of 'debasing the minds of these poor people with his spiritual haberdashery'. Since the almshouse and its chapel were the property of Earl de la Warr, the bishop could not unseat Neale, but he was banned from officiating in any other church in the diocese. As his work on the Byzantine Church became known, he was invited to preach in many other dioceses. Today J. M. Neale is best known for his translations of ancient and medieval hymns from Latin into English. These include Peter Abelard's 'Brightest and best of the sons of the morning', *Venantius Fortunatus' 'The royal banners forward go' and other favourites to be found in many hymn books. [7 August, A.]

Neri, Philip (1515–95) was born in

Florence, where he was much influenced by the Dominicans. Though his family had intended him to become a merchant, he spent some time as a hermit near Monte Cassino, and then went to Rome, where he visited the catacombs, prayed with the martyrs, and met *Ignatius Loyola. Neither the Society of Jesus nor the Franciscan movement attracted him. Gentle and shy, he wandered the streets of Rome, talking to young people, and formed a group which looked after pilgrims in Rome and cared for sick people. He was ordained in 1551, and settled in San Girolamo, a college for secular priests who received board and lodging, but no stipend. Many people, rich and poor, came to him for spiritual guidance. His informal confraternity was the start of the Oratory. Though it initially met with suspicion and hostility, he attracted the support of the archbishop of Milan, and eventually of the reforming Pope Gregory XIII. The centre of Philip's ministry, and that of the priests who joined him, was one-to-one spiritual direction, focused on the confessional. Unlike the other religious Orders, his movement had very few rules, and simply concentrated on the things of the spirit. By the time Philip died, there were seven Oratorian houses in Italy. After his death, the movement spread to many other countries. The Oratorian movement in England was founded by *John Henry Newman after his conversion to Roman Catholicism. [26 May, A. R.]

Newman, John Henry (1801–90) and *John Keble were the original founders of the Oxford Movement. *Dr Pusey joined them later. Newman had the inspiration which led to *Tracts for the Times* and gave the High Church reformers their title of Tractarians. He became vicar of the University church of St Mary the Virgin, Oxford, and his sermons on the Apostolic Succession and the Book of Common Prayer packed the church as dons and students alike came to hear him. He wrote a series of books defending the Anglo-Catholic position; but while Keble retreated to his country parish, and Pusey took over the leadership of the movement, Newman began to have agonizing doubts. His work on the Early Fathers of the Church gradually convinced him that the Roman Catholic view of authority was right. In 1844 he resigned his living and was received into the Roman Catholic Church. This was a serious blow to the Anglo-Catholics, and indeed to the Church of England at the time. He went to Rome, and returned with a commission: to establish a community of the Oratorian Fathers in England on the lines established by *Philip Neri. The first such community was founded in Birmingham, and this was followed by what is now Brompton Oratory. Newman lived in comparative obscurity for many years. It was not until he was seventy-eight years old that he was created a cardinal. A course of lectures which he gave in Dublin became *The Idea of a University*, a seminal book which has inspired subsequent generations of university teachers. [11 August, A.]

Nicholas of Myra (early fourth century) is the original of Santa Claus. He is an historical figure, a bishop of Myra in Asia Minor who was thrown into prison during the persecutions of Diocletian, but was able to return to his diocese after the Edict of Milan (314) brought religious toleration to the Roman Empire. He was at the Council of Nicaea in 324–5, and strongly opposed the Arian view of the nature of the Person of Christ. Some Greek accounts say that he actually struck Arius of Alexandria, and was suspended from his episcopal office for a time as a result. He preached the Athanasian doctrine of the Trinity, and had a great reputation for justice and

generosity. He is thought to have died in Myra, and to have been buried in a magnificent shrine in the cathedral. When the Saracens swept into Asia Minor in the eleventh century, his relics were rescued and taken to Bari in Italy, where there was a Greek colony. He is sometimes known as Nicholas of Bari for this reason. Legends have clustered around his name: the best known is that of the gift of three bags of gold to a man who had lost all his money, to provide dowries for his three daughters. This is the origin of the pawnbroker's three golden balls. Crivelli's painting of the incident, showing the daughters in bed and the bags of gold on the floor, is in the National Gallery in London. Nicholas is the patron of sailors in the Eastern Orthodox Church. Sailors in the Eastern Mediterranean used to invoke him with the prayer, 'May St Nicholas hold the tiller.' He is also the patron of children, but his association with Christmas and Christmas presents comes from a Dutch (Protestant) custom in the Low Countries. The Dutch took it to New Amsterdam, which the British renamed New York when the Dutch ceded the colony. [6 December, A. R. O.]

Nightingale, Florence (1820–1910):

the Victorian image of 'the lady with the lamp' does less than justice to a woman of remarkable will and intellect who virtually founded the nursing profession and became a major social reformer. She wanted to offer her life to the Church of England, but there were no opportunities for women when she was young. She studied nursing for a short time with the Sisters of Charity in Paris and with the Lutheran deaconesses at Kaiserswerth in western Germany; but it was not until she was over forty that she found her true vocation. The Secretary of State for War, Sidney Herbert, asked her to take a group of nurses to the hospital in the Crimaea, where more men were dying of cholera, dysentery and sheer neglect than from battle. She trained and directed nurses, cleaned the hospital, supervised Turkish workmen, fought the prejudices of the medical administration, and came home a heroine. Her health was shattered, and she refused all publicity. She never made a public statement or attended a public function. She lived for another fifty years, and wrote a mass of minutes, memoranda and directives on health and nursing matters from her sickbed. She interviewed all the witnesses for a Royal Commission on the Health of the Army, provided facts and figures for Queen Victoria and the Prince Consort, advised the Union government in the American Civil War and both sides in the Franco-Prussian War. She saw the Nightingale School of Nursing opened at St Thomas's Hospital in London in 1860, and knew every nurse personally. She wrote *Notes on Nursing*, beginning with the celebrated dictum that the first duty of a hospital is to do the patient no harm. She is known to have read and pondered the works of the mystics, and she wrote, 'Where shall I find God? In myself. That is the true mystical direction.' [13 August, A.]

Ninian (fifth century): according to *Bede, when *Columba came from Iona to evangelize the 'northern Picts', the 'southern Picts' had already received the Gospel from Ninian, 'a very reverend and holy man of British race'. He had a 'stately church' called *Candida Casa* (the White House) because it was built of stone, and that was unusual among the British. Ninian became bishop of the area, and his see was named after St Martin (*Martin of Tours). It is not entirely clear what Bede meant by 'Picts', a term he uses freely for all the Scottish tribes, but he says (writing from Jarrow in Northumberland) that the 'southern Picts' lived 'on this side of the mountains', which seems to mean southern and western Scotland. Nor is it clear what he means by 'British' – a term he often applies to the Welsh. However, he says that Ninian had been 'regularly instructed in the mysteries of the Christian faith' in Rome, and that he brought back from his travels a relic of St Martin. Archaeological excavations at Whithorn in southern Scotland have uncovered the stones of an early stone church, painted white, which is thought to be *Candida Casa*. In Bede's day, Ninian's church was a place of pilgrimage. St Ninian's, near Stirling, commemorates his name, and there were many church dedications in Scotland until John Knox and his followers abolished them in the sixteenth century. [16 September, A. R.]

Nino of Georgia (early fourth century) was, according to Byzantine tradition, a slave girl who was taken to Georgia as a captive. Nobody knows her name. The Byzantine Church called her Nino, and the Roman Church called her Christiana. She made a great im-

pression among the barbarians by her gentleness and her faith in Christ, and she acquired a reputation for healing. She saved the life of the queen, and both king and queen became Christians, and were instructed by her. This story comes from the late fourth century, by which time Georgia was Christian, and in contact with Rome. It was told to the historian Rufinus by a Georgian prince, who was recounting events which took place in the lifetime of his parents or grandparents. There is a whole cycle of extravagant Nino legends, but the basic belief that Christianity came to Georgia through the faith of a nameless slave girl is firmly held in the Georgian Church. [15 December, R. 14 January, O.]

Occam, William of (1349) probably came from the village of Occam or Ockham in Surrey. He became a philosopher, studying at Oxford and at the Sorbonne in Paris, and specialized in the history and nature of logical thought. He is best known for the formulation of 'Occam's razor' – the philosophers' theory that explanations of phenomena should involve as few prior assumptions as possible. He became a Franciscan friar, vowed to absolute poverty, and was involved in a conflict with the papacy for his criticisms of the great wealth of the Church. William was summoned before a papal commission to account for his anti-papal writings, and imprisoned for a time. He fled to the protection of the Holy Roman Emperor Ludwig of Bavaria, and went first to Padua, where he is thought to have influenced the papal critic Marsiglio of Padua, and then to Munich, where he wrote a treatise accusing the pope of seven heresies and seventy-seven errors, arguing that papal government had been set up by Christ not for the sake of popes and clergy, but for the sake of the people. He embarked on a major work in ten treatises on the nature of authority, though only two (on the authority of the pope and the authority of the emperor) were completed by the time of his death. [10 April, A.]

Oengus the Culdee (Angus, ninth century): 'Culdee' was a Celtic term, meaning 'God's vassal', and originally applied to monks who followed the strict Celtic Rule, with its extreme penitential practices, including such curbs to the flesh as lengthy fasts, sleep deprivation and standing up to their necks in running water. It was not until two centuries later that the Culdees in Scotland were found to be lax, and *Margaret of Scotland brought them into conformity with Benedictine practice. Oengus is thought to have been the first of the Culdees, an Irish ascetic who studied in the monastery of Clonenagh in Ulster. He became a hermit, settling in the neighbourhood of the monastery of Tallaght, near Dublin, where he collaborated in writing the Martyrology of Tallaght, and later wrote his own long metrical poem on the saints, known as the *Félire* in Ireland and *Festilogium* in Latin. This is one of the chief sources of information for the early Irish saints. It is said that he later returned to Clonenagh, becoming abbot and consecrated as a bishop. [11 March, R.]

Olga of Kiev (c. 879–969) was the grand duchess of Kiev, then the most important city in Russia. When her husband, the grand duke Igor, was assassinated in 945, she ruled in his place. She was ruthless in hunting down Igor's murderers, but proved a just and competent ruler. She re-established trading links with Constantinople, and about the year 941, she became a Christian. Byzantine monks were sent to instruct her, and she took

the name Helen at her baptism. She made a state visit to Constantinople in 957. She attempted to convert her people to Christianity, but with little success. She sent to the German emperor for missionaries, but a mission led by Adalbert of Magdeburg failed, and his companions were murdered. Her son, who succeeded her, was not a Christian, but her grandson *Vladimir completed the official Christianization of Russia. When Olga died, he built a church for her shrine. The destruction of Kiev by the Mongol invaders brought an end to the pilgrimages, but in 1574, a council of bishops confirmed her as a saint of the Russian and Ukrainian Churches. [11 July, R. O.]

Olympias of Constantinople (361–408) was a wealthy widow who became a deaconess. She established herself in a large house with a community of single women devoted to serving God and the poor. She lived very frugally, and founded a hospital and an orphanage. When *John Chrysostom became patriarch of Constantinople, he warned her against excessive generosity, saying that she must save her money for those who needed it. She supported John in his conflicts with the emperor and empress, and with Theophilus, patriarch of Alexandria. When John was driven from his see, she shared in the persecution which followed. She was brought before the prefect and accused of setting fire to the great basilica of St Sophia, to which she replied contemptuously that she contributed to the building of churches – she did not destroy them. She defended herself with such spirit that the case was dismissed; but her community was broken up, and all her charitable works were stopped. John Chrysostom's letters to Olympias from his distant places of exile were written in deep pastoral concern for a woman who had lost her wealth, her health and her life-work. She carried out commissions for John in Constantinople, and sent him money when she could. When she died, a year after his death, she was not much more than forty years old. [25 July, R. 17 December, O.]

Osmund of Salisbury (1099) is thought to have been a nephew of William the Conqueror. He came to England after the Norman Conquest, acted as William's chancellor for two years, and became bishop of Salisbury in 1078. He was one of William's commissioners for the Domesday survey, and responsible for the collection of information for the Midlands and most of the north of England. He was, like all *Lanfranc's bishops, both erudite and an able administrator. The books of liturgical services in the Salisbury diocese were old and incomplete: Osmund drew up regulations for the celebration of Mass and other services in a form which has become famous as the Sarum Use, and it was adopted by most of the dioceses of England and Wales. He took charge of the building of the cathedral, and re-ordered the cathedral chapter, binding the canons to residence. (This was the practice in Normandy, but not in England.) His cathedral was completed and consecrated in 1092 – and was struck by lightning five days later. Brushing aside prophecies of disaster, he had it repaired, and the worship at Sarum became a model for other cathedrals. Osmund was a scholar, and happiest when working in his large and well-stocked cathedral library. Unlike most of Lanfranc's bishops, he had some knowledge of Anglo-Saxon religious traditions, and he is credited with saving *Aldhelm's name from being removed from the Calendar. He was a quiet man who had no worldly ambi-

tions. Though his shrine was destroyed in Henry VIII's reign, there is a stone slab which was saved from it in Salisbury cathedral, bearing the date of his death. [16 July, A. 4 December, R.]

Oswald of Northumbria (c. 605–42) was forced into exile when he was about ten years old, and went to Iona, where he lived for eighteen years, being educated by the monks in the Celtic tradition. He returned to Northumbria as king to do battle against the heathen Penda of Mercia and his ferocious ally, Cadwalla of Wales. On the night before the battle at Hexham, he set up a wooden cross, praying before it for victory, and his forces defeated their enemies. One of his first acts in his kingdom was to send to Iona for missionary monks. *Aidan became his bishop and his friend. Because Aidan, raised in a community of Irish monks, could not speak English fluently, the king, who was virtually bilingual after his long stay on Iona, often went with him on his travels in the locality, and interpreted for him. He realized that Aidan could not live in a palace, and gave him Holy Island, opposite his own castle of Bamburgh, as a refuge. Oswald is said by *Bede to have been a merciful and just king, who promoted peace in the kingdom. He died in battle against Penda of Mercia when he was thirty-eight years old. [5 August, A. R.]

Oswald of Worcester (902) was one of that great triumvirate of bishops who revived learning and monastic life in England in the ninth century. With *Dunstan and *Ethelwold, he founded monasteries and re-ordered monastic observance. He came of a Danish military family, and was related to two previous archbishops. He studied at Fleury-sur-Loire, and became a priest and a monk of Cluny. He was a canon of Worcester for some years before his appointment as bishop in 961 on the recommendation of Dunstan, then archbishop of Canterbury. Edgar of Wessex found him a wise adviser and a diplomat, and gave him extensive lands for his monasteries. Oswald brought scholars over from the Continent, including Abbo of Fleury, a celebrated mathematician and astronomer. His greatest foundation was the monastery of Ramsey in Huntingdonshire, which was his favourite place of residence. He became archbishop of York in 972, holding the office in plurality with the see of Winchester. Following the earlier depredations of the Danes, the Northern Province was desperately poor, while Winchester was a wealthy diocese, so this seems to have been a case of accepting extra responsibility at the king's request rather than of preferment. It was his custom to wash the feet of twelve poor men each day throughout Lent, and in 992, he performed this task until Leap Year Day, when he kissed the feet of the last man, pronounced a blessing, and died. [28 February, R.]

Pachomius (c. 292–346) is celebrated as the founder of community monasticism, while *Antony is regarded as the founder of solitary monasticism. Both came from Upper Egypt, and they were contemporaries. Pachomius was conscripted into the Roman army, and turned to the religious life when he had completed his military service. He had a talent for administration, and set up houses of about forty monks in the Thebaïd. By the time of his death, there were nine houses for men and three for women. The day was divided into liturgical observance and work, with periods of meditation. The work included agriculture, weaving, mat-making and other crafts, and the goods were sold to provide an income for the monasteries. The Rule was extremely austere. Each house had a superior, and the superiors met with Pachomius, who was superior-general, twice a year, to pray, discuss their affairs, and go through their accounts. There was much interest in this system in Jerusalem, where monasteries were also developing. *Jerome found a copy of the Rule and Letters of Pachomius, and translated them into Latin. Through him, the monastic system of the Thebaïd reached Rome, where it had a profound influence on Western monasticism. [9 May, R. 15 May, O.]

Pancras (?304) was a Roman martyr, probably killed in the persecutions of Diocletian. Beyond these facts, little is known about him. Legend says that he was a Phrygian orphan who came to Rome with his uncle, and was executed for his faith at the age of fourteen. It seems that he became a popular saint as a kind of male counterpoint to *Agnes, the girl martyr. There have been a number of dedications in Pancras' name: an ancient church on the via Aurelia in Rome was built over his tomb, a monastery in Rome was dedicated by *Gregory the Great, and *Augustine of Canterbury dedicated a church soon after his arrival in Kent. Augustine would have been familiar with the Roman cult of Pancras. There were six other ancient dedications in England, of which the most enduring has been the London church which gives its name to the nearby railway terminus and the borough. [12 May, R. O.]

Pandita Mary Ramabai: see **Ramabai.**

Papua New Guinea, Martyrs of (1901 and 1942): European missionaries began to arrive in Papua New

Guinea in the 1870s, as the country opened to trade. Two missionaries, James Chalmers and Oliver Tomkins, were sent out by the London Missionary Society, and were killed by tribesmen with some Papuan companions in 1901. Thereafter there was a great increase in missionary activity, principally by Anglicans and Methodists. By the time of World War II, there were over a million Christians. In 1942, the country was invaded by Japanese troops. Many Papuan Christians escaped into the dense forests of the highlands, but mission stations were burned and over three hundred Christians of all denominations were killed, mostly Papuans, but also including a few missionaries. The Martyrs' School in Papua New Guinea honours their memory. The statue of Lucien Taipedi, a Papuan catechist, on the west front of Westminster Abbey, is one of the series of statues of modern martyrs. The Japanese soldier who killed Lucien subsequently became a Christian, was baptized in his name, and built a church at Embi in his memory. [2 September, A.]

Patrick (c. 460) is the patron saint of Ireland, but he came from the west coast of Britain, probably from either the Severn estuary or the Dumbarton area, at the western end of Hadrian's Wall. At the age of about sixteen, he was taken captive by Irish raiders and became a slave in pagan Armagh. He must have come from a Christian family, because he prayed desperately, and he records in his *Confessions* that 'the Spirit seethed in me'. After some six years he escaped, determined to enter the priesthood and return to Ireland to take the Gospel to a land of tribal wars and savagery. All we know of his life comes from his Confession. He says nothing about his subsequent life until 'after many years', he re-

turned to Ireland with a party of clergy and went as a missionary bishop into areas where Christianity was unknown, baptizing and founding churches in

dangerous circumstances. His simplicity, his humanity and, above all, his faith made him a central figure in the development of what became a distinctively Celtic monastic system. *Columba took this system to Iona, and *Aidan took it from there to Lindisfarne. Subsequently, many writings were attributed to Patrick, but the only two generally recognized as authentic are the *Confessions* and the *Letter to Coroticus* – a tribal chief from Dumbarton who captured and enslaved some of his converts. The prayer (or hymn) known as *St Patrick's Breastplate*, in the translation of Mrs C. F. Alexander, may be partly written by him, with additional verses added later. The shamrock has become the symbol of 'the strong name of the Trinity' which this most celebrated of the Christian missionaries of Ireland proclaimed. [17 March, A. R.]

Patteson, John Coleridge (1871), the curate of Ottery St Mary in Devon, went out to Melanesia to join the young bishop *George Augustus Selwyn, whom he had known at Eton. He sailed the islands, learned the many different languages, and started a school on Norfolk Island for Melanesian boys. It was said that he treated them exactly like Etonians. In 1861 he became bishop of Melanesia, taking charge of all the missions and devoting his inheritance from his father to the work. Trouble came with the arrival of planters from Fiji and Queensland, Australia, who visited the islands, persuading the young men to accept indentures and to work on their plantations. Few of the young men ever returned to the islands: low wages kept them in debt. The islanders, angry at the depopulation of the islands, became hostile. On 18 September 1871, Bishop Patteson landed at the island of Natapu, unaware that it had recently been raided by planters and that five islanders had been killed. He went ashore alone and unrecognized in a small boat. When they attempted to follow, the rest of the party were kept off by a hail of poisoned arrows. Later, a small canoe was pushed out towards the ship where the others waited. It contained Bishop Patteson's body, covered by a palm frond bearing five knots: one for each of the murdered islanders. In a society where 'payback' is part of the local culture, that was a moderate revenge. Three of Bishop Patteson's companions died of tetanus from poisoned arrows – one on the same occasion, and two in a separate attack. In England, the news of their death was met with shock; and within a year, the British Parliament regulated the labour trade in Melanesia, ending the indenture system. [20 September, A.]

Paul the Apostle (?64 or 65): Saul of Tarsus, later Paul, was a city man from Asia Minor. He was a Roman citizen, well educated in Jewish law, which he had studied in Jerusalem under the great rabbinical teacher Gamaliel. He was a Pharisee, trained in the meticulous observance of the law, and he collaborated with the temple authorities in hunting down the Christians. When Stephen was stoned, he

guarded the coats of his executioners, and approved of the killing (Acts 7:58, 8:1). Afterwards, he was 'ravaging the church by entering house after house, dragging off both men and women and committing them to prison' (Acts 8:3). He went off to Damascus, 'still breathing threats and murder against the disciples of the Lord'; but he arrived in that city blind and confused, having met Christ on the road, a vision 'as to someone untimely born' (1 Cor. 15:8). The Christians of Damascus were kind to him, baptizing him in the name of Paul, and helping him to escape when he, in his turn, was hunted by the temple authorities. It is not surprising that the disciples in Jerusalem, when he returned, were more suspicious. They thought he was a spy. The Hellenists wanted to kill him, and only *Barnabas, who was a Greek Cypriot and an outsider like Paul, spoke for him. Paul undertook his first great missionary enterprise to Cyprus with Barnabas. He was to make three great missionary journeys round the eastern Mediterranean area in the years 46 to 48, 49 to 52 and 53 to 57, founding and visiting the churches in Greece and Asia Minor. He spent very little time in Jerusalem.

He never held any authority in the Church there, and he wrote vehemently to the Corinthians, saying that he thought he had done as much as any of the brethren, cataloguing what he had suffered in his travels (2 Cor. 11:21–27). He had 'anxiety for all the churches' in the Middle East. He wrote to them – to the Romans, Corinthians, Philippians, Galatians and probably many others. Of the Letters which are now preserved in the New Testament, those mentioned above are certainly his, though the authorship of the Letters to the Ephesians and the Colossians has been disputed, and the Letter to the Hebrews is thought to be by another hand. He was in Rome for a time, and was kept under house arrest. Though he was released, he was arrested again, and executed at Tre Fontana, probably in 64 or 65. [29 June, A. R. O.]

Paul the Hermit (c. 235–345) is traditionally regarded as the first of the Desert Fathers. He came from the

Lower Thebaïd in Egypt, and the main source for his life is a biography by *Jerome, which contains elements of popular fable. He is said to have been orphaned at the age of fifteen, to have fled from the persecutions of the Roman emperor Decius, and to have decided to live in a permanent state of withdrawal from the world. *Antony of

Egypt visited him, broke bread with him, and was with him when he died at a great age, burying him with the help of two lions, who dug a pit for his body. They were sometimes represented together, with the lions, in medieval art. [15 January, R. O.]

Paula of Rome (347–404) was a Roman widow who became a Christian, gave most of her wealth to the poor of the city, and joined the circle of devout women who were taught by *Jerome in his three years as the papal secretary. She was looking for theological and spiritual guidance, and became involved in his great work of translating the Bible. Her mother was a Roman, her father of Greek stock, so she spoke both languages fluently, and she learned Hebrew – more quickly than Jerome did. When Jerome had to leave Rome, Paula and her daughter Eustochium followed him to Jerusalem with a small group of women. At the church of the Nativity she knelt by the grotto and quoted Psalm 131: 'This is my rest, for I have chosen it.' The party visited other holy sites in Judaea, stayed in Alexandria, then a great centre of theological learning, and went on into the Thebaïd to visit the successors of the Desert Fathers, the monks and the solitary hermits. Then Paula, with Eustochium, returned to Jerusalem, where she continued to assist Jerome with his translations, and had a hostel built for pilgrims, saying that if Mary and Joseph came back to Bethlehem, there would at least be a decent inn to receive them. She founded two monasteries on the pattern of those established by *Pachomius – one for men, which Jerome directed, and one for women, which she directed for nearly twenty years. Jerome wrote her epitaph: 'The first in the series of noble Roman matrons, she preferred the poverty of Christ and the humble fields of Bethlehem to the splendours of Rome.' [26 January, R. O.]

Paulinus of York (644) was sent from Rome by *Gregory the Great with the second group of monks to support *Augustine of Canterbury on his English mission. When *Edwin of Northumbria wished to marry the Kentish princess Ethelburga, he was told that as a Christian, she could not marry a pagan. Edwin agreed to give Ethelburga and her household freedom to practise their faith, and to consider becoming a Christian himself. Paulinus led the party of monks who accompanied the princess north. Edwin, who seems to have been a thoughtful and open-minded king, was converted, and he and all his household, including the young *Hilda of Whitby, were baptized. Many large-scale conversions followed, and the first stages of a cathedral were built; but when Edwin died in battle at the hands of Penda of Mercia and Cadwalla in 633, Paulinus escorted the princess back to the royal court in Kent. Only *James the Deacon remained in the north. After his return to Kent, Paulinus became bishop of Rochester. [10 October, A. R.]

Perpetua and Felicity (303) were two young women of Carthage, arrested during the persecutions of Diocletian. Vivia Perpetua was the wife of a Roman citizen of standing, and had a baby whom she was breast-feeding. Felicity, her slave, gave birth to her child in prison. We have Perpetua's own account of the trial and the horrors of imprisonment. Both women steadily refused to sacrifice to the emperor in order to save their lives. Their children were taken by the Christian community, and they were marched to the amphitheatre with three men, 'rejoicing as if on their way to heaven'. Perpetua's account is continued by an eye-witness (possibly Tertullian) who describes their sufferings in the arena in detail. There were murmurings of revulsion in the crowd against the barbarous treatment of the two girls. Their names have been honoured in the Roman martyrology since the end of the persecutions. They both appear in the procession of twenty-two virgins in the church of San Apollinare Nuovo in Ravenna, and are mentioned in the canon of the Roman Mass. In 1907, an excavation team found a stone inscription referring to them in the remains of the great basilica at Carthage. [7 March, A. R. O.]

Peter the Apostle (64 or 65) was the brother of *Andrew. The two worked as commercial fishermen on the Lake of Galilee. Peter's original name was Simon or Symeon, and Jesus called him '*Képa*', which means a rock

or stone in Aramaic. This became Cephas or Petrus in Greek. He was married, and lived at Capernaum with his wife and her mother, whom Jesus cured of a fever (Mark 1:30–31). At an early stage he became the spokesman for the group of apostles. When Jesus asked them at Caesarea Philippi, 'Who do people say that the Son of Man is?', he said, 'You are the Messiah, the Son of the living God'; and Jesus replied, 'Blessed are you, Simon the son of Jonah. And I tell you, you are Peter, and on this rock I will build my church, and the gates of Hades shall not prevail against it' (Matt. 16:17–18). Peter is courageous and impulsive. He tried to walk on the water; he wanted to build tents for Jesus, Moses and Elijah on the Mount of the Transfiguration; and he was prepared to stay with Jesus if everyone else deserts him. But all four Evangelists tell the story of how he denied his Lord after he was arrested, saying, 'I do not know this man you are talking about.' The triple denial before the cock crew was matched by a triple questioning after the Resurrection: 'Simon, son of John, do you love me?' Three times he affirmed his love for Jesus, and was told, 'Feed my sheep.' It is recorded in the Acts of the Apostles how he led the election of Matthias as a new apostle to replace Judas, and was the first to address the crowd on the day of Pentecost in the power of the Spirit. He performed the first healing after Pentecost (of the lame man at the Gate Beautiful), and undertook the first mission outside Israel, going into Samaria to lay hands on the converts of Philip the Deacon. He had the revelation that Gentiles must be received into the Church as well as Jews, was delivered from prison, and went on further missions to Antioch and Corinth. At some point, he went to Rome. It is no longer accepted by scholars that he ruled the Church there for twenty-five years, but it is accepted that he was martyred there about the year 64 or 65. *Irenaeus, writing in the second century, calls the Church at Rome 'the greatest and most ancient Church, founded by the two glorious apostles, Peter and Paul'; and Irenaeus had learned from *Polycarp, who sat at the feet of *John the Evangelist. Recent excavations in the Vatican establish beyond reasonable doubt that Peter's tomb lies beneath the great basilica. From early times, Peter has been portrayed as the heavenly doorkeeper, and the keys are his most familiar emblem in art. [29 June, A. R. O.]

Peter the Venerable (?1092–1156): in 1122 Peter became abbot of Cluny, the mother house of many other Benedictine monasteries in western Europe. He was a scholar with wide academic interests who encouraged his monks to study, and built up an outstanding library for the period. Since he had been born in the Auvergne, he was very conscious of the threat posed to Christianity by the Moors, who were then pressing up through Spain. He set up a team of interpreters to translate the Koran into Latin so that it might be better understood. He came to the conclusion that Islam was a heresy, and that Mohammed's personal failings made him unworthy to be called a prophet. Abbot Peter is probably best known for his championship of Peter Abelard. When Abelard's theological works were condemned, he offered him shelter at Cluny, and helped to reconcile him with his fiercest critic, *Bernard of Clairvaux. Abelard died two years later. Abbot Peter sent his body to Heloïse (by then abbess of the nunnery of the Paraclete) for burial, with the assurance that he had died after full repentance for his sins, and in communion with the Church. He was equally liberal in his defence of Jews and heretics against persecution, though he did not agree with them. The Emperor Frederick Barbarossa named him 'the Venerable' – that is, the greatly respected. [25 December, R.]

Petroc (sixth century) is well known in Devon and Cornwall, where his monastery was at a place later called Padristowe and later Padstow. Little Petherick, where he is said to have established a second community, and Trebetherick also commemorate his name. A medieval life of Petroc written at the monastery of Saint-Méen in Brittany is apparently based on an earlier one from Bodmin Priory. This says that he and his followers came from Wales and settled in Cornwall, and that he lived a most austere and holy life there for thirty years. He made two pilgrimages to the Holy Land, and is said by John of Tynemouth, who recounts many unlikely marvels, to have reached 'India' and 'the East Ocean' (possibly the Persian Gulf). In his old age, he retired to a hermitage on Bodmin Moor, and he died at the house of a man named Rovel, which may have stood on the site of the present farmhouse of Treravel. The story of his reliquary is an interesting one. His relics were stolen by a canon of Bodmin named Martin, and taken to Saint-Méen in the early twelfth century. The prior of Bodmin appealed to King Henry II, who ordered their return. They came back in a splendid ivory shrine of Sicilian-Islamic workmanship which was probably a gift from Count Walter of Coutances, keeper of the Great Seal. This shrine was seen and much admired by William Worcestre, who writes of it in the fifteenth century. It was hidden during the Reformation, and rediscovered, empty, in the eighteenth century. It may now be seen in the British Museum. [23 May, A. 4 June, R.]

Philip the Apostle (first century) is usually bracketed with *James the Less: they share a feast day and many dedications. He was the third apostle to be called, after the brothers *Peter and *Andrew. Like them, he came from Bethsaida. He was probably a Greek Jew – his name is Greek, and when a group of Hellenes who had come to worship at the festival in Jerusalem wanted to meet Jesus, they asked Philip

first, and he went to Andrew (John 12:20–22). He was at the feeding of the five thousand – a practical man who

looked at the crowd, and said that six months' wages would not be enough to feed them all; and he was at the Last Supper, where he said to Jesus, 'Lord, show us the Father, and we will be satisfied.' Jesus answered, 'Have I been all this time with you, Philip, and you have not known me? He who has seen me has seen the Father' (John 14:8–10). He is thought to have preached in Phrygia and died at Heliopolis. He is shown in art either carrying a cross (in the traditional belief that he was martyred by crucifixion) or with five loaves, to recall the feeding of the Five Thousand. [1 May, A. 3 May, R. 14 November, O.]

Philip the Deacon (first century) was one of the seven Hellenic deacons chosen by the Apostles (see *Stephen). He became an evangelist who 'went from place to place spreading the good news', and it was while he was travelling south from Jerusalem to Gaza that he met the chief treasurer of the *kandake* or queen of Ethiopia, probably an African convert to Judaism. He had drawn up his chariot by the side of the road, and was pondering over the messianic prophecies of Isaiah. Philip explained the fulfilment of the prophecy in the life, death and Resurrection of Jesus Christ, and the official asked to be baptized. After baptism, he 'went on his way rejoicing' (Acts 8:26–40). He is said to have been a eunuch, and was probably black. Philip seems to have realised, even before the Apostles, that the Christian faith must spread beyond the borders of Israel. This incident may have been the foundation of the Church in Ethiopia. [6 June, R. O.]

Phoebe (first century): *Paul writes in his letter to the Romans, 'I commend to you our sister Phoebe, a deacon of the Church at Cenchreae, so that you may welcome her in the Lord as is fitting for the saints, and help her in whatever she may require of you, for she has been a benefactor to many, and of myself as well' (Rom. 16:1–2, RSV). This is the only biblical reference to Phoebe, and its main interest lies in the fact that for centuries, the word *diakonos* has been translated 'servant' in relation to her, but 'deacon' in relation to men. This is the case in the Authorized Version of the Bible, and also in the Roman Catholic Douai Version, though the Greek is quite clearly the same. The scriptural argument in favour of deaconesses in the Church of England relied heavily on the use of *diakonos* for Phoebe (see *Elizabeth Ferard). Modern versions of the Bible, both Anglican and Roman Catholic, translate *diakonos* as 'deacon' for Phoebe as for the men, and she is described as a deacon in Orthodox Calendars. There was a legend in the Middle Ages that Phoebe was Paul's wife, but this is now emphatically discounted. [3 September, R. O.]

Plunket, Oliver (1629–81): in the reign of Charles II, Roman Catholics were still suspected of treason. The fact that the queen, Catherine of Braganza, was a Catholic, and was allowed by the terms of her marriage contract to prac-

tise her faith, was widely resented. Oliver Plunkett – trained by Jesuits, a lecturer in theology and apologetics at the Propaganda College in Rome, and archbishop of Armagh from 1669 – was a marked man. He met the queen, and urged her to try to mitigate the severity of the punishments to which Catholics were subject in both England and Ireland. He was one of only two Catholic bishops in Ireland, a country suffering from neglect, sectarian violence and bigotry. He is said to have confirmed 10,000 people. For most of the time, he was able to work openly with the consent of a friendly and tolerant viceroy, but there were periods of persecution when he had to use an alias, disguise himself as a layman, and hide in country houses. The false allegations of Titus Oates in 1678, alleging the existence of a Catholic plot to assassinate the king and take over England, led to a panic in which a number of innocent Catholics were condemned and executed. Archbishop Plunkett was arrested and taken to London. He was certainly innocent of the charges made against him: that he had plotted to bring 20,000 French soldiers into Ireland and to tax the clergy in order to raise a standing army. He was imprisoned in Newgate, and tried in London in 1681. The trial was heavily biased against him, and he was convicted of treason. He was martyred at Tyburn. [1 July, R.]

Polycarp (c. 69–c. 155): a letter about Polycarp, bishop of Smyrna, written from the Church at Smyrna to the other Christian churches after his death, and reproduced by the fourth-century historian Eusebius of Caesarea, gives most of the available information about him. He is also mentioned in the writings of *Irenaeus of Lyons, who was his disciple. Polycarp had learned directly from *John the Evangelist, and in his old age, he could remember

John's words and even the inflexions of his voice. He became bishop of Smyrna in about 107, and was noted for his defence of the Christian faith against the Gnostics, a defence carried on by Irenaeus in his *Adversus Haereses*. He was much given to peace and reconciliation, and he travelled to Rome to meet Anicetus, bishop of Rome, to try to heal the growing breach between the Eastern and Western Churches. The two could not agree, and finally decided to differ in charity. Polycarp died in one of the sporadic riots stirred up by Roman governors against Christians from time to time. He refused to escape, and sat calmly waiting for his pursuers to find him. Taken before the governor, he refused to sacrifice to the Roman gods, and said that he had been a Christian for eighty-six years: he would not deny his master in his old age. He was despatched by a sword-thrust. The letter from the Church at Smyrna concludes by saying, 'He was the twelfth to die at Smyrna, but he alone is specially remembered by all, so that even the heathen everywhere speak of him.' [23 February, A. R. O.]

Pusey, Edward Bouverie (1800–1882): when *John Keble and *John Henry Newman founded the Tractarian movement in Oxford, Pusey (who, like them, was a Fellow of Oriel College) was senior to both – already a renowned Oriental scholar and Regius Professor of Hebrew. He joined the movement two years after Keble's Assize Sermon of 1833; and, as Keble retired to his country living and Newman began to have doubts about the Anglican position, he took charge of the movement. Though by nature a somewhat retiring and absent-minded man, he had a clear view of the Church of England as part of the Catholic Church, without the accretions and abuses of Rome. He founded 'The Oxford Library of the Holy Catholic Church anterior to the Division of East and West', which indicated the breadth of his view of the Church; and he took the Tractarian movement beyond the universities of Oxford and Cambridge, into the parishes. He paid £6,000 out of his own resources for the building of St Saviour's church, Leeds, which was staffed by Anglo-Catholic priests. He revived the use of sacramental confession, and encouraged the use of ritual in liturgical services. He also revived the idea of women's religious communities, which had disappeared from England ever since the Reformation, and he was instrumental in the formation of communities at Devonport (see *Priscilla Lydia Sellon) and Clewer (see *Harriet Monsell), among others. Dr Pusey endured much conflict: he was accused by the bishops of London and Oxford of 'Romish tendencies', and was forbidden to preach in the Oxford diocese; he had a bitter feud with Dr Jowett of Balliol, whom he considered a 'latitudinarian', and defended the Athanasian Creed against Archbishop Tait. Pusey House, the Oxford theological college, was founded in his memory, and he left it his extensive library. [16 September, A.]

Ramabai, Mary (1858–1922): this Indian scholar is often called 'Pandita', which is the feminine form of the Indian 'Pandit', a term of respect. She was the daughter of a Brahmin, a Sanskrit scholar who travelled from village to village in South India, reading aloud the Hindu scriptures. In a great famine in 1876–7, Ramabai's father, mother and sister all died of starvation. She and her brother barely survived, and were taken in by Christian missionaries in Calcutta. Her father had taught her the Hindu scriptures, and she was asked to lecture to groups of Hindu women about their duties; but she realized increasingly that the status of women in Hinduism was very low. They were forbidden to read the scriptures for themselves, and were taught that they could only reach salvation through complete subservience to their husbands. Ramabai began to work for the education of women, and lectured in the University of Calcutta. She married in 1870, and had a child. Her husband died young of cholera, and for the rest of her life, she wore the white sari and cropped hair of a Hindu widow. With the help of the Wantage Sisters, whom she met in Poona, she came to England, and then went on to the United States, where she wrote a book, *The High Caste Indian Woman*, which was a considerable success. She returned to India in 1889 with American financial support, and set up a school in Bombay for the neglected and uneducated women of Indian society – child widows, temple prostitutes and unwanted wives and daughters. Ramabai became a Christian, but she was unwilling to ally herself with any one Christian group, because she was impatient of the sectarian divisions which often caused dissension in the mission field. She translated the Bible into her own first language, Marathi, while still managing the school and setting up other institutions. She was the first woman to address the Indian National Congress, and the first woman leader in Indian public life. [30 April, A.]

Remigius (Rémi) (533) is known as 'the apostle to the Franks'. He was the bishop of Rheims who, at the request of *Queen Clothilde, personally prepared Clovis, king of the Franks, for Christian baptism. Clovis, formerly a hardened and bloodthirsty warrior, was baptized in a magnificent ceremony in Rheims cathedral, and mass conversions followed. With the king's support, Remigius was able to establish other bishoprics and to build churches. He was famous for his learning and eloquence. In France, many place-names, such as Saint-Rémy de Provence and Saint-Rémy-sur-Durolle preserve his name. [1 October, A. 13 January, R.]

Richard of Chichester (1197–1253) was a renowned thirteenth-century scholar who studied in Oxford, Paris and Bologna, specializing in canon law, and became chancellor of the University of Oxford. His appointment as bishop of Chichester in 1254 was opposed by Henry III and part of the cathedral chapter, and was only accepted when Pope Innocent IV threatened excommunication. He was a devout bishop who restored Church discipline, insisting that Mass should be said in a dignified manner (in contrast to the slovenly mumbling of some clergy) and that the people should receive Holy Communion without payment. He is best known for his prayer: 'Thanks be to thee, my Lord Jesus Christ, for all the pains and insults thou hast borne for me. May I know thee more clearly, love thee more dearly and follow thee more nearly.' [16 June, A. 3 April, R.]

Richard Rolle (1349) was born at Thornton-le-dale in Yorkshire. He is sometimes referred to as 'Richard of Hampole' because he spent his last few years directing a small community of nuns at Hampole near Doncaster. He ran away from home to become a hermit. A succession of patrons allowed him to live on their land. He was frequently rude to visitors, and scathing in his comments on the clergy and monks of the area. There is no evidence that he was ever licensed as a hermit, received into a monastic Order or ordained priest, though he is widely known in Yorkshire as 'St Richard, Hermit'. He lived an austere life of fasting and penance, contemplating the glory of the Godhead. He wrote prolifically – a series of works in Latin, English and his own Northumbrian dialect. Opinion differs as to whether he was a true mystic or primarily a poet and a man of letters. There is no sign in his work of the spiritual desolation and anguish which is part of the mystical experience. His best-known work is *The Fire of Love,* which became a spiritual classic and is still in print. [20 January, A. 29 September, R.]

Ridley, Nicholas (1500–1555) was one of the 'new men' in the Tudor Church, open to the new insights of the Protestant reformers, though loyal to the existing order. After finding a ninth-century treatise (written at the request of the pope) which argued that Christ's words used in the consecration of the bread and wine at Holy Communion were allegorical, and not meant to be taken literally, he came to the conclusion that the current Roman doctrine of the Mass was blasphemous and dangerous. In the reign of Edward VI, he came to prominence. He was a member of the Prayer Book Commission which drafted and authorized the Prayer Book of 1549. He became bishop of Rochester in 1547 and bishop of London in 1550. When Mary Tudor became queen, he was deposed from his office and sent first to the Tower of London and then to prison in Oxford, with *Thomas Cranmer and *Hugh Latimer. Younger and more learned than either, he was the sharpest in debate in the Great Disputation in Oxford in 1554. He went to the stake wearing the robes of a bishop, calling on God to receive his spirit as he died. He is commemorated by Ridley

Theological College, Cambridge. [16 October, A.]

Robert Grosseteste (c. 1170–1253) was a scholar and a polymath. He translated Greek classical and theological works, wrote biblical commentaries, and produced original writings on canon law, medicine, natural science and astronomy. He was elected chancellor of the University of Oxford, and held many livings; but when he was appointed bishop of Lincoln at the age of sixty, he resigned all his other appointments and set to work to reform a wealthy diocese which had grown lax and neglectful of the needs of the faithful. He reformed the cathedral chapter, visited all monasteries and convents, and drew up his *Constitutions,* telling the clergy in detail what their duties were. He took the view (some sixty years after the murder of *Thomas Becket) that the king had no power over the Church: clergy should not hold any office of state, and the ecclesiastical courts should be free of secular interference; but he also went to Rome and attacked the power of the papacy, complaining that English benefices were being given to absentee Italian clerics, and that the pope was abusing his power. He was temporarily suspended from his episcopate, and lived thereafter under a threat of excommunication. In the last year of his life, he was instructed to promote the pope's nephew to a Lincoln canonry. He refused. It is not clear whether he was actually excommunicated, or whether he died before the threat could be carried out. *John Wyclif and the Lollards frequently quoted his views, and in the nineteenth century, Bishop Stubbs wrote of him as a champion of the liberties of the Church. [9 October, A. R.]

Romero, Oscar (1917–80): this quiet and unassuming Roman Catholic priest, with his devotion to Our Lady of Peace, seemed a safe choice as a bishop in the corrupt and crime-ridden country of El Salvador. Born of a peasant family in a rural area, he knew the needs of the ordinary people of his country, and the poverty and oppression which they suffered. He graduated at the Gregorian University in Rome, became secretary to his home diocese, and was unaffected by the liberation theology which developed in Central and South America in the wake of Vatican II. He became bishop of Santiago de Maria in 1974; but he was moved to public protest when military forces raided a village in his diocese and killed five peasants. He wrote to the president and started a newspaper, *El Apostól*, which championed the poor against an unjust government. He became a controversial figure: when he preached, government agents sat in his congregation with tape-recorders, and a smear campaign was started against him in the government-controlled newspapers. He made it plain that he was not a revolutionary, but a witness for social justice. He was appointed archbishop of El Salvador in 1974, and five years later he went to Rome, where he had an audience with Pope John Paul II, and deposited seven dossiers containing information about crimes against humanity in El Salvador. In October 1979 there was a military coup which increased the terrorization by the National Guard and the police. Archbishop Romero continued to preach openly against the oppressors, and on 24 March 1980 he was gunned down at the altar during a funeral Mass. His steadfast resistance to evil made him a world figure, and he is one of the modern martyrs on the west front of Westminster Abbey in London. [24 March, A. R.]

Rossetti, Christina (1830–94): her father was a Dante scholar and a member of the *Carbonari*, the revolutionaries of Naples who fought against the Bourbons; her brother was Dante Gabriel Rossetti, the wild Pre-Raphaelite artist who painted her many times as the Virgin Mary, and whom she and her mother cared for in his declining years when he was addicted to laudanum. Her sister became an Anglican nun, but Christina lived the quiet life of a Victorian spinster in London, immersed in family responsibilities and domestic chores, with a strong sense of duty. She lived under considerable emotional strain, frequently depressed, and referring to herself as 'a poor dove that must not coo' and 'an eagle that must not soar'; but her faith held together the contradictory elements in her life, and helped her to find expression in writing poetry. Some of her religious poems, such as 'Does the road wind uphill all the way?' and 'In the bleak midwinter' are well known. She had at least one unhappy and unfulfilled love affair – expressed in 'I took my heart in my hand, O my love' and possibly in 'Remember me'. Christina's mixture of Italian passion and Anglo-Catholic ideals led her to a life of consecration devoted to her family. [27 April, A.]

Ruysbroeck, John (1293–1381): Jan van Ruysbroeck (otherwise known as Johannes Rusbrochius, anglicised as John Ruysbroeck), came from the village of Ruysbroeck near Brussels. He lived a quiet life of contemplation with two other priests in the forest of Soignes. They were received as Augustinian canons, and built up a monastery with their followers. John spent many hours in the forest, listening to the voice of God, and writing notes on a waxed tablet. He was well read in theology, but his books were written in the local Brabant dialect of Flemish, so that laymen could read them and profit from them as well as clergy. It was not until a century after his death that the Carthusian monk Laurence Surius translated them into Latin, and they were published in Cologne. Like many of the works of the mystics in the Low Countries, they were slow to reach England, and have only become well known in the twentieth century. They are now published in the series 'Classics of Western Spirituality'. Ruysbroeck did not give his writings titles, so that titles like *The Spiritual Espousals*, *The Sparkling Stone* and *The Ladder of Spiritual Love* have been assigned to them by translators. Ruysbroeck's writing on the nature of God – 'inaccessible height and fathomless depth, incomprehensible breadth and eternal length, a dim silence and a wild desert . . . a Fathomless and Unconditional Good' – and on the Trinity – 'ever working in a living differentiation' in 'waves of endless love' – is strikingly different from the formularies of the medieval schoolmen, linking it to the much older work of the Neo-Platonists. [2 December, R.]

Sadoc (1260) was one of a band of friars sent to Hungary (then dominated by the Tartars) by *Dominic in 1221. He was probably himself Hungarian, from a family which had become Christian in the time of *King Stephen. He moved on from Hungary to Sandomir in Poland, where he founded a Dominican priory, and became the superior. In 1260, the Tartars besieged and overwhelmed Sandomir, and Sadoc told the friars to prepare for death. Forty-nine friars were present at Compline in the priory chapel, singing the Salve Regina, when the Tartars broke in, and they were all cut down save one, who hid in the belfry and was able to report the massacre. [2 June, R. 2 February, O.]

Sampson of Constantinople (Samson, fifth century) was a wealthy philanthropist who became a priest and founded a great hospital for the sick poor. He is said to have been a Roman, and a relative of the Emperor Constantine, and to have trained as a physician. He worked in his hospital with all who suffered in body, mind or spirit – a holistic ministry. He was known in his lifetime as 'Samson the Hospitable' and 'Samson Xenodochus' ('Samson who cared for strangers'). His hospital was burned down in the sixth century but rebuilt by Justinian, and later it came under the jurisdiction of the Knights Templar. [27 June, R. O.]

Scholastica (547) was the sister of *Benedict of Nursia. She was probably the founder of a small women's monastery a few miles from Monte Cassino, where Benedict had his larger foundation. According to *Pope Gregory the Great, who is the sole source on their lives and work, brother and sister met only once a year for prayer and meditation. When Scholastica died, Benedict had her body placed in the tomb which had been prepared for himself, and was later interred with her. Scholastica is the patron of Benedictine nuns. Her name in religion encourages the belief that she was a scholarly woman. [10 February, A. R. O.]

Seabury, Samuel (1729–96) was the first bishop consecrated for the United States of America after the American War of Independence. The manner of his consecration and its consequences had a considerable importance for the development of the Episcopal Church of the USA, which is part of the Anglican Communion. A group of clergy elected Seabury as their

first bishop, but he could not be consecrated in England, because that would
have involved an oath of allegiance to
King George III. Seabury had studied
in Scotland, and knew that the small
Episcopal Church of Scotland had non-
juring bishops, so, with the consent of
the archbishop of Canterbury, he
was consecrated in Scotland by four
Episcopalian bishops. When he returned to America, he found that there
were objections to this 'back door'
process. A synod had been held, and Dr
William White, the rector of George
Washington's church and a strong supporter of American independence, had
been elected in his place. The American clergy wanted full validation, and
recognition from Canterbury that they
formed an independent branch of the
Anglican Church. After some three
years of negotiation, a legal formula
was found. Dr White and another
bishop were consecrated in the chapel
at Lambeth palace by the archbishops
of Canterbury and York and two other
bishops. They worked in harmony with
Bishop Seabury, and the Episcopalian
Church has continued to keep the
Scottish title. [14 November, A.]

Sellon, Priscilla Lydia (1821–76):
when in 1848 *Dr Pusey appealed to
the bishops of the Church of England to
establish religious houses for women,
the bishop of Exeter was the first to
respond. A small group of women were
constituted as Sisters of Mercy in
the dockland areas of Plymouth and
Devonport, where they visited families,
nursed the sick, and started an orphanage and a school. Dr Pusey was their
spiritual director, and Lydia Sellon was
their superior. She disposed of her own
considerable inheritance, contributing
a large sum towards buying housing
properties, to be run on *Octavia Hill's
system of management. At first the
Sisters faced suspicion and some re-

sentment from the local population, but
their work in the three great cholera
epidemics of 1854, 1866 and 1871
brought them respect and approval.
In 1856, the community joined with
the Holy Cross Sisters at Ascot, and
foundations were made in a number of
other cities. [20 November, A.]

Selwyn, George Augustus
(1809–78) was an Old Etonian, and had
a distinguished career at Cambridge.
He was ordained into the Church of
England, served a curacy at Windsor,
and took a doctorate in Divinity.
Shortly after the Treaty of Waitangi
(1840), which led to the colonization of
New Zealand by Britain, he expressed
an interest in ministering there, and
was offered the bishopric at the age of
thirty-two. He had a keen intellect,
immense enthusiasm and great energy.
He learned Maori, travelled the North
and South Islands under very rough
conditions, and explored Melanesia,
where *John Coleridge Patteson was
sent as bishop largely as a result of his
efforts. He went to England with a
detailed plan for the Anglican Church
in New Zealand, including two bishops
and synodical government, and returned as archbishop of New Zealand.
He championed the Maoris against
land speculators, and acted as a peace-
maker in the Maori War in 1854. He is
regarded as one of the founders of
modern New Zealand. Archbishop
Selwyn returned to England in 1867 to
become bishop of Lichfield. His son
John Selwyn became the second bishop
of Melanesia after the death of Bishop
Patteson. Selwyn College, Cambridge
was founded from subscriptions raised
in John Selwyn's memory; but the college fittingly forms a memorial to the
father as well as the son. [11 April, A.]

Seraphim of Sarov (1759–1833)
was a monk in the monastery of Sarov,

103

near Moscow. He was canonized by the Russian Orthodox Church in 1903 for his holiness, his austerity of life, and his capacity for physical endurance. The harsh regime at Sarov, which combined heavy labour with long hours of liturgical worship and little food, broke his health, and he was very ill for three years, during which time he had visions of the Virgin Mary. After he recovered, he went to live in the forest as a hermit, chopping wood for fuel in the bitter winters, and growing his own food. His love of the natural world and his care for the foxes, wolves and other animals of the forest became legendary. At one point he lived in complete silence for three years, but eventually he went back to the monastery, where he looked after visitors and acted as chaplain to a community of nuns. Seraphim's mysticism, and his teaching on the importance of combining prayer with service to others, have become well known in both the Eastern and the Western Churches. [2 January, A. R. O.]

Sergei of Radonezh (1314–92) was a much earlier example of the ideals of Russian monasticism than *Seraphim. Born in Rostov, the son of a noble Christian family at the time of the Tartar invasions of Russia, he sustained his parents by his own labour after their financial ruin. After their death, he led a life of seclusion in the forest, often going without food for days. When others came to join him, they formed the house of the Holy Trinity. Sergei insisted that each man should subsist by his own labour, tilling his own field, and that they should meet together only for worship. The monks were not allowed to beg, and were often so poor that they had no bread or wine for the daily Eucharist. Sergei resigned as abbot after a time, devoting himself to the spiritual direction of the many people who were drawn to him by his warmth and simplicity. Among them were Russian princes whose resistance to the Tartars was weakened by their own feuds. Sergei travelled long distances on several occasions to bring them to reconciliation. When they were united, he sent them into battle against the Moslems under the sign of the three-barred Russian cross. Though they faced overwhelming odds, they defeated the Tartars in the battle of Kulivoko Polik, which marks the first step in the freeing of Russia from Moslem domination. Sergei went back to his monastery, and inspired younger monks to found monasteries on the pattern of the House of the Holy Trinity. [25 September, A. R. O.]

Sigfrid (?1045) was sent to Scandinavia as a missionary bishop some two years after the death of *Anskar. The ravages of heathen tribes had destroyed Anskar's work, but when Olaf Tryggveson, king of Norway, became a Christian during a visit to England, the time seemed ripe for rebuilding his work. Sigfrid is thought to have been an Anglo-Saxon monk of Glastonbury, though he may have been of Danish stock. York has also laid claim to him. The death of King Olaf some five years after the beginning of the mission meant that little was achieved in Norway, but Sigfrid established missionary bases in Sweden, consecrated bishops for east and west Gothland, and established a monastery at Växjö before extending his work into Denmark. He is commemorated as the Apostle of Sweden and Denmark: both countries remained in communion with Rome until the Reformation. [15 February, A. R.]

Silvester I (335) became pope in 314, shortly after Constantine decreed religious toleration throughout the

Roman Empire. Since his pontificate lasted for twenty-two years, almost until Constantine's death, it has long been assumed that he played a major role in the influence which the Church acquired during this period; however, Roman Catholic sources now cast considerable doubt on this thesis. Religious toleration for all the many creeds then found in the Roman Empire did not amount to the establishment of Christianity as a state religion. The story of 'the Donation of Constantine' – that the emperor suffered from leprosy, was miraculously healed and converted by Sylvester, and gave him most of central Italy as a thank-offering – has been shown to be a medieval invention to justify the expansion of the papal states. Constantine was not baptized until he was on his death-bed in Asia Minor, after Silvester's death. The equally miraculous story that Constantine saw a flaming cross in the sky with the words 'In this sign conquer', before the battle of the Milvian Bridge is similarly discounted: it was not recorded during his lifetime. Constantine was generous to the Christian community in Rome: his mother Helena was a practising Christian. He started the building of the first basilica of St Peter, gave Silvester the Lateran Palace, and provided gifts of farms and land; but when he called the bishops of the Church together to settle the Arian heresy in 324 at the Council of Nicaea, they met in what is now Izmir in western Turkey, near his birthplace and Helena's home. Pope Silvester did not even attend the Council, and only one Western bishop was present. There is no evidence that Silvester ever ratified its findings. In 330, Constantine took his court to Asia Minor, building a new capital for the Roman Empire at Byzantium, which others came to call Constantinople. The departure of the imperial court left a power-vacuum in

Rome which Silvester and his successors were able to fill; but the main architect of Vatican authority appears to have been *Pope Damasus, some decades later. [31 December, R.]

Simeon, Charles (1759–1836), the son of a wealthy lawyer, went to King's College, Cambridge as an undergraduate, and stayed there for the rest of his life. At the age of twenty, he had a powerful conversion experience. He was ordained, and was appointed to the living of Holy Trinity, Cambridge, while continuing to live in college. He directed all his efforts towards fostering vocations among the students. At first the students mocked his pedantry and his eccentricities, and once he was pelted with rotten eggs; but as the Evangelical wing of the Church of England became stronger, he attracted followers, who called themselves 'Simeonites' or 'Sims'. He was a compelling preacher, and his huge church was crowded Sunday by Sunday: even the more rowdy element in King's came to call him 'the old Apostle'. He was an active member of the Church Missionary Society, and influenced many former students in their decision to go to the mission field. He was the founder of the Simeon Trust, using his considerable wealth to acquire the patronage of livings, and to appoint Evangelical clergy. [13 November, A.]

Simeon Stylites (390–459) was the first and most famous of the Middle Eastern pillar-saints: while other hermits sought seclusion and privacy in the forests or the mountains, he lived on his pillar in full view of passers-by, enduring heat and cold and storm, fasting and praying, often remaining in one position for many hours. The pillar was only a few feet wide (though probably surrounded by railings), and he was dependent for necessities on devoted followers, who reached him by ladder. Simeon was the son of a Syrian shepherd. He practised various forms of mortification of the flesh before deciding on this extreme form of penance. His first pillar was only nine feet high, the second and third were taller, and his fourth and last (built by his devotees) was sixty feet high, effectively removing him from the curious crowds which flocked to see him. He wrote many charitable letters of counsel and advice to those who could not visit him. He is said to have been a gentle and kindly man, exhorting the people below to peace and justice, and showing no signs of fanaticism. [5 January, R.]

Simon the Apostle (first century) is known as Simon Zelotes, to distinguish him from *(Simon) Peter, Simon of Cyrene and other Simons in the

Gospels. He is referred to as 'the Canaanean' or 'the Canaanite' (Matt. 10:4; Mark 3:18) or 'the Zealot' (Luke 6:15; Acts 1:13). He may have been a member of the Zealot party, a strict Jewish sect who looked for the overthrow of the Roman occupation. Nothing certain is known about him after the events of Pentecost. He is usually associated with *Jude in commemoration. There is a sixth-century Western tradition that he preached in Egypt, and then joined Jude in a mission to

Persia, where they were both martyred on the same day; but in the earlier Eastern menology of St Basil, he is said to have continued his ministry for some years, and to have died peacefully at Edessa. In art, he is usually shown holding a fish, indicating the belief that he was among the Apostles who were fishermen on the sea of Galilee. [28 October, A. R. O.]

Simon Metaphrastes or 'the Metaphrast' (c. 1000) was the main compiler of the lives of the early saints in the Eastern Church. Greek menologies and Byzantine synaxaries depend heavily on his work. He is thought to have been a court official at Constantinople, but nothing is known about his life. [28 November, R. O.]

Singh, Sundar (1889–1929): as his name indicates, Sundar Singh was a Sikh, brought up in the proud tradition of that reformed and monotheistic form of Hinduism. He went to an American Presbyterian school, but rejected Christian teaching, looking for truth in the sacred books of his own faith. He was sixteen when he realized that he must become a Christian, though this meant the rejection of his own culture, and social ostracism. The local Sikh community became angry, and the American mission had to close. Sundar's wealthy landowner father disowned him, and he went to a mission station at Simla, where he was allowed to study and pray. He was baptized there by an Anglican priest. A month later, he gave away all his possessions and adopted the saffron robe of a *Sadhu*, or Indian holy man. He worked in a leper asylum and a plague camp, and undertook a dangerous preaching mission in Tibet before further study at St John's College, Lahore. He refused to take Anglican Orders because he believed that he must have the freedom to speak directly to Hindus and Buddhists without an ecclesiastical label. He continued his lonely ministry, accepting no disciples and facing many hazards: death from frostbite, drowning, and poisonous snakes and a puma; torture and imprisonment from hostile people. From time to time he would appear in the mission centres, and talk to groups of Christians. He was invited to other countries in Asia, including China and Japan, to preach his message; but he always returned to the mission field. In 1929, he went back to Tibet, and did not return. He was reported missing, presumed murdered. [19 June, A.]

Slessor, Mary (1848–1915) came from a very poor Presbyterian family in Aberdeen which went through great poverty and hardship. She was working in the mills at the age of eleven. She was fascinated to hear of the mission to the Calabar in Nigeria, where the people were said to be 'the most degraded in Africa' – in a state of constant tribal warfare, inflamed by the rum or gin which white traders gave them in return for slaves. Mary went to night school and Bible classes, and when she was thirty, she was given special training, and achieved her ambition of being sent to the Calabar as a missionary. She was only five feet tall, with a mop of flaming red hair; but she was tough and wiry. She picked up Efik, the *lingua franca* of the area, made trips to the out-stations, and talked to the chiefs as easily as she had talked to the mill girls in Aberdeen. She was sent to work among the Okoyong, a fierce Bantu people who practised ritual sacrifice, trial by ordeal and twin-murder. The second-born of twins was thought to be the devil's child, and ritually killed. Mary opposed the 'heathen practices', saved the children and started an orphanage for them. She is said to have beaten one chief over the head with her umbrella. The people were in awe of her, and came to love her. In 1891, she was appointed as the British agent for the Okoyong, and became the magistrate for the district. She died in Nigeria shortly after the outbreak of World War I, and was mourned as *Eka kpukru owo*, 'everybody's mother'. [11 January, A.]

Spiridion (Spyridon, fourth century) was a shepherd in the 'pan-handle' of Cyprus, the north-eastern peninsula. When he was consecrated bishop of Tremithus, he continued to tend his flock, and a story is told of how two robbers tried to steal it. He prayed with them, set them free, and gave them a ram, because he said they deserved it after working all night for nothing. This gentle, humorous bishop was present at the Councils of Nicaea and Sardica, where he upheld the faith against heretical views. In the persecutions of the Eastern emperor Galerius (305–11), he was hamstrung, lost his right eye and was sent to work in the mines. He is the principal patron of Corfu, and a well-loved saint in his native Cyprus, easily recognized by his blue shepherd's cap. [14 December, A. R. O.]

Stein, Edith (1891–1942): Dr Edith Stein was a distinguished German philosopher who became a Christian at the age of thirty as a result of reading the autobiography of *Teresa of Avila. She came of an orthodox Jewish family, but she said, 'This is the Truth', and on the following day, she bought a catechism and asked for Christian baptism. As a Roman Catholic, she studied the texts of *Thomas Aquinas, translated *John Henry Newman's *Letters and Journals* and *The Idea of a University* into German, and wrote *Wahrheit der Dinge* ('The Truth of Things'), in which she attempted to reconcile the insights of the medieval schoolmen with those of twentieth-century philosophy. In 1933, she became a Carmelite nun as Sister Teresa Benedicta of the Cross. Hitler was in power in Germany, and Jews were being persecuted: because she was of Jewish race, she was in danger. Through the writings of the Carmelite friar *John of the Cross, she sought a life of abnegation and prepared for sacrifice. She wrote her most powerful work, *Endliches und Ewiges Sein* ('Finite and Eternal Being'), at this time. In 1937, her superiors sent her to a convent in the Netherlands which was thought to offer her greater safety. There she wrote the *Kreuzeswissenschaft* ('Knowledge of the Cross'). She did not live to revise it. Germany overran Holland, and in 1942, following a protest by the archbishop of Utrecht about the treatment of the Jews, she was one of many who were arrested in reprisal. She died in Auschwitz concentration camp about a week after her arrest. [9 August, R.]

Stephen (first century) is the proto-martyr or first martyr of the Christian faith. He was a deacon, one of the seven Hellenists who were appointed to care for the Greek Christians. He is mentioned first, and described as 'a man full of faith and the Holy Spirit' (Acts 6:5). In the ensuing passages, we are told that he was 'full of grace and power, and did great wonders and signs among the people', but he spoke with such force and clarity that he was brought before the Sanhedrin, and accused of blasphemy. He made a learned and eloquent defence (Acts 7:2–53). He ended by calling the Sanhedrin 'stiff-necked people', 'betrayers' and 'murderers'. The elders became enraged and ground their teeth at him. He was condemned to death, dragged outside the city walls, and stoned. He fell on his knees, asking God to forgive his attackers, and died. This seems to have

been a judicial execution rather than an act of mob violence, because there were official witnesses. They left their

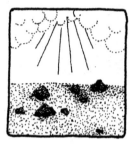

outer garments with a young man called Saul, who 'approved of their killing him'; but the execution must have had a powerful effect on Saul, who would be converted on the road to Damascus and would become the apostle *Paul. Artistic representations of Stephen often show him with a stone, to indicate the manner of his death, and a palm, to indicate martyrdom. [26 December, A. R. O.]

Stephen of Hungary (c. 975–1038) married Gisela, sister of the Holy Roman Emperor Henry II, and brought Hungary into Christendom. Pope Silvester II sent him a crown, and his coronation took place in 1001. He established Benedictine monasteries and appointed bishops. The pagan customs of the Magyar tribes were prohibited. He had a care for the poor and oppressed, and went out to distribute alms, sometimes in disguise. *Margaret of Scotland was brought up in his court as a relative of Queen Gisela, and learned her own strong faith and charity from the royal couple. This period is known as 'the golden age of Hungary', and King Stephen is a national hero. There is a curious story about the Crown of Stephen: Hungary subsequently suffered many invasions and many vicissitudes. The crown was lost, and it was said that Hungary would never be free until it was returned to Budapest. In the 1970s, it was discovered in the United States, in Fort Knox. Apparently the American Forces at the end of World War II had found it and placed it in safe keeping, though it was not identified. President Carter returned it to Hungary some time before the country was finally freed from Soviet rule, and it is now on display in Budapest, though some doubts have been cast on its authenticity. [16 August, R.]

Studdert Kennedy, Geoffrey

(1883–1929): better known to the troops in World War I as 'Woodbine Willie', Geoffrey Studdert Kennedy was an Army chaplain who went through the horrors of trench warfare on the Western front. He was criticized by senior officers for his informality, his slangy sermons and his complete disregard of rank and status; but he had a gift for communicating with the ordinary soldiers, who respected his honesty and his total lack of hypocrisy. He never told them that war was glorious. He went into the front line talking, arguing, praying and handing out the comforts, such as cigarettes, which gave him his nickname. He wrote to his wife, 'I see Gethsemane. I always see it these days.' The agony of Christ was central to his faith, and he brought the suffering Christ to the bewildered young men in the trenches. In 1917, he was awarded the Military Cross for gallantry under fire: he had risked his life to fetch morphia for the wounded, and rescued two men from shell-holes. After the war, he was appointed a King's Chaplain, and went to St-Martin's-in-the-Fields in London to work with the homeless and unemployed men who came to the Crypt. His friend *William Temple described him

as 'one of God's greatest gifts to this generation'. He moved to a City living as a base for intensive work with the Industrial Christian Fellowship, trying to make the Christian faith relevant to the needs of the modern world in the period of the post-war slump and the General Strike of 1926. There were many requests for him to preach and speak at public meetings, and he did not spare himself. He died on a mission to Liverpool at the age of forty-six. [8 March, A.]

Sumner, Mary (1828–1921): known as 'the mother of the Mothers' Union', Mary Sumner was fifty-seven years old and the wife of an archdeacon when she spoke at a Church Congress in 1885 and called for a new movement for women 'to raise the Home life of our Nation'. Her own children were all married and independent: the Mothers' Union was to be her 'youngest child'. The call was a timely one, because the birth rate was dropping rapidly, and infant deaths (many of them caused by faulty rearing practices) were very common. Mary travelled all over England, addressing meetings, forming committees and drafting rules, leaflets and membership cards. The movement grew rapidly. Its principles were the duties and responsibilities of motherhood, which its founder described as a profession requiring 'faith, love, patience, method, self-control and some knowledge of the principles of character-training', and the indissolubility of marriage. By 1892, there were 28 diocesan branches, 1,550 branches and over 60,000 members. In 1895 a central organization was set up, with Mary Sumner as president, and two years later, Queen Victoria became its patron. It spread to other countries: first to Australia, Canada, India and other parts of the British Empire, and then to the West Indies, Japan and South

America. Mary Sumner's campaign for recognition of the dignity and importance of motherhood and the values of family life had a great impact on the status of married women. [9 August, A.]

Swithun (862) was a Wessex man, educated at the Old Minster in Winchester, who became chaplain to King Egbert of Wessex, and bishop of Winchester, the royal capital, in 852. The monk-chronicler William of Malmesbury describes him as 'a treasury of all the virtues', especially commending his pastoral care for his people and his charity and humility to the poor. The tradition that if it rains on St Swithin's day, it will rain for forty days afterwards seems to be a compound of three separate elements. Before he died, Swithun asked that he should be buried in the ordinary cemetery outside the west door of the Old Minster, 'where his grave might be trodden on by passers by, and the rain fall upon it'. He died on 2 July 862. During the rebuilding of the cathedral in 971, the walls were extended to bring his tomb, which had become a place of pilgrimage, into the structure; and there was a period of very heavy rainfall, which was attributed to Swithun. When a new cathedral was constructed in the eleventh century, his shrine was moved again, on 15 July 1093. The Roman Catholic Church now celebrates the anniversary of his death as his feast day, but the Anglican Church celebrates it on the traditional date. [15 July, A. 2 July, R.]

Taylor, Jeremy (1613–67): the author of *Holy Living* and *Holy Dying* was a High Churchman who attracted the attention of *Archbishop Laud and became chaplain to *Charles I. He acted as a chaplain to the Royalist troops during the Civil War, and then retired to remote livings, first in Wales and later in Northern Ireland, during the Cromwellian period. After the Restoration, Charles II made him bishop of Down and Connor, presumably in the hope that he could help to heal the divisions of Northern Ireland. Taylor had written of 'the unreasonableness of prescribing other men's faith, and the iniquity of persecuting different opinions', and hoped to pursue a middle way; but the appointment proved to be an unhappy one. The Roman Catholic community treated him as a Protestant, while the Presbyterians were vituperative about what they considered to be his Romish tendencies. He called them 'Scotch spiders', and had thirty-two benefices declared vacant because the incumbents had not been episcopally ordained. He spent the last nine years of his life in acute controversy, and his chief achievement was the rebuilding of the cathedral at Dromore in County Down, after taking over the administration of that diocese. Taylor was a prolific writer, combining theological scholarship with a depth of religious experience in his devotional works, which have remained classics of spirituality. [13 August, A.]

Temple, William (1881–1944): the son of Archbishop Frederick Temple, William Temple had an even more outstanding career than his father: President of the Oxford Union and first class honours in 'Greats', headmaster of Repton; rector of the fashionable church, St James's Piccadilly; bishop of Manchester; archbishop of York; and archbishop of Canterbury. He broke new ground through his strong commitment to the achievement of a more just society. As a student, he spent much time in the university settlements – Oxford House, Bethnal Green and the Bermondsey Mission. As headmaster of Repton, he told the Governors that the public schools represented 'class divisions in an accentuated form'. He left St James's Piccadilly to devote his considerable energies to the Life and Liberty movement, which led to the setting up of the Church Assembly, forerunner of the General Synod of the Church of England, and gave the laity a voice in the affairs of the Church. As bishop of Manchester, he made contacts with both industry and the trade unions, drew crowds at his missions on the Blackpool beaches, and acted as chairman for the great Malvern Conference of 1940, which laid the foundations for a more egalitarian society after the war. He went to Canterbury in 1940, and gave the public inspiration and guidance for a Christian approach to the war against Nazism. His many newspaper articles and broadcasts, his emphasis on Christian citizenship, his contribution to ecumenical movements, his understanding of the forces of social change, made him a key figure in the plans made for social reconstruction in the post-war world; but he died in October 1944, after only two and a half years at Canterbury, at the age of sixty-three. He had influenced many leading churchmen and politicians of his time, and his books, particularly *Nature, Man and God*, *Christianity and the Social Order* and *Readings in St John's Gospel*, have continued to influence subsequent generations. [6 November, A.]

Teresa of Avila (1515–82), the daughter of a wealthy family of that city, spent twenty years as a Carmelite nun before she was able to carry out the reform for which she is celebrated. In 1562, reacting against the laxity and worldliness of the unreformed Carmelites, she founded the small convent of St Joseph at Avila with the aim of returning to the primitive Carmelite Rule. Her nuns, many of them from noble Spanish families, wore plain habits and rough leather sandals: they

were known as the *Carmelitas Descalzas* ('discalced' or shoeless). Their life was one of contemplation, prayer and solitude. They ate peasant food and had no servants. One of Teresa's favourite sayings was 'The Lord walks among the pots and pans.' She was never afraid of hard work or the most menial of tasks, but she also taught the nuns to dance and sing and to be joyful. She insisted in selection that they should be women of intelligence and good judgement, saying, 'God preserve us from stupid nuns!' She wrote to the devout Philip II of Spain, had an audience with him, and thereafter worked under his protection. She was distressed by the uncompromising rejection of her work by some of the older Carmelite houses: on at least one occasion, she had the convent door slammed in her face; but she travelled all over Spain in spite of increasing age and illness, founding new houses and reforming existing ones. She was responsible for the foundation of a parallel Order for friars in association with *John of the Cross, who became chaplain of the Avila convent and her personal confessor. John, trained at the University of Salamanca, had a greater knowledge of theology, but they read the Bible together and learned from each other. Teresa combined great practical ability with a deep contemplative experience. Her writings, particularly *The Way of Perfection*, *The Interior Castle* and her autobiography, are classics of spirituality. She made her final foundation at Burgos in 1582, and died on her way back to Avila, probably of exhaustion. [15 October, A. R. O.]

Teresa of Lisieux (1873–97) was a French Carmelite nun, born some three and a half centuries after Teresa of Avila. She came of a devout family.

Her mother died young, and she and her three sisters were cared for by an aunt. Teresa followed her two elder sisters into the convent at Lisieux at the age of fifteen, and the youngest, Céline, joined them some years later. Teresa's life was short, and without events apparent to the outside world; but she faithfully performed all that was required of her in a very austere régime. She hoped to become a missionary in Indo-China, but in 1895 she had a haemorrhage: the first sign of tuberculosis. She suffered in silence until the summer of 1897, when she was moved to the convent infirmary, and she died in October of the same year at the age of twenty-four. Her short life might have passed unnoticed if she had not been told, during her illness, to write the story of her spiritual experiences. This was edited by one of her sisters, and published as *L'Histoire d'une âme*. A simple account of total obedience to the will of God and to her superiors, lived out heroically in conditions of pain and suffering, it has been translated into many languages. Teresa of Lisieux is the 'dove' of Vita Sackville-West's book *The Eagle and the Dove*, which contrasts her life with that of *Teresa of Avila. [3 October, R.]

Theodore (841) and **Theophanes** (845): these two brothers are known as the *Graptoi*, which means 'the Written-on'. They grew up in Jerusalem and became monks. When the emperor Leo the Isaurian supported the Iconoclasts in the second wave of the movement to destroy images in churches, the patriarch of Jerusalem sent them to exhort him not to 'disturb the peace of the Church'. Leo had Theodore scourged, and sent them both to an island off the coast of the Black Sea, where they suffered severely from the conditions of their imprisonment. They were released on the emperor's death, but his successor, Theophilus, was even more violent in his iconoclastic beliefs. He had them scourged and banished again. When they returned to Constantinople in protest for a third time, he commanded that twelve lines of iambic verse describing them as 'vessels full of the iniquity of superstitious error' should be inscribed on their faces. The records say that the message was cut into their faces; but in view of its length, it seems more likely that it was pricked or tattooed. Whatever the nature of the process, it took two days, and was both painful and disfiguring. Theodore died in their subsequent banishment, but Theophanes survived, and outlived the emperor Theophilus. When *Methodius became patriarch of Constantinople, and the images were restored to churches, Theophanes became bishop of Nicaea. [27 December, R. O.]

Theodore of Tarsus (602–90) was born in the same city as *Paul. When Islam took power in Asia Minor, he went to Italy, and became a monk-scholar in Rome, working in Greek and Latin in the Greek Orthodox tradition. He was sixty-six years old when Pope Vitalian, anxious to heal the divisions between the Celtic and Latin clergy which still persisted in England after the Synod of Whitby, decided that his appointment as archbishop of Canterbury was the only way to heal the breach. Like the Celtic monks, the Orthodox did not keep the Latin date of Easter, or wear the circular Latin tonsure. This surprising appointment proved to be an inspired one. Theodore set out with his abbot *Hadrian in support, and spent a year on the journey to England, staying at Frankish monasteries to become accustomed to the ways of the Western Church, and learning English. When he finally arrived, his actions were decisive. *Bede says that he 'visited every part of the island'. He called two episcopal synods, reorganized the dioceses, appointed new bishops, and deflated the ambitions of *Wilfrid, who was sent from York to a smaller diocese at Hexham. He was sometimes ruthless, but highly efficient. Bede's account of how he dealt with *Chad – first declaring that his consecration to York was invalid, but then, pleased with his humility, consecrating him personally and sending him to Mercia – is indicative of his pastoral ability. The story of how he told Chad that he must ride a horse in order to cover the ground in his large new diocese, and then hoisted him bodily into the saddle when he demurred, says much about his determination – and perhaps his sense of humour. The old

Celtic ascetic must have been light in weight. Theodore died 'old and full of years' at the age of eighty-eight. He had set up the structure which *Gregory the Great originally envisaged when he sent *Augustine on his mission in 597, and had created the basis for a national Church. [19 September, A. R. O.]

Thomas the Apostle (first century) is generally remembered as Thomas Didymus ('the Twin') or 'Doubting Thomas'. He is the apostle who, faced with the resurrected Christ in the Upper Room, insisted that he would not believe the evidence of his own eyes unless he could touch the marks of the nails and feel the wound in Christ's side. He was allowed to do this, and his response was 'My Lord and my God' (John 20:19–28). The tradition that Thomas carried out a mission in India is a very strong one. There are apocryphal accounts of his travels – *The Acts of Thomas, The Apocalypse of Thomas, The Gospel of Thomas* and many others – and the fact that some of them seem to have come from Gnostic or Manichaean groups does not necessarily invalidate their account of his travels. There was an established trade route from the Red Sea to south India, and though the journey was long and hazardous, he could have travelled with merchants. When the Portuguese arrived in south India, they found existing Christian communities, and they were shown Thomas's tomb at Mylapore. Though the Portguese obliterated most traces of the older form of faith, the Mar Thoma Church still exists, chiefly in the United States. [3 July or 21 December, A. O. 3 July, R.]

Thomas   Aquinas   (1225–74), scholar, philosopher and theologian, studied under the Benedictines in Monte Cassino and Naples, and became a Dominican friar against the wishes of his noble family. He went on to work in Paris, where the Dominicans were attempting to reconcile the

thought of Aristotle to Christian theology, and later to Cologne, where he developed the scholastic system of thought which is set out in his *Summa Theologica*. This exhaustive and highly intellectual work (an English translation runs to twenty-two volumes) deals with the nature of God, the creation of the world, the earthly life of Christ, the work of the Church, Christian morality and the sacraments in a totally logical and rational manner. Each topic is divided into questions and answers, with subdivisions of the questions, answers to the questions, objections to the answers and answers to the objections. No allowance is made for the emotions, human affections or natural impulses. Thomist thought became so basic to Western theology until Vatican II that all Roman Catholic schools and colleges were required to teach according to its principles. Thomas also wrote many other works – the *Summa contra Gentiles*, directed to the conversion of Jews, Muslims and members of heretical sects; the *Questiones disputatae*, dealing with the nature of truth, power and evil; biblical commentaries and philosophical works on classical Greek philosophy and the Neo-Platonists. His extraordinary intellectual grasp and his orthodox teaching earned him the title

of 'the Angelic Doctor'. [28 January, A. R.]

Thomas Becket (1118–70) was archdeacon of Canterbury. He was involved in a mission to Rome to secure the pope's approval to the accession of Henry II, and became the king's

chancellor and friend. He was a highly competent statesman and diplomatist; but when the king, exasperated by clerical resistance to his incursions on the rights and privileges of the Church, determined to make him archbishop of Canterbury, he resisted, warning the king that, as archbishop, his first loyalty would be to God. When both pope and king continued to press him to take office, he did so, and changed his way of life completely. Turning from his former magnificence, he lived in near-monastic simplicity, and fearlessly opposed the king's depredations on the Church. Under extreme royal displeasure, he left England secretly in 1163, and asked Pope Alexander III to relieve him of office; but the pope refused to do so. Thomas was exiled for six years. When he returned to England bearing the pope's authority to suspend the archbishop of York and six bishops who had collaborated with the king, he told the archbishop of Paris that he knew he was going home to die. On Christmas Day 1170 he publicly carried out the suspensions, and the king, in a fit of rage, asked who would rid him of his troublesome archbishop. Four knights went to Canterbury, and he was hacked down in his cathedral. The universal horror caused by his martyrdom led to severe penances for Henry II, and to the pilgrimages to Thomas's shrine which are celebrated in Chaucer's *Canterbury Tales*. T. S. Eliot's *Murder in the Cathedral* tells the story in poetic form. [29 December, A. R.]

Timothy and Titus (first century): Timothy, whom *Paul calls 'my loyal child in the faith', was the son of a Jewish mother and a Greek father. He accompanied Paul on his mission to Philippi, and subsequently carried out missions in other Greek cities. He was working with Paul when the Letters to the Philippians, the Colossians and the Thessalonians were written, and his name is mentioned in all three. Paul's two Letters to Timothy were written when Timothy was in Ephesus, where he directed the Christian community, and according to Eusebius of Caesarea, became bishop. The apocryphal *Acts of Timothy* record that he was killed at Ephesus during a pagan Greek festival. Titus, who was a Greek, worked with Paul at a later stage in his ministry, and was sent to visit a number of churches in Greece and Dalmatia. Paul wrote to the Corinthians, describing him as his partner and associate, and commenting on Titus's eagerness to carry out the work. The single Letter to Titus is written to him in Crete, where he apparently had a very difficult ministry; but there is some doubt about the authenticity of this Letter. Eusebius of Caesarea records that Titus eventually became bishop of Crete. [26 January, A. R. O.]

Traherne, Thomas (?1636–74) was known only as an obscure seven-teenth-century cleric until a hand-written manuscript of his poems was found on a London bookstall, and published in 1903. The poems were at first attributed to the metaphysical poet Henry Vaughan, but have been established conclusively as Traherne's work. Traherne was chaplain to Sir Orlando Bridgman, Lord Keeper of the Seal to Charles I – a position which brought him into contact with the leading literary men of his age, and gave him time for prayer and writing. Like many of the religious poets of his age, he was overwhelmed by the majesty and glory of the universe as revealed by physical science, and he celebrates the wonder of the Creator and the Creation. Some commentators have suggested that he was influenced by Neo-Platonism or Gnosticism, but his work is essentially part of the spiritual and literary development of his time. [10 October, A.]

Tyndale, William (c. 1494–1536) was a biblical scholar who studied at both Oxford and Cambridge, and deter-mined to make a new translation of the Bible into English direct from the Greek. Existing translations had been derived from *Jerome's much earlier work, and he was told that direct trans-lation was forbidden by papal decree. After being rebuffed by Cuthbert Tunstall, bishop of London, he went to Germany to work with Lutheran scholars. His translation of the New Testament was smuggled into England, and publicly burned in 1526. He con-tinued to work on the Old Testament in hazardous circumstances, being obliged to move house frequently to evade arrest. He was arrested in Antwerp in 1535 and imprisoned in a castle near Brussels. In 1536 he was publicly executed by the secular authorities. It is said that his last words were 'Lord, open the king of England's eyes.' As the Reformation took hold, the beauty of Tyndale's language became recognized, and Cranmer's Great Bible of 1539 consists largely of Tyndale's translation from Genesis to 2 Chronicles and for the whole of the New Testament. The latter part of the Old Testament was translated by Miles Coverdale, who revised Tyndale's work. Much of the Authorized Version of the Bible, first published in 1611, derives from this work. Tyndale's translation of the New Testament was republished in 2000 by the British Library, which holds the 1526 edition. [6 October, A.]

Uganda, Martyrs of (1886 and 1971–9): the earlier martyrdoms in Uganda occurred shortly after the murder of *Bishop James Hannington. The young *kabaka* (king) of Buganda, the southern province, was both unstable and irrational in his behaviour. The witch doctors, whose hold over him was threatened by the missionaries, told him that the foreigners would 'eat the country'; and when the missionaries forbade Christian boys to agree to his homosexual practices, he ordered a massacre. Some forty-six of them, Anglicans, Roman Catholics and Free Churchmen, were marched to Namugongo, the place of ritual sacrifice, and burned alive to the sound of the ritual chants of executioners. Two magnificent shrines at Namugongo now commemorate them. In the twentieth century, the military dictatorship of Idi Amin from 1971 to 1978 led to many more Christian deaths, including that of *Archbishop Janani Luwum. Clergy, university teachers, judges and many others who opposed a régime of terror were arrested by the state police and disappeared. Christianity is a strong force in Uganda today, based on the blood of two sets of martyrs. [3 June, A. R.]

Underhill, Evelyn (1875–1941): after taking a degree at King's College for Women in London, and marriage to the barrister Hubert Stuart Moore, Evelyn Underhill, who kept her family name, devoted herself to religious study and writing. She had been brought up as an Anglican, and though she was strongly attracted to the Roman Catholic Church, particularly when she was under the spiritual direction of Baron Friedrich von Hügel, she returned to the Anglican Communion, commenting that 'it seems to be a respectable suburb of the City of God'. Her early book *Mysticism* was followed by a series of scholarly works on mystics such as the anonymous author of *The Cloud of Unknowing*, *John Ruysbroek, *Jacopo da Todi and Jacob Boehme. Her thinking was greatly influenced by von Hügel, and by the writings of *Teresa of Avila. Her best-known work, *The House of the Soul*, in many ways reflects Teresa's *The Interior Castle*. Evelyn Underhill was much in demand as a retreat leader and a spiritual director at a time when women were debarred from taking Holy Orders in the Anglican Church. [15 June, A.]

Valentine (?third century): the fact that St Valentine's Day is a traditional day for lovers may owe more to the Roman spring festival of Lupercalia than to a Christian martyr. Holy days were often based on earlier festivals, and some sort of spring festival occurs in almost all cultures; but there was a real St Valentine. The seventeenth-century *Acta Sanctorum* records two – St Valentine 'of Rome' and St Valentine 'of Terni', a city some sixty miles north of Rome. Modern commentators have concluded that they are one and the same: that Valentine was bishop of Terni, and that he was taken to Rome, where he was martyred in an imperial persecution about the year 270. [14 February, A. R. O.]

Vedanayagam, Samuel Azariah

(1874–1945) was the son of an Anglican village priest in south India, and became one of the leaders of the movement for a united Church of South India. He served for some years as secretary for the YMCA in south India, and was ordained priest in 1909, when he took charge of a mission station in the state of Hyderabad. He became an assistant bishop in the Madras diocese in 1913. His aim was to create an educated indigenous clergy for India – people who could take the gospel out into the villages of a predominantly rural economy. Like many priests in the mission field, he regretted sectarian differences, and he became a powerful voice for Christian unity in the World Council of Churches. He made links with the other great faiths of India, and his great cathedral at Dornakal combines European architecture with that of Hindu and Moslem traditions. Like his contemporary, Mahatma Ghandi, he was a strong supporter of the peasant way of life, and did much to improve the condition of the Untouchables, then the lowest rung in the ladder of the Hindu caste system. He died two years before the Church of South India was finally established. [2 January, A.]

Vedast

(539) was a priest who worked in the Toul region of northeastern France. Clovis, king of the Franks, defeated the Allemanni in 496, and decided to become a Christian. Vedast accompanied him to Rheims to be baptized by *Remigius. Vedast became bishop of Arras in 499. When he arrived at the town, he found that it had been devastated by the Vandals, and the cathedral had been turned into a bear-pit. He ministered there for forty years, and as a result of his missionary

labours, he was able to add the district of Cambrai to his diocese about the year 510, and to extend the work of the Church into what is now southern Belgium. Many churches in this area were dedicated in his name, which also survives in the names of roads and mountains. In Belgium, he is usually known as St Vaast, and in England as St Foster. Three English churches, including one in London, still bear his dedication. There are stained-glass representations of him in two Suffolk churches, at Long Melford and Blythburgh. [6 February, R.]

Venn, Henry the Elder (1725–97), John Venn (1758–1813) and Henry Venn the Younger (1796–

1873): three generations of clerical Venns – father, son and grandson – are commemorated in the Anglican Calendar. Henry Venn the Elder was the fourth in a clerical dynasty: he became curate of Clapham, where his son John was born, and then moved to be rector of Huddersfield, where he had a great reputation as an Evangelical preacher. His son John became rector of Clapham at the time when the Clapham Sect was a power for social reform (see *William Wilberforce). He virtually acted as chaplain to the group, which included several leading Members of Parliament and the governor of the Bank of England. John Venn was a founder of the Church Missionary Society, and of the British and Foreign Bible Society. His son, Henry Venn the Younger, born in the rectory at Clapham, continued the family tradition. He became a prebend of St Paul's cathedral, and was secretary of the Church Missionary Society for thirty-two of its most formative years. His progressive policies of insisting that missionaries should learn the languages of the areas to which they were sent, rather than relying on interpreters, and of working towards indigenous leadership in churches overseas, contributed greatly towards the Society's success. [1 July, A.]

Vianney, Jean-Baptist (1786–1859): better known as the Curé d'Ars, Father Vianney was sent as parish priest to the small and remote village of Ars-en-Doubes in 1815. The French Revolution and the upheavals of the Napoleonic era meant that France had suffered from a quarter of a century of secularization, and the ministry to the rural population had been neglected. The new priest at Ars proceeded to preach hellfire from the pulpit. He forbade dancing, immodest dress, obscenity and swearing, and the village inns had to close because of his opposition to heavy drinking. Curious things happened in the clergy-house; objects were moved, smashed or burned, and whether this was the work of the devil, poltergeists or protesting villagers was never resolved. With the passing of the years, he mellowed and developed a reputation for spiritual counsel and healing. The railway station at Lyons had to open a special booking office to cope with the travellers to Ars. Father Vianney spent up to sixteen hours a day in the confessional, weeping at his penitents' accounts of their sins, and giving wise and gentle advice. He never left Ars, and by the time he died in 1859, there were over a thousand pilgrims a week. He became a model of the simple, devout country priest who lived close to God in humility. [4 August, A. R.]

Vincent de Paul (1580–1660) had a ministry which crossed the class barriers of seventeenth-century France. He was born of a peasant family in Gascony, was educated by the Franciscans, and became a chaplain at the French court; but despite the fact that he became a spiritual director to wealthy and noble families, he never lost his devotion to the poor. He worked in prisons and hospitals, with the sick poor of Paris and the depressed and neglected peasantry of the rural areas. In 1625 he founded a Brotherhood of priests to extend his work, and in 1633 he collaborated with Louise de Marillac to set up the Daughters (later Sisters) of Charity to work in the villages. The wealthy and noble were directed to provide for his good causes for the good of their souls. His priests were carefully and systematically trained by Vincent himself, both in prayer and meditation and in the relief of human suffering: they went to work with convicts and galley-slaves, in infirmaries and lazarettos, and on the field of battle. An excellent administrator, he initiated many schemes for new seminaries and missions. The Brotherhood, like much of his other work, was abolished at the time of the French Revolution, but it was refounded in 1833 by a Catholic scholar, Antoine Frédéric Ozanam, as the Society of St Vincent de Paul. [27 September, A. R.]

Vincent of Saragossa (304) was a deacon in Spain in the time when Dacian, known for his great cruelty, was the Roman governor. Vincent was related to Valerius, bishop of Saragossa, and was arrested with him on a charge of refusing to worship the Roman gods. They were imprisoned and tried. Since Bishop Valerius had a speech impediment, Vincent spoke for him, and died under torture. His story was probably taken to Rome by Prudentius, the Spanish-Roman poet, who composed poems on him and *Agnes, the young Roman martyr who died in the same persecution. Vincent became the protomartyr of Spain. King Henry VII had a devotion to him (possibly because his own claim to the English throne involved his descent from John of Gaunt and his second wife, Blanche of Castile) and he is represented on the elaborate Henry VII tomb in Westminster abbey. [22 January, A. R. O.]

Vitus (?c. 304) was an early Sicilian saint who was probably martyred in the persecutions of Diocletian, like *Lucy. Nothing certain is known about his life, though he is said to have been the son of a Roman senator, and martyred with his tutor and his nurse, who were both Christians and taught him the faith. There was a very early cult of St Vitus, which spread to the Slavs and to Germany, where he became one of the Fourteen Holy Helpers of the Rhineland tradition. 'St Vitus' dance' was a popular name in the Middle Ages for any condition involving spasmodic and jerky movements. This seems to have originated with the troops of the Norman King Roger II in Sicily in the eleventh century, who are thought to have suffered bites from a particularly poisonous species of local tarantulas. Later it was applied to various toxic states which caused 'dancing mania', and which seem frequently to have originated from food poisoning, rabies or snakebite, as well as from epilepsy and neurological conditions. Vitus became the patron saint of sufferers from all these conditions, and also of actors and dancers. [15 June, R.]

Vladimir of Kiev (955–1015) was the grandson of the *Grand Duchess Olga of Kiev, who attempted to convert her people to Christianity, but was largely unsuccessful. She died when Vladimir was only twelve years old. When he succeeded as ruler of the province of Russia, which was then Viking territory, he was at first as brutal and bloodthirsty as most of his contemporaries; but in 989, in return for military help from the Byzantine

Emperor Basil II, he agreed to become a Christian, and married the emperor's daughter. His conversion was wholehearted: he put away his former wives and mistresses, forbade the worship of idols, and welcomed missionaries to his court. He gave alms to the poor (a practice then unknown among his people), and became a just and honourable ruler. Later, he made close links with the Western Church. He and his grandmother Olga are regarded as the Christian pioneers of Russia. [15 July, R. O.]

Walburga (779) was the daughter of 'King' Richard of Wessex and his wife Winna, and sister to *Willibald and *Winnibald. She was educated in the double monastery at Wimborne, became a nun, and went out to join her mother's brother, Boniface, in the evangelization of Germany. Winnibald became abbot of the great double monastery of Heidenheim, and summoned Walburga to take charge of the nuns. When he died in 761, Willibald, who had become bishop of Eichstätt, appointed her as superior over the whole monastery. The nuns in a double monastery were usually noblewomen, and enclosed, while the monks dealt with external affairs and directed the labourers and craftsmen. Walburga is reputed to have been an excellent abbess, with skills in medicine and a gift for healing. The unhappy association of her name (of which Walpurgis is a German variant) with the witches' sabbath or *Walpurgisnacht* seems to be fortuitous: it may derive from the fact that her feast was traditionally on 1 May, the date of pagan spring festivals, or from an ancient pagan goddess named Walborg. [R. now 25 February.]

Walter Hilton (?1396) was an Augustinian friar in the priory at Thurgarten, near Southwell. His Order was a scholarly one, devoted in his day to translating and expounding the Scriptures and to countering the wilder claims of the Lollards (see *Wyclif). Hilton's main work, *The Ladder of Perfection* (later translated into Latin as *Scala Perfectionis*), has become a spiritual classic, one of the great fourteenth-century English mystical works, which also include the writings of *Julian of Norwich and *Richard Rolle. Hilton begins by stressing *Gregory the Great's distinction between the active life and the contemplative life, one or the other being necessary to salvation. Those who lead the active life are counselled to self-discipline, bodily continence and good works; but the contemplative life is the higher path. Those who follow it climb the 'ladder of perfection', passing through 'a glowing darkness' as they progress towards 'Love uncreated' – God himself. Hilton's thought is very close to that of the author of the anonymous mystical work, *The Cloud of Unknowing*, which has sometimes been attributed to him; but most scholars now think that this is the work of another writer in the same tradition. [24 March, A.].

Watts, Isaac (1674–1748): this celebrated hymnologist was a Dissenter – at a time when Non-Conformists were no longer persecuted, but were still not admitted to the ancient universities. Though a wealthy local philanthropist offered to pay for his education at Oxford or Cambridge, he refused, because he felt he could not subscribe to the Thirty-Nine Articles. This meant that he was barred from the professions: he became tutor to the son of a baronet, and then acquired titled patrons. He wrote prolifically, both prose and poetry, but his *Hymns and Spiritual Songs* earned his considerable literary reputation. The hymns include

'O God, our help in ages past', 'Jesus shall reign where'er the sun' and 'When I survey the wondrous Cross'. A man of learning and piety, Watts was awarded an honorary degree of Doctor of Divinity by the University of Edinburgh. There is a monument to him in Westminster abbey. [25 November, A.].

Wenceslas (?907–29): the 'Good King' whose Christian charity is celebrated in *J. M. Neale's Christmas carol was actually a duke of Bohemia. He succeeded to the dukedom when

he was very young, and was killed by the pagan followers of his brother Boleslav, probably when he was in his early twenties. He had been taught by his Christian grandmother, Ludmilla, and in his short reign he strengthened the contacts between the duchy and the Holy Roman Empire, and worked for the Christianization of Bohemia. After his death, he was immediately venerated as a martyr. His relics were taken to the cathedral church of St Vitus in Prague, and became a pilgrimage centre. He became the patron saint of Bohemia, and a focus for Czech nationalism. His feast came to England through the Roman Missal, but relatively little is known about his life, and no source has been found for the events described in the carol. Commentators have suggested that the carol celebrates

Victorian ideas of benevolence rather than those of early tenth-century Bohemia. [28 September, R. O.]

Wesley, John (1703–91) and **Charles Wesley** (1707–88): the Wesley brothers, who both studied at Oxford and were ordained into the Anglican Church, were much influenced by the Moravians – German Lutherans in the tradition of John Hus, who took their inspiration from the Bible, and showed a zeal which was then often lacking in the Anglican Church. It was at a Moravian meeting that John Wesley had an overwhelming conversion experience on 24 May 1738. The foundation of Methodism is usually dated from that day. He began to preach in the open air, and the labouring classes flocked to hear him. His preaching tours (often accompanied by Charles, his loyal supporter) took him from Cornwall to the Scottish borders, through rural areas where the enclosure movement and the denudation of the countryside had brought much social distress, and into the squalor of the crowded and disease-ridden towns. He is said to have travelled 26,000 miles (most of the time on horseback, though he used a chaise in his later years) and to have preached 40,000 sermons. Though he preached in a plain, dry style, the crowd reactions roused by his sermons were often extreme. Both brothers regarded themselves as being in Anglican Orders, but the churches closed their doors against them, and they were accused of rabble-rousing and causing insanity. The Methodists separated from the Moravians in 1745, and sent out lay preachers; but it was not until John Wesley ordained missionaries for the United States and Scotland in 1784 – against the wishes of Charles – that separation from the Church of England became inevitable. The final break occurred three years after the death of Charles, and in the year in which John died at the age of eighty-eight. John Wesley's sermons, letters and journal, which describes his spiritual experience, have been a source of inspiration to many Christians. Charles Wesley wrote over 3,000 hymns, including 'Love divine, all loves excelling', 'Jesu, lover of my soul' and 'Hark, the herald angels sing'. [24 May, A.]

Westcott, Brooke Foss (1825–1901): Westcott House, Cambridge, commemorates the name of this Victorian theologian who became Regius Professor of Divinity at Cambridge and initiated a revival of biblical scholarship through his commentaries on the Bible, which became essential reading for successive generations of theological students. He did much to raise the standard of divinity studies in the university, and became examining chaplain to the archbishop of Canterbury. He steadfastly refused all promotion, apart from a canonry at Westminster abbey, until he reached the age of sixty-five. Then, on being offered the bishopric of Durham, he came to the conclusion that it was his duty to enter public life and to speak about national problems. He opposed the build-up of armaments in the 1890s, and became involved in labour relations. He investigated the causes of industrial unemployment, resolved disputes between employers and the trade unions, and addressed thousands at the Durham Miners' Gala. His tradition of social concern for the mining communities of Durham county has been long remembered, and the Industrial Christian Fellowship later drew much of its inspiration from his work. [27 July, A.]

Whiting, Richard (1539) was abbot of Glastonbury, and one of the three abbots executed under the orders of Henry VIII at the time of the dissolution of the monasteries. In 1535, following the Act of Supremacy, Thomas Cromwell's commissioners visited Glastonbury and reported that the monastery was in good order; but they returned in 1539, by which time Glastonbury was the only monastery left in Somerset. Abbot Richard was accused of 'having shown his cankerous and traitorous mind towards the King's Majesty and his succession'. It is not known what the specific charges were. Cromwell noted in his *Remembrances*, 'Item, the abbot of Glaston to be tried at Glaston and executed there', which indicates that the case was prejudged. Abbot Whiting asked permission to say a farewell to his community, but the community had already been dispersed. He was executed on the Tor, a nearby hill. [1 December, R.]

Wilberforce, William (1759–1833) was Member of Parliament for Hull, a member of the Clapham Sect (see *John Venn) and an indefatigable parliamentary reformer, sitting on committees, making speeches, piling up evidence of abuse and writing memoranda. He led the movement for the abolition of the slave trade in Charles James Fox's Ministry of All the Talents in 1807; but slavery in the colonies remained legal under British law, and the condition of the slaves, particularly the Africans who had been transported to the West Indies to run the sugar plantations, was still a national scandal. After decades of opposition by slave-owners, abolition was finally achieved during Wilberforce's last illness in 1833. His other interests included many Anglican causes: the Church Missionary Society and the London Missionary Society benefited from his assiduous support, and he was one of the founders of the British and Foreign Bible Society. [30 July, A.].

Wilfrid (c. 633–709) studied at Lindisfarne under *Aidan, and undertook a pilgrimage to Rome with *Benedict Biscop. He spent three years at Lyons with Bishop Annemundus, and came back as a monk, convinced that the Latin Rite was superior to the Celtic Rite. He became abbot of Ripon, where he introduced the Benedictine Rule and the Latin date of Easter. At the Synod of Whitby in 664, he was the chief proponent of the Latin Rite, and argued successfully against his former teachers that authority in the Church rightly belonged to the pope as successor to *Peter, Prince of the Apostles. He was appointed bishop of York, and went to Gaul to be consecrated by twelve Frankish bishops in a magnificent ceremony; but he was away for over a year, and the conflicts between the Roman and the Celtic Church were by no means over. He returned to find that *Chad, abbot of Lastingham, had been nominated in his place. Though Chad gave way to him willingly enough, there was much resistance to his return to York, and the matter was finally settled by *Theodore, archbishop of Canterbury, who divided the York diocese into three, and later into five dioceses, and sent Wilfrid to the smallest at Hexham. Wilfrid appealed to the pope and travelled to Rome. At one point he was shipwrecked on the coast of Friesia, and spent a year in missionary work, later carried on by *Willibrord. Though his Saxon biographer Eddi (who took the Latin form of his own name as Eddius Stephanus) insists that Wilfrid was twice restored to York by papal decree, he never carried the confidence of the kings of Northumbria. He died in a monastery of his own foundation in Mercia. [12 October, A. R.]

William of Occam: see **Occam**

William of York (1154) was the son of Emma, half-sister to King Stephen and the bishop of Winchester. In an age when nepotism was not only acceptable but considered laudable, his appointment was strongly supported by Stephen's party, though it was unacceptable to those who considered Stephen a usurper. In the subsequent civil war, when the supporters of Stephen were challenged by those of Matilda, daughter of Henry II, William's fortunes fluctuated with the political situation. It is difficult to disentangle his own character from the adulation and invective which were directed at him. Henry of Winchester consecrated him without consulting the pope; the pope, Innocent II, died two days later, and William was deposed by his successor. He was removed from his archdiocese for six years until another pope reinstated him, but he returned to York, which solidly supported Stephen against Matilda, to a rapturous welcome. The crowds were so great that the Ouse bridge collapsed under their weight (though nobody was killed, which was accounted a miracle). The event is commemorated in the St William Window in York Minster. Less than three months after his return to York, William was poisoned. It is said that the poison was in the chalice when he celebrated Mass at the high altar, and placed there by the archdeacon of York, Osbert. In that same year, King Stephen died, and was succeeded by Matilda's son, Henry II. Osbert fled to Normandy, where he was laicized, and became a baron under the new régime. [8 June, R.]

Willibald (761) and **Winnibald** (786) were the sons of the West Saxon 'King' Richard and his wife Winna, and brothers to *Walburga. They accompanied their father on his pilgrimage; but Richard died at Lucca, and Winnibald, who was delicate, became ill in Rome, so Willibald went on alone to the Holy Land. The account of his travels, dictated to a nun named Hugebure, is the earliest known travel book by an English writer. It can be read in translation in C. H. Talbot's *Anglo-Saxon Missionaries in Germany* (1954). Subsequently, Willibald was a monk at Monte Cassino for ten years before going to join *Boniface in Germany. In 742, he became bishop of Eichstätt, and one of his first acts was the foundation of the monastery at Heidenheim. Winnibald was already working with Boniface: Willibald appointed him abbot of Heidenheim, and Walburga came out from England to act as superior to the nuns. Willibald outlived them both, and served as bishop of Eichstätt for forty-five years. [Willibald 7 June, R. Winnibald 18 December, R.]

Willibrord (658–739) is the patron of the Netherlands and is known as 'the apostle of Friesia'. A Yorkshireman, he studied under *Wilfrid at Ripon, and determined to follow Wilfrid in evangelizing the Friesians. He obtained the support of the Frankish king Pippin, and the approval of the pope, and in 692 returned to Rome, carrying Pippin's recommendation that he should be consecrated. He was given a mission to develop the work, and was consecrated as archbishop of the Friesians. He built churches and monasteries, and consecrated bishops to work in new dioceses. His most famous monastery was at Echternach, in what is now Luxembourg. For the most part, he worked under the protection of Pippin's troops, though at one point he was driven out of Utrecht by Radbod, the pagan king of Friesia. *Boniface joined him, and though Willibrord hoped that Boniface would be his own successor, he carried out missions among the pagans without Frankish protection, and so met his death. Willibrord, described by *Alcuin as 'venerable, gracious and full of joy', lived to the age of eighty-one, and his tomb at Echternach became a centre for pilgrimage. [7 November, A. R.]

Wilson Carlile: see Carlile

Winifred (Winfrede, Gwenfrewi, c. 650) is the much-loved saint of Ellis Peters' 'Brother Cadfael' mysteries. She was a real person, and there are two medieval lives of her, though the oral traditions were not committed to parchment in Latin until some five centuries after her death. It seems that she came from Clwyd, her father was wealthy, and her mother was the sister of a holy man named Beuno. A young chieftain wanted to marry her, but she refused him. Subsequently she became an abbess, according to one account. The details of her martyrdom, her resuscitation after Beuno's prayers and her miraculous spring at Holywell (Tre Ffynnon) may be the stuff of legends, but great veneration was paid to her in the Middle Ages. Her relics were translated to the Benedictine abbey at Shrewbury in 1138, and from 1148 her feast was kept throughout the province of Canterbury. Many pilgrimages were made to her well, and miraculous cures were claimed. Henry V made a pilgrimage there after the battle of Agincourt, and Lady Margaret Beaufort, the mother of Henry VII, enclosed the well in its present buildings. In 1917, when mining works threatened the supply of water to the well, there was considerable local anxiety, until further excavation reconnected it to a subterranean reservoir. Winifred was included in the Roman Martyrology of 1596 by Cardinal Baronius, though he erroneously described her as an English virgin saint rather than a Welsh one. [3 November, R.]

Wyclif, John (1324–84), otherwise Wiclif or Wycliffe, was a scholar of Balliol College, Oxford, and according to some accounts, briefly master of the college. A Yorkshireman from Richmond, he was successively the incumbent of three college livings at Fillington, Ludgershall and Lutterworth. He was frequently at the court of King Edward II, and wrote pamphlets and other statements defending the Church in England against papal domination and ecclesiastical abuse. In his *De Domina Divina* (1376), he argued that all authority, both religious and secular, could be forfeited by unjust rulers. Though a series of papal Bulls demanded that he be imprisoned by the king, the bishops and the university, he continued to express his views freely in writing and from his pulpit at Lutterworth, arguing that the Church had no need of a pope or bishops, and that the clergy had no power of absolving sins. The latter was particularly alarming to the papacy, since (long before *Martin Luther's attack) it threatened the lucrative trade in indulgences. Wyclif also maintained that the elements in the Eucharist continued to have the character of bread and wine, and that the common people should be able to read the Bible in the vernacular. With a group of scholars, he translated the Bible, and sent out 'poor priests' to preach throughout the kingdom. Thanks to the support of the king's powerful son, John of Gaunt, he escaped arrest and trial for heresy; but many of his followers, known contemptuously as 'Lollards' (from the Dutch *lollen*, 'to mumble'), suffered the penalties for heresy. Wyclif's movement died out in England after his death, but deeply influenced John Hus, who in turn was to influence Martin Luther. [31 December, A.]

Xavier, Francis (1506–52) was one of the first six members of the Society of Jesus, formed by *Ignatius Loyola in 1533. He was born in the castle of Xavier, near Pamplona, and his first language was Basque. In 1541 he was appointed apostolic nuncio to the East, and set sail for the Portuguese colony of Goa. He was to spend the rest of his life in the East, carrying out missions to Goa (where he opposed the colonial oppression of the Portuguese), in southern India, in Malacca (also a Portuguese colony), and in the Spice Islands (now Indonesia). His frugality of life and his care for the poor and oppressed peoples of Asia brought him many converts. He described their sufferings as 'a permanent bruise on my soul'. When he reached Japan, which was not then closed to Europeans, he represented himself to the local rulers as the emissary of the king of Portugal, presented them with such Western novelties as spectacles and a clock, baptized over two thousand people, and left priests and catechists to carry on his work. The Church in Japan continued to expand and flourish until the persecutions at the end of the sixteenth century drove Christianity underground (see *Martyrs of Japan). Francis undertook a final mission to China; but he became ill off the coast near Guangzhou (now Canton), and died on the beach with only a catechist in attendance. His example inspired the Society of Jesus and other religious Orders to send missions to the East. His tomb is in the cathedral in Goa. [3 December, A. R.]

Youville, Margaret d' (1701–71): when Margaret was left a widow in French Montreal, she was twenty-eight years old, pregnant and had four young children. She was left in great poverty.

Her new baby and two of her other children died. Her well-born but dissolute husband, François d'Youville, had been a fur trader who illicitly supplied the Indians with brandy and died in debt with his name dishonoured. When Margaret began to help sick and disabled women, people even poorer than herself, other women came to join her, but they were subjected to mockery and cat-calls in the street, and on one occasion were denounced from the pulpit as public sinners. Margaret was accused of carrying on her husband's liquor trade with the Indians, and the group became known as the *Soeurs Grises*. In French, *gris* means 'grey', but it is also slang for 'tipsy'. In spite of the opposition, the group gradually won public respect. King Louis XV of France confirmed their status in 1753, and two years later they were officially instituted as the Sisters of Charity. In 1757 they took over the derelict City Hospital in Montreal. This became of vital importance to the city during the Seven Years' War. Margaret accepted many war casualties, French and English alike, in addition to the civilian patients. She saved several British prisoners from the Indians, paying £200 to ransom one and helping four others to escape, dressed improbably as Grey Nuns. When Montreal finally fell to General Wolfe's troops in 1759, she found that the new British administration also appreciated her work. Her loyalty was to 'our masters, the poor', without distinction of race, colour, or status. She had a special care for the Indians because of the way in which her husband had corrupted them and nursed them herself during a smallpox epidemic. When she died in 1771, her epitaph, spoken by one of her first Sisters, was 'She loved greatly, Jesus Christ and the poor.' Margaret became the first native-born Canadian saint in 1990. [R. 23 December].

125

Key Dates

The Roman Empire

64–5	Persecution of Christians under Nero. Sporadic persecutions in both Eastern and Western Empires until
304–5	Persecutions under Diocletian.
312	Constantine's Edict of Milan. Religious toleration throughout the Empire.
324–5	Council of Nicaea. Formulation of definition of the Trinity. First agreed draft of the Creed.
330	Constantine moves his capital to the Eastern Empire.
366–84	Pope Damasus claims jurisdiction over the whole Church as the heir to St Peter, opens up the catacombs, and erects shrines to martyrs.
380	Christianity proclaimed the official religion of the Eastern and Western Empires.

The Celtic Church

c. 434	Patrick's mission to Ireland.
565	Columba founds a Celtic monastery on Iona.
635	Aidan goes from Iona to Lindisfarne.
597	Augustine and the Roman mission arrive in England.
664	Synod of Whitby: the Celtic bishops accept the Latin Rite.
715	The Irish Church accept the Latin Rite.

The Eastern Orthodox Church

328	Constantine establishes his court in New Byzantium (Constantinople).
800–999	Conversion of the Slavs.
900–999	Foundation of the Russian Church.
800–1099	The Eastern Orthodox Churches separate from papal jurisdiction.
1096–1271	The Crusades: struggle for control of the Holy Land between Saracens and Western European military forces. Jerusalem left under Moslem control.
1204	Sack of Constantinople.
1439	Final separation of the Eastern and Western Churches (the Florentine Council).
1453	Fall of Constantinople to the Ottoman Turks.

The Anglican Church

1517	*[Outbreak of the Reformation on the Continent: Luther's protest in Wittenberg, followed by his excommunication].*
1534	Henry VIII rejects papal jurisdiction (Act of Supremacy).
1536	Dissolution of the monasteries
1545–63	*The Council of Trent (the Counter-Reformation, tightening the discipline of the Roman Catholic Church).*
1553–8	England is returned to Roman Catholic jurisdiction under Mary Tudor.
1559	The Elizabethan Settlement. Establishment of the Church of England.
1570	Elizabeth and all who accept her as head of the Church excommunicated by a papal Bull.
1571	The 'English Mission', led by Jesuits.
1611	Authorized Version of the Bible.
1649	Execution of King Charles I.
1649–59	The Commonwealth. Roman Catholicism proscribed, Anglicanism discouraged.
1660	Restoration of the Anglican Settlement under Charles II.
1689	The Toleration Act (applied to Dissenters, but not to Roman Catholics).
1784	Samuel Seabury consecrated first bishop of the Episcopal Church of the United States of America.
1828	Roman Catholic Emancipation.

The Non-Conforming Churches

1560	Establishment of Presbyterianism in Scotland.
1612	First Baptist Church in England.
1649–59	Development of Congregational churches in Cromwell's time.
1668	Organization of the Society of Friends.
1738	John Wesley's experience at Aldersgate: commencement of his preaching tours.
1788	Separation of Methodists from the Church of England.
1972	The Congregational Church and the Presbyterian Church in England combine to form the United Reformed Church.

Reunion?

1948	Formation of the World Council of Churches, based in Geneva. The WCC represents branches of the Anglican Communion, and most of the Eastern Orthodox Churches, and all the major Free Churches (except the Unitarians)
1961	The Roman Catholic Church first sends accredited observers to the WCC.
1964	The Vatican II decrees on Ecumenism first recognizes members of other Churches as 'separated brethren'.
1968	The Roman Catholic Church becomes a full member of the WCC's Faith and Order Commission.

Glossary

The Anglican Communion includes the Church of England, the Episcopal Church of the United States of America, the Anglican Churches of Canada and Australia and their equivalents in Asia, Africa and South America, more than thirty Churches in all. Each has a General Synod which makes major decisions on faith and order, and a structure of diocesan synods and parish councils. The Churches keep in touch with one another through the Anglican Consultative Council and the ten-yearly Lambeth Conferences, hosted by the archbishop of Canterbury.

The Roman Catholic Church is governed by a complex and interacting set of Congregations, Councils and Committees centrally based in Rome. All major decisions come from the Vatican in the name of the pope, and papal pronouncements on matters of faith and morals (such as the doctrine of the Immaculate Conception) are binding on all Catholics. There have been calls from some cardinals for a more 'collegiate' form of government following the Second Vatican Council (Vatican II) of 1962–5.

The Eastern Orthodox Churches have fourteen major jurisdictions, including the historic patriarchates of Constantinople, Alexandria, Antioch, and Jerusalem, the patriarchate of Moscow, and a number of national Churches in Eastern Europe, North and South America, Australia and Asia. The Greek and Russian Churches are now the largest. All this 'family' of Churches are in communion with one another, and acknowledge the primacy of the patriarch of Constantinople, the Ecumenical Patriarch. Each is independent in its internal administration.

The Free or Dissenting Churches, often called 'Non-Conformists', include the Methodist Church, the United Reformed Church (formerly Presbyterians and Congregationalists), the Baptist Church, the Salvation Army and the Society of Friends. They are Protestant Churches or groups which do not accept the reformed and modified Catholic practice established by the Church of England and the Lutheran Churches of Northern Europe in the sixteenth century. Though they have their own ways of honouring great Christians, they are generally reluctant to call them 'saints', because of the past dangers of superstitious practices.

Feasts, festivals and commemorations: in the Roman Catholic Church, there are four grades of observance for saints: Solemnity, Feast, Memorial and Optional Memorial. In the Anglican Church, the four grades are Feast, Festival, Lesser Festival and Commemoration. In general terms, these are often referred to as saints' days, feast days, holy days or commemorations, irrespective of the actual grade of observance.

Common Worship: the Common Worship Calendar, introduced in 1998, and the Common Worship Prayer Book, introduced in 2000, are approved for use in the Church of England. Other parts of the Anglican Communion may develop their own versions.

Fractured Calendars: the world-wide spread of the Churches and the different forms of organization mean that there is no *consolidated* list of saints. The Revised Roman Universal Calendar issued in 1969 consists of a central core of saints' days, and observance of those noted as days of obligation is enjoined on all Roman Catholics. In addition, the Vatican issues national Calendars. That for Britain, published in 2000, accords St George a Solemnity (the highest degree of observance) in England, while St Andrew has an equivalent honour in Scotland, St David in Wales, and St Patrick in Ireland. The Churches of the Anglican Communion and the Eastern Orthodox Churches have their own individual Calendars, though there are of course many overlaps. There is a considerable amount of agreement for the first thousand years of the Christian era, but thereafter, Western and Eastern Calendars divide. Roman Catholic Calendars are restricted to saints of the Roman Catholic Church since the Reformation in the sixteenth century, and do not include any Anglicans, Lutherans or members of the dissenting Churches.

Naming (or proclaiming) Saints: In the **Roman Catholic Church**, the procedure is called *promoting a cause*. Causes are examined by the Congregation of Rites (a process which can take many years, and is increasingly expensive), and the pope proclaims the name in a service of *beatification* or *canonization*. Beatification, recognition as 'Blessed', is usually the first stage, and canonization, with the title of 'Saint', often comes later. The present procedure was instituted in 1723, and many earlier saints have never received formal recognition. In the **Church of England**, names of people to be honoured by inclusion in the Calendar are examined by the Liturgical Commission of General Synod, which makes recommendations to the full Synod, and these are subject to a vote. This is a modern equivalent of the ancient practice by which saints were recognized *e consensu gentium*, by the will of the people. Other Anglican Churches follow a similar procedure.

Saints' days: each saint has a date for commemoration (often known as a feast day). Traditionally, this was the date of the saint's death, but the uncertainty of many such dates, the necessity of avoiding major Holy Days such as Christmas or Easter, and the attempt to space commemorations fairly evenly through the year, mean that this is now not always the case. On that day, special prayers and collects (known as 'propers') may be used, and in the case of major saints or patronal festivals, processions and other customs observed.

Patron saints: the practice of adopting a saint as patron of a place or a trade is traditional and wide-spread. St George, St Andrew and St Patrick, respectively the patron saints of England, Scotland and Ireland, were all martyrs, and their crosses form the Union Flag. St Eligius, himself a goldsmith, is the patron of metalworkers,

Glossary

and St Crispin and St Crispinian of shoemakers. Many churches have dedications in the names of saints, and keep their patronal festival. By canon law, the allocation of patronage in the Roman Catholic Church is now regulated from Rome. It is understandable that St Matthew is the patron of accountants and St Stephen the patron of deacons, but why is St Clare of Assisi the patron of television?

Saints and their emblems: in medieval art, many of the saints are shown with recognizable emblems: St Agnes with a lamb, St Laurence with a gridiron, St George with a dragon. There were two reason for this. Artists had not yet learned how to draw portraits, so that one saint looked very much like another under the halo; and most people were illiterate, so that there was little point in adding names. An emblem clearly identified the saint by referring to a well-known legend. The problem was that many of the legends were inaccurate and corrupted: 'Agnes' comes from a Greek word meaning 'pure', and not a Latin word meaning 'a lamb'; Laurence, as a Roman citizen, would have been executed with a sword-thrust, not on a gridiron; and the dragon legend, of Eastern origin, has been drawn into the story of the martyrdom of St George in a confused oral tradition. However some emblems – St Peter's keys, and the symbols from the Book of Revelation which characterize the writers of the four Gospels (Matthew the man, Mark the lion, Luke the ox and John the eagle), have acquired an enduring significance.

Miracles are events which cannot be explained by natural laws as we understand them. Medieval people, with a much more limited knowledge of science than we have today, were apt to see miracles on all sides: tales of saints who flew through the air, foretold events like battles, saw visions and resurrected the dead or dying multiplied with the telling – and there is still a public appetite for such tales, though today they are more likely to be about flying saucers than flying saints. Christians cannot deny the *possibility* of the miraculous: God can intervene in his own world, though he may not do so as often as some people claim, and will not be manipulated to produce seemingly magical answers to our problems; but any claim to the miraculous is now rigorously investigated by medical practitioners, physical scientists and psychologists before being tentatively accepted – with the reservation that there may still be natural laws which we do not fully understand.

'Headless' saints: in the medieval period, it was the custom for martyrs who had been beheaded to be shown on statues and in paintings carrying their heads in their hands. This gave rise to some absurd legends, like the eleventh-century Abbot Herluin's assertion that St Denys of Paris walked two miles from Montmartre (the place of his execution, which is named for him) to the site of his tomb carrying his head, and accompanied by a choir of angels. In the sixteenth century, Protestant extremists often unwittingly encouraged these legends by lopping off the heads of statues which had originally been intact.

Tolerating diversity: there can be few better examples of the acceptance of extreme religious differences than that offered by Thomas More (now commemorated in both the Roman Catholic and Common Worship Calendars). When he was sentenced to death following his trial in 1535, he reminded the court that St Paul had persecuted St Stephen – 'and yet they be now both twain holy saints in heaven, and shall continue there friends for ever, so I verily trust'. He went on to express the hope that he and his judges might similarly 'in heaven merrily all meet together in everlasting salvation'.

Further Reading

The following publications give further information and details of source documents for the saints in this Dictionary:

Paul Burns (ed.), *Butler's Lives of the Saints*, Burns and Oates, (12 volumes, 2000) [RC].
The New Catholic Encyclopaedia, (14 volumes, New York, 1967) [RC].
David Hugh Farmer (ed.), *The Oxford Dictionary of Saints,* 3rd edition, 1992 [RC].
Brother Tristam, SSF, *Exciting Holiness: Collects and Readings for the Festivals and Lesser Festivals of the Church of England*, Canterbury Press, 1997 [A].
Robert Atwell, *Celebrating the Saints: Daily Spiritual Readings for the Calendar of the Church of England*, Canterbury Press, 1998 [A].
Kathleen Jones, *The Saints of the Anglican Calendar,* Canterbury Press, 2000 [A].

For ecclesiastical and theological terms, see:

E. A. Livingstone, *The Oxford Concise Dictionary of the Christian Church,* Oxford University Press, 1977, revised edition, 1996.
Tony Meakin, *A Basic Church Dictionary,* Canterbury Press, 1990, revised edition, 1999.
Michael Walsh, *A Dictionary of Devotions*, Burns and Oates, 1993 [RC].
Nicholas Zernov, *Eastern Christendom*, Weidenfeld and Nicolson, 1961.